In Praise of F*[...]*

Riveting, harrowing and completely inspiring: Flying to Extremes is a treasure for aviation fanatics, Northerners and for everyone looking for the one book to remind you that life is to be lived and celebrated. Dominique Prinet, mahsi cho for documenting your northern adventures for all future generations. WOW! What a life! What a read! BRAVO!

Richard Van Camp, Indigenous Tlicho writer from Fort Smith, NWT. Author of international reputation, and recipient of numerous awards. The Lesser Blessed has been adapted into a film. Richard taught creative writing at UBC for eight years.

I have never seen, in all my years, a more tenacious, ingenious, obstinate, durable, fantastic young man, whether it be in the Armed Services or in civilian life...His capacity for work is unlimited, his concern for his passengers was almost fatherly, and his sense of responsibility toward his plane and the company which employs him is outstanding.

Dr. Seymour Wishnick, M.D., Chicago (passenger); see Chapter 7, *Sinking with a Floatplane in the Arctic Ocean.*

Flying to Extremes *is an incredible account which many might classify as humanly impossible. Often without daylight and running out of fuel, hindered by unreliable maps, and beaten down to a few feet above the barrens by blotted windshields, Dominique Prinet manages to get the job done with skill and courage. These pages should be compulsory reading not only for aviation enthusiasts, but for by anyone thinking of throwing in the towel and screaming "I quit!" Dominique Prinet never does.*

Robert Grant, Northern Bush Pilot, 12,000 hours, author of three successful books on bush flying in the North (see Bibliography).

Flying in the polar night by minus 55° F, finding a fuel cache of a few barrels dropped off during the previous summer, filtering the gas and pumping it by hand into the wing tanks, using a gyrocompass reset from sights on the moon and stars, ..., and trying to navigate way beyond the reach of radio beacons, such is the daily job of the bush pilot. Blessed with the talent of a great raconteur, Dominique Prinet gives us a first-hand testimony of life as a bush pilot, with the unabashed enthusiasm of a young man of 25.

Michel Didier, Ph.D., B-747 captain, Air France

I have known Dominique Prinet since 1966 when I helped him out with a mechanical problem along the Arctic coast at Coppermine. Flying to Extremes is one of the most insightful books on aviation prior to the 1970's in the polar regions of Canada. This was typically flying by the seat of your pants. During those early days, navigation was by astrocompass, the odd radio beacon, and paper charts which left large blank areas where you made notes and drew in the land marks as best you could. Amazing!

Ron Sheardown, Northern Bush Pilot, 20,000 hours, Canadian and US Airline Pilot, Alaskan Aviation Hall of Fame. Found pilot Bob Gauchie on April 1, 1967 who had survived two stressful winter months stranded on the tundra in a Beaver on skis.

Flying to Extremes

Memories of a Northern Bush Pilot

Flying to Extremes

Memories of a Northern Bush Pilot

By Dominique Prinet

hancock

house

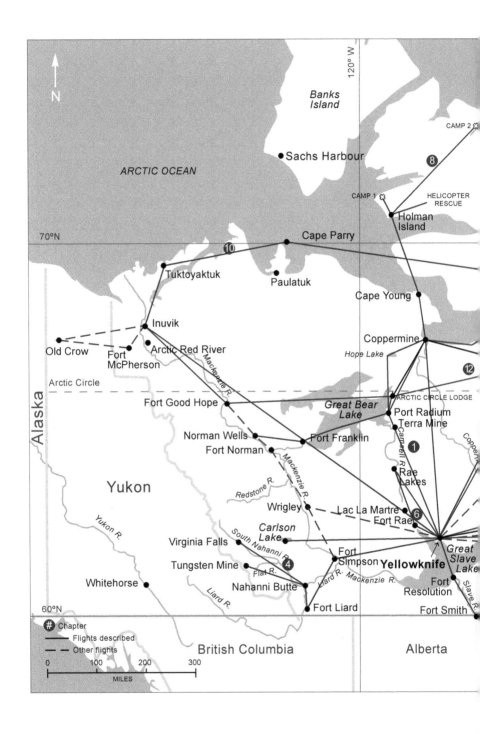

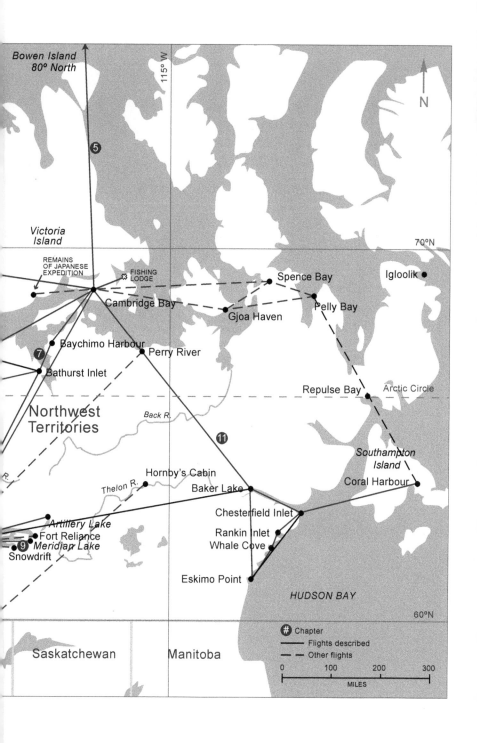

Bowen Island
80° North

115° W

N

Victoria
Island

70°N

REMAINS
OF JAPANESE
EXPEDITION

FISHING
LODGE

Spence Bay

Igloolik ●

Cambridge Bay

Gjoa Haven

Pelly Bay

⑦ ● Baychimo Harbour
● Perry River

Bathurst Inlet

Repulse Bay

Arctic Circle

Northwest
Territories

Back R.

⑪

Southampton
Island

Hornby's Cabin

Coral Harbour

Thelon R.

Baker Lake

Artillery Lake
● Fort Reliance
⑨ ● Meridian Lake
Snowdrift

Chesterfield Inlet

Rankin Inlet
Whale Cove

Eskimo Point

HUDSON BAY

60°N

⑤

❼

Saskatchewan

Manitoba

🄲 Chapter
——— Flights described
– – – Other flights

0   100   200   300

MILES

Sunk along the Arctic Coast with three passengers in a Cessna 185, near an abandoned Inuit community. It took three days to get the plane out, in freezing waters. Painting by Hélène Girard.

ISBN-13: 978-0-88839-145-2 [paperback colour]
ISBN-13: 978-0-88839-755-3 [paperback b&w]
ISBN-13: 978-0-88839-234-3 [epub]
Copyright © 2021 Dominique Prinet

Library and Archives Canada Cataloguing in Publication
Title: Flying to extremes : memories of a northern bush pilot / by Dominique Prinet.
Names: Prinet, Dominique F., author.
Description: [Colour edition] | Also issued in a black & white edition.
Identifiers: Canadiana (print) 20200407880 | Canadiana (ebook) 20200353349 | ISBN 9780888391452
(softcover) | ISBN 9780888392343 (EPUB)
Subjects: LCSH: Prinet, Dominique F. | LCSH: Bush pilots—Northwest Territories—Biography. | LCSH:
Bush flying—Northwest Territories—Anecdotes. | LCGFT: Autobiographies.
Classification: LCC TL540.P75 A3 2020 | DDC 629.13092—dc23

*Cover Photo: Noon in February 1969 near the North Pole,
at latitude 80° N and –60° F. The flight was atrocious (Chapter 5).*

Editor: Audrey McClellan
Main translator: Nonta Libbrecht-Carey
Production, Cover and Maps: Linda Mitsui
Cover photograph: Dominique Prinet
Other photographs: Dominique Prinet except as noted.

Printed in Canada

*We acknowledge the financial support of the Government of Canada through the Canada Book Fund
and the Canada Council for the Arts, and of the Province of British Columbia through the British
Columbia Arts Council and the Book Publishing Tax Credit.*

*Hancock House gratefully acknowledges the Halkomelem Speaking Peoples whose unceded
traditional territories our offices reside upon.*

HANCOCK HOUSE PUBLISHERS LTD.
19313 Zero Avenue, Surrey, B.C. Canada V3Z 9R9
#104-4550 Birch Bay-Lynden Rd, Blaine, WA, U.S.A. 98230-9436
Phone (800) 938-1114   Fax (800) 983-2262
www.hancockhouse.com   info@hancockhouse.com

Contents

Cover Photo: Noon in February 1969 near the North Pole,
at latitude 80° N and –60° F. The flight was atrocious (Chapter 5).

Dedication

To my wife, Dominique, who not only came to Canada
and joined me in Yellowknife, but flew with me on
many Arctic trips, remaining graceful after our crash
through the ice with a ski plane.

Foreword

Flying to Extremes is based on five years of intensive commercial flying for Gateway Aviation in bush planes on wheels, skis, and floats, from 1967 to 1971, mostly from a base in Yellowknife, Northwest Territories. I took copious notes on some of the most striking flights and published their descriptions in 15 or 20 issues of *Aviasport*, a French aviation magazine, between 1967 and 1972. These stories have now been translated into English and collected in this book. There was no reason to place them in chronological order, since the socio-economic environment in the North did not change dramatically during my years of flying, and I remained with the same airline. For a while I thought of ordering the stories by season, but there were too many flights in summer and winter and not enough in the spring and fall, during breakup and freeze-up. I finally ordered them in a way I thought would bring a little variety.

One word, now, on names of people and places. At the time, the Northwest Territories extended north from latitude 60° N all the way to the North Pole, right across Canada except for the fairly narrow Yukon triangle along the B.C. and Alaska borders. The region is now divided into the Northwest Territories to the west (capital: Yellowknife) and Nunavut to the east (capital: Frobisher Bay, now Iqaluit).

In *Flying to Extremes*, the words used to describe the Indigenous people have been changed from what they were at the time as a matter of respect for their traditions and culture: those living in the boreal forest are the "First Nations," and those near the shores of the Arctic Ocean, the "Inuit." However, the European names of the small northern communities have been left as they were in the '60s, although they now have reverted, rightfully so, to their traditional Indigenous names. A table of name conversions for northern communities is given at the end of the book.

At the time I was flying in the North, we used the old British system of measurement. I subsequently applied the metric system in the stories since it is now the legal system in Canada, but I was advised to return to the British system for the North American edition in order to make the book more readable for senior Canadians and Americans of all ages. For the usual winter temperatures of –40°, the units don't matter anyhow: –40° F = –40° C.

Words of a technical nature are explained in the Glossary.

Acknowledgements

I am grateful to **Sylvie Tordiff** of Yellowknife, NWT, for reviewing these stories and distributing them to friends and relatives across several northern communities for evaluation. In particular, she asked **Vern Christensen** and **Walt Humphries** of Yellowknife to review the background history of the town (Chapter 2). To verify that I was telling the truth, the whole truth, and nothing but the truth in a way that would not offend anyone, she also gave a copy of the text to others such as **Richard Van Camp** of Edmonton, a published Dogrib Tlicho writer; **Dan Marion** of Behchoko; **Rob Tordiff** of Yellowknife, former president of the NWT Métis Association; and two Métis elders from the South Slave (Fort Smith), **Tony Whitford**, former Commissioner of the NWT, **Deana Twissell**, and **Gord Bohnet**.

My pilot colleague **Joe McBryan** at Gateway Aviation, airline pilot and owner of Buffalo Airways in Yellowknife (Chapter 3), reviewed the text and gave it his blessing. Other pilots provided great support and wise advice, such as **Michel Didier**, PhD, B-747 captain with Air France (retired); and **Ron Sheardown**, a bush pilot with 20,000 hours in the North, holder of airline pilot licences in Canada and the US, and member of the Alaska Aviation Hall of Fame, who used to fly from Hope Lake, found Bob Gauchie after he had disappeared in the tundra for two months of winter (Chapter 3), and rescued me out of Coppermine (Chapter 10).

A number of private, commercial, and military pilots also reviewed the stories, including **Alain Roellinger**, who flew around the North Pole and published his story;[1] **Patrick Dubois**, flight instructor who used to train airline pilots out of Montreal; **Hannes Knopf**, electrical engineer and Canadian wilderness frequent traveller; **Jochen Spengler**, computer engineer and pilot in Germany; and **William Liddell**, Canadian graphic designer and pilot. **Des Ramsay, PhD**, former military pilot and physicist, and his wife, **Shirley**, an English teacher, also made very helpful suggestions.

I wish to also express all my gratitude to **Pat Carney**, former federal cabinet minister and senator. When I stopped flying, I joined her economic consulting company, Gemini North, in Yellowknife as an economist. A former journalist, Pat Carney has written two best-selling books,[2] and she reviewed my stories from a former northerner's point of view. Her son John Dickson, raised in Yellowknife, was also an Arctic bush pilot and is presently a captain with Cathay Pacific, flying 747 aircraft around the globe.

My wife, **Dominique**, who witnessed several of these flights and knew all about the others, verified their contents to prevent me from telling too many lies. **Linda Mitsui**, graphic designer, put the book together. She configured the text in its entirety from the Table of Contents to the Index, drew all the maps, edited and inserted some 200 images, and designed the covers.

These stories first appeared as articles, but, for this book, I have expanded some descriptions to provide additional historical background, for which I relied on outside sources. For instance, I had heard many times about the shooting of the two ducks at the "Rapids of the Drowned" on the Slave River, near Fort Smith, which caused several canoes to go down the rapids and flip over in 1786 (Chapter 3). It was only in 2018, with the help of Sylvie Tordiff, that I found the expert, historian **Jim Green**, also of Fort Smith, who was familiar with all the details and told me the true story.

[1] **Alain Roellinger**, *De l'Alaska à l'Oural* (France: Éditions Jean Pierre Otelli, 2015).

[2] **Pat Carney**, *Trade Secrets* (Toronto: Key Porter Books, 2000); and *On Island* (Victoria, BC: TouchWood Editions, 2017).

Similarly, I knew about the loss of five prospectors forgotten in the Nahanni River a few years before my arrival (Chapter 4), but could only find the details recently with the help of Joe McBryan, who connected me to one of his old pilots, **Robert Grant**, and his wife, **Linda**. They, in turn, sent me the transcript of the public hearing held in Yellowknife in 1960 to review the accident, as well as an exhaustive article published originally in *Weekend Magazine*, vol. 10, no. 41 (1960), explaining the whole disaster.

In Chapter 13, the description of the rescue of one of my colleagues grounded on the **Redstone River** with an Otter on floats comes from the book written by the man who flew there to repair the plane and make it usable again, **Denny McCartney**.[3]

[3] **Denny McCartney**, *Picking Up the Pieces* (Victoria, BC: Trafford Publishing, 2002).

Introduction

Life in Paris was hard during the German Occupation, which lasted until 1944, and for the following 10 or 15 years. I remember walking to school in snow with my wooden clogs while the fountains were frozen. We could warm up in one room around a coal stove during the evening, but there was otherwise no heat. Food was scarce, there was sometimes no gas for cooking, and occasionally no electricity.

Unfortunately, for several generations my family, on both my father's and my mother's side, has featured prominent academicians, some of them pretty smart, and I was expected to uphold the tradition. As a result, I had to be the youngest of my class in the best French high school, in the toughest programs, which combined the full classical program of French, Latin, and Greek, plus the full science program of math, physics, and chemistry. At around age 14 I broke down and had to

The Lycée Henri IV in Paris.

repeat a year. Then, it was off to the dreaded college classes of Mathématiques Supérieures and Mathématiques Spéciales to prepare for the entrance test to the top French university, the École Normale Supérieure. I failed but was admitted to a less prestigious engineering school.

A degree from the École Normale opens virtually every door throughout one's life. That was to have been my destiny since the day I was born. What I really wanted to do was fly airplanes, but I wore out my eyes during endless nights of study and could no longer pass the very stringent medical required to join either Air France or the French air force. I obtained my glider's licence at 16, two years before I was allowed to drive a car, and got my airplane licence at 17 in order to join an Air Cadet exchange program. Through that program I did a VIP tour of the United States and met President Eisenhower at the White House. A few years later I managed to attend a dozen free, two-week sessions on advanced piloting and aerobatics at the national flight centre in Carcassonne, and then took additional training at the national flight centres of Saint-Yan, to get my professional pilot licence, and Challes-Les-Eaux, to become an instructor. Flying with students north of Paris on weekends and holidays allowed me to survive for a few years while pretending to train as an electrical engineer.

My failure at the École Normale turned into my own personal Great Depression at the thought that I had proven to be the family idiot. I spent the next few years in complete disarray: I wrote off a car in northern Norway while on holidays with friends; damaged a light aircraft while trying, with a cast around my ankle, to recover from a poor landing by a student; demolished my father's car by driving over the dotted line of a highway and smashing into a truck while coming home at 75 mph, as if I were taking off in the Messerschmitt 108 (the civil version of the 109) that I had been flying all day; and eventually flew upside down close to the ground with a student in an open cockpit biplane over the river Oise, near Paris, until the engine stopped. We landed on a field of young wheat, but the plane flipped over on its back.

It was either jump off a bridge or renounce the world as I knew it, which I chose. I decided to retire from civilization and hide in the deep forests of British Columbia, as far from home as I could go, to work as a logger. I arrived in Vancouver at 25 with $200 in my pocket and no return ticket, knowing nobody in the city.

In January 1965, the logging camps in B.C. were closed because of snow, but I found a job as a pilot and flight instructor. I had suddenly entered Heaven. British Columbia was spectacular, the people kind and open-minded, and the opportunities limitless.

Mid Atlantic, January 15, 1965, emigrating to Canada on a CP Air DC-8. I never imagined that, 20 years later, I would become the airline's V.P. By then, it had been renamed Canadian Airlines.

Civil servants at the Ministry of Transport actually helped me convert my French commercial and instructor licences to their Canadian equivalents, after many ground and flight tests, instead of explaining why flying commercially in Canada was not an option for a new immigrant!

I decided that this was going to be my country and that I would be flying for a living, since pilots were allowed to wear glasses in Canada. One day I took a group of passengers over the Rocky Mountains from Vancouver to Edmonton in a small plane. While waiting for them, I was offered a job in the Northwest Territories. This was the First-Class Lounge area of Heaven, reserved for the lucky ones. And they were going to pay me to fly up there? I was absolutely thrilled.

From the spring of 1966 to the winter of 1971, except for four winters spent at university, I flew up North in a state of total bliss, earning more than enough money in three months of flying around the clock during the summer to pay for lodging, food, transportation, and tuition.

After my first fascinating summer of flying in the Arctic, I had regained enough confidence to return to university to finish an electrical engineering degree at UBC. Then, after one full year of Arctic flying, I spent two winters at McGill in Montreal to get an MBA, earning a living from flying in the Arctic during the summer.

During these years I was writing up some of my flying adventures for publication in *Aviasport*, an aviation magazine in France.

These stories obviously struck a chord with young French pilots. The 100 or 200 of them who contacted me to ask about opportunities to come over and fly were obviously feeling as uncomfortable as I was with the education and social environment of the time in France, perceiving themselves as misfits or pariahs. This prevalent malaise culminated in a general student explosion during the May 1968 Revolution, three years after I had run away from it all and sought refuge in Canada.

The stories describe some of my flights across the North and in the Canadian Arctic, in conditions that I thought were thrilling because they were at the limit of what an airplane and a pilot can do. My work in the North gave me back some confidence, and after a few years I was able to step back into civilization and carry on from there.

The winter of 1971 was slow. I lost my job as a pilot one Friday evening, but the following Monday morning I joined, as an economist, the consulting company recently established in Yellowknife by Pat Carney, a future Member of Parliament and senator, to conduct a number of studies on the proposed Mackenzie Valley gas pipeline. That job was completed after a couple of years, so I joined Nordair in Montreal, where I became VP. The company was doing very well and Nordair was eventually purchased by Canadian Pacific Airlines (CP Air) whose president asked me to move to Vancouver and become his marketing VP. The CP Air-Nordair amalgam became Canadian Airlines which, in turn, was purchased by Pacific Western Airlines who promptly threw out the president and a few VPs, starting with me, and brought Canadian Airlines to its knees within a few years. I went on to Tanzania for five years to turn around and manage the national airline, and finished my career in Vancouver as a sailing instructor.

Flying to Extremes tells stories of crazy flying in the Northwest Territories in the 1960s. During the long Arctic winter nights, when there was no daylight for weeks, I would carry passengers in temperatures as cold as −60° F, in blizzards and fog, over endless and obscured frozen terrain in a very remote area where the compass does not work. I landed on sandbars, on rivers and lakes, and on the tundra, and once I even broke through the ice when landing close to the treeline in the middle of nowhere in November, coming out from under water and surviving by pure miracle. During the summer, my floatplane sank one day in the Arctic Ocean, and on another flight it fell out of the sky with a full load of ice on the wings, hitting the surface of a lake at great speed in zero visibility.

I lived those years with passion. I was enthused, thrilled, and proud. I had arrived in Canada a broken young man from an old conservative and academic family, and this flying to extremes turned me around and saved my life.

So, to young people who feel lost and desperate, I say: "Not to worry! You are not alone. This is normal. Hang tough and show your resilience! Just pull up your socks, challenge yourself to do something with passion, and prove to the world that while you may not be what everyone expected, you are unique anyhow, and you can accomplish things that few people could."

1. Taking Off with a Bang

Yellowknife, October 1968, Cessna 180 on skis.

The weather was rather miserable, as it always was at that time of the year, with low ceilings and occasional light snow, and we had switched to skis a couple of weeks earlier because the small lakes were already frozen. On this day I was off to Terra Mines in a Cessna 180, bringing the miners some supplies.

Terra Mines was a small silver mine along the Camsell River, near Port Radium, just southeast of Great Bear Lake. Since I had to unload a fair amount of food and gear at the mine, load some bags of ore, and then refuel with a small hand pump, I took along our young dock boy, Danny Pappas.

The flight was close to 300 miles, and the skis slowed us down, so it took us close to two and a half hours to get there. The final stretch was painful, since the area close to Great Bear Lake is rough and hilly, and the tops of the hills were in the clouds. We eventually managed to sneak in and reach the small lake by the mine, but the far end of the lake was still wide open. We had been told, over the high-frequency radio, that whatever ice was there would be thick enough for a Cessna 180, and we made a slow approach over the frozen part, trying to land on skis in as short a space as possible.

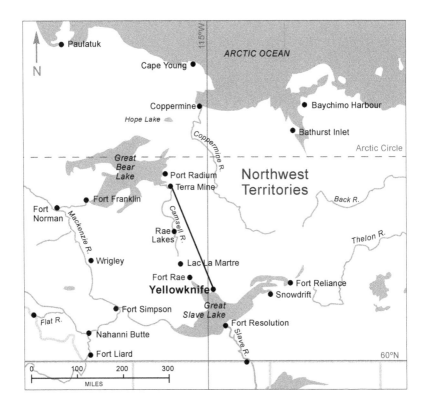

As we touched down I heard a loud *bang* just behind me, a sharp, metallic noise.

"What the hell was that?" Danny asked.

I had no idea, but a pilot has to display calm at all times. "I think the tail fell off, but let's take a look."

I stopped the plane and walked around to the back. Everything looked just right: the tail, the controls, the fuselage, the undercarriage, and the skis.

"We must have hit a piece of equipment under the snow on landing. It doesn't seem to have caused any damage."

I grumbled to myself as we taxied to the mine, wondering why the folks here weren't more careful. They should know not to leave equipment frozen under the snow right where airplanes landed.

At the mine, the manager, Hank Sanche, came over to meet us.

We dropped off the supplies and equipment we had brought, loaded a dozen bags of ore, and emptied two 10-gallon kegs of aviation fuel into the wing tanks. I was glad to have Danny along.

Now it was time to go. Even though it was early afternoon, the sky was getting dark already, the ceiling was below the hilltops, and visibility was fine but not great. We taxied to the end of the lake which had recently iced up. I followed our landing tracks but still couldn't see what we had hit. I adjusted the gyrocompass from the known orientation of the lake. There were no red lights on the instrument panel, and the needles were all in the green: ready for takeoff. Full power, and we started sliding smoothly on the thin layer of fresh snow towards the open end of the lake and the hills. Liftoff!

Bang!

Again? This was a different noise, not as sharp and brief as the first one.

We were just coming off the ice when the left ski rotated 90 degrees around the axis of the wheel, coming to rest vertically against the wing strut next to me. We had one ski horizontal, as it should be, and the other vertical, with its flat surface facing forward and acting like a giant air brake. We were airborne, with full power and takeoff flaps, but could hardly gain any speed or altitude.

Resupplying Terra Mines, near Great Bear Lake, with a Cessna 206.

Danny Pappas, the Gateway Aviation dock boy, de-icing an Otter wing in Yellowknife.

We were reaching open water at the other end of the lake, and the question was: do I shut down the engine, do some water-skiing across the end of the lake, and finish the run in the rocks and trees at the foot of the hill, or do I keep on going flat-out in the hope of climbing over the trees and the hill? I thought about it for a while and after carefully weighing the pros and cons I lost the option to land on the water. It was too late for that, so we continued going flat-out.

Another question soon came up: do I shut it down now and fly straight into the trees under control, or do I keep my fingers crossed and see if we can miss the treetops, at the risk of stalling and tumbling down?

While I was in deep thought, pondering the merits of each option, the trees were coming at us with great velocity, and the hill and rocks behind them. This stressed Danny, who suddenly screamed and leaned back, crossing both arms in front of his face. By then it was again too late to make a decision, so I did nothing and continued at full power.

Because of the engine roar and Danny's scream, I didn't hear the prop and the skis chopping off some treetops, but I'm sure they did. This brush with the trees did not affect the (poor) flying characteristics of the plane: at about 80 mph, with the nose up, full power, and some flaps, we continued straight on and entered the clouds. I dropped the nose to try to gain a little speed. A few minutes later, when I was sure we had cleared the hills, we slowly turned towards Yellowknife on the gyrocompass.

We obviously could not feel our way down between the hills to return to the mine; we simply had to continue in the clouds and try to reach Yellowknife. It was quite cold outside, so I was not worried about freezing on the wings, but I rapidly became concerned about our speed. We were managing only 90 mph at cruising power, rather than the traditional 120 mph with skis. The return trip would take over three hours, and I didn't believe we had enough fuel.

By now Danny was feeling better. His face was red and his eyes wide open. He smiled. "Gee! That was close!"

"Yes! Sometimes it does get very close. This is why it is important to enjoy each flight while it lasts."

He shook his head in disbelief.

The flight continued without any difficulty except for our very slow speed: we were still staggering along at barely 90 mph. After an hour and a half we emerged out of the low clouds, and I could find out where we were. Only about 20 miles off-course, not too bad. We corrected the heading back to a direct flight toward Yellowknife. An hour later we could finally pick up the Yellowknife radio beacon. Nice: our radio compass would show us the way. But the gas gauges were now showing very low levels, perhaps 20 percent of capacity or less. Danny was happy and relaxed, and I was increasingly worried.

It was getting dark, but navigation was still easy because of the contrast of white lakes against the black spruce trees and the pull from the Yellowknife radio beacon.

When we had flown nearly three hours and had about half an hour to go, I called the Yellowknife airport on high-frequency radio. "Yellowknife radio, this is Cessna 180 CF-JWT. We are about 35 miles north, inbound from Terra Mines, with the left ski in the upright position. Our speed is quite reduced and we might run out of fuel. Please remain on standby."

"JWT, roger. Good luck! Standing by."

I checked the fuel gages: they were at zero, but I could get them moving halfway across the dial by kicking the rudder pedals. This meant there was still fuel left in the tank. But ten minutes later the needles hardly moved when I kicked the rudder; a moment after that they no longer moved at all, no matter how hard I kicked the rudder pedals. The engine was going to quit at any minute.

"Yellowknife radio, JWT, we are now running on fumes. I will let you know when the engine quits. We are about 10 miles north."

I could see the lights of the town in the distance. I headed straight for the middle of the airport without worrying about any runway or joining the official circuit for planes lining up to land. Five miles to go. I was keeping my altitude. I would be really mad if the engine quit now!

"Yellowknife, JWT, if we can reach the airport, we will be making a straight-in approach, landing on the snow parallel to the runway."

"Roger, JWT. The fire truck is on its way. Hang tough!"

As we came in over the snow, not far from a runway, the fire truck was rushing along with us. The heel of the ski touched first, which put it back in the horizontal position, and we finished the landing nicely, just off the runway.

I stopped the engine, then climbed out and went to thank the firemen before walking back to check the airplane. I discovered that

Yellowknife airport terminal and control tower.

Yellowknife airport.

the rear cable holding up the back of the left ski to keep it horizontal had caught on a piece of mine equipment during landing and snapped, allowing the back of the ski to drop down after takeoff, while the front was pushed up by the air flow. The cable hanging from the fuselage had fallen back into place on the ski when I checked it at the mine, so I never noticed the break.

I got back into the plane, moved it over to the runway, raised the skis, and started taxiing towards the control tower. It was a triumphant arrival, like a presidential motorcade: the big fire truck was following us with all lights flashing, and I felt terribly important. In the dark I couldn't see the crowds cheering, but I was sure they were there.

In the tower I shook a few hands, thanked the men for their encouragements and support during the approach, and closed my Flight Notification. I returned to the plane to move it to the parking lot, but no matter how I tried, the engine would not start. We had totally run out of gas—not a drop left. We pushed the Cessna by hand across the tarmac to the parking lot, and I invited Danny to the bar for a stiff drink. He told me he would never fly with me again, but he did.

2. Prospectors, Alcohol and Fights in Yellowknife

Yellowknife, in 1966, was a small mining town at the end of a two-day drive on a gravel road of 900 miles from Edmonton. The Mackenzie River had to be crossed by ferry, or on the ice during winter. That spring, a truck taking wine and spirits to the government liquor store had fallen through the ice and sunk. The fish, it was said, were in an advanced state of intoxication, swimming around in circles and upside down—they had the hiccups and were making bubbles.

The town itself was built on solid ground. Founded in the 1930s, it had developed on a rocky plateau at the end of a bay on the north shore of Great Slave Lake. Soil was scarce and the few trees were mostly stunted spruce and birch that had managed to slide their roots through the cracks of the rocky landscape. Moraines and large polished rocks scattered across the countryside were remnants of the Ice Age. The rock was pink and grey, veined with white quartz. Dynamite was the only way to carve out a few sections of road. Between the rocks were lakes, an endless series of small lakes stretching to the horizon.

When I arrived, the Northwest Territories government was

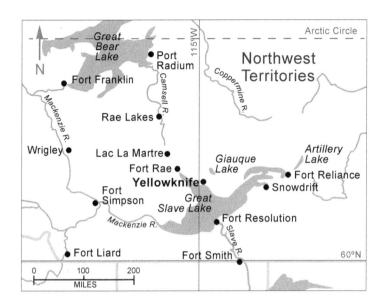

building a new prison in Yellowknife to cool down unpredictable and irrational hotheads. Stanton Hospital had burned to the ground on May 22. Only ashes remained, so patients had to be flown to Edmonton. The main street was now paved and lined with real sidewalks.

Yellowknife in 1967.

Yellowknife officially became the capital of the Northwest Territories in September 1967 and gradually lost its northern "bush town" charm. Concrete buildings were erected to house offices and apartments, and a traffic light was even set up at the main intersection—the first sign of an advanced civilization. Pedestrians and snowmobilers completely ignored it, but taxis and trucks did slow down a little. Four months earlier, the entire government council team had arrived from Ottawa in a DC-7, led by the new Commissioner, Stuart Hodgson, and his deputy, John Parker. Until this great leap forward, Yellowknife had been almost exclusively a mining town.

Gateway Aviation crew at the float base in front of a Beech 18 on floats. From left to right: Ed Logozar, pilot; Danny Pappas, dock boy; a seasonal pilot; and pilots Cedric Mah, Dominique Prinet, and Paul Weston.

The community was a hub at the end of the road, the last stop before the Arctic. To travel farther north one had to take a plane, either from the airfield with two runways, where men like Bob Engle (NWT Air), Bob O'Connor, Don Burnett, and Duncan Grant flew with airplanes on wheels, or from the protected bay, where companies like Ptarmigan Airways (Chuck and Jimmy McAvoy, Bill Hettrick, Clem Beckham), Northward Aviation (Dunc Matheson, Paul and Bryan Hagedorn), Gateway Aviation (John Daykin, Bob Warnock, John Langdon, Ed Logozar), and Wardair (Max Ward) were based with ski planes or floatplanes, depending on the season.

In Yellowknife, alcohol flowed freely, at least for the adults of European origin and during the days and hours when the bars were open. The locals, especially in winter, were often "half seas over," as good Father René Fumoleau liked to say. Then again, winter in Yellowknife was horrific. It was dark almost all the time, and the temperature hovered around −40° F. Fortunately, the wind did not rise too often. The previous year, a man had died when his car broke down on the outskirts of the city and the cold got him before he could reach the first house. One of my neighbours, too, was caught by the cold and died outside his door on his way home from a friend's house. A third man, who was returning from the bar late at night, was found stiff the next morning, his head stuck to the sidewalk.

The Yellowknife Inn and its saloon were located on Franklin Avenue, the main street, in the town centre. On one side of the street were the post office; YK Foods, a grocery store that sold vegetables brought in by plane; a small cinema; and a pelt, moccasin, parka, and snowshoe merchant. A block farther along, Didi Woolgar sold very nice memorabilia, mostly artifacts made in the North. On the other side of the street was the studio of photographer Gerry Reiman, along with another hotel, a motel, a travel agent, a small hardware store run by Peter Bromley, and the Hudson's Bay Company store, which sold a bit of everything. That was where I bought my rifle, a .303 Lee-Enfield from World War II. The HBC sold rifles of all types and calibers displayed between the umbrellas and the brooms, no questions asked. Explorers and adventurers heading north would come to this Hudson's Bay store to gear up. A block south was another small hardware store run by Walter England, the coroner who conducted the investigation when my colleague Marten Hartwell crashed during the winter of 1972 in one of Gateway Aviation's Beech 18s that I used to fly. Marten was found after a month-long search.

The small cinema was equipped with a soundproofed room for young mothers and their babies. When people were not at the bar,

Franklin Avenue, downtown Yellowknife.

they would go to see a film. Television only ran for four hours in the evening, showing programs recorded on tape and broadcast locally one or two days after they aired in the South—the time it took to get them to Yellowknife by plane. When people went to see a film in the winter, they sometimes left their car engine running for two hours—for comfort and to be sure they would be able to open the door. For longer stops during the day, you had to start up your car and run it for a while every three or four hours, or you were guaranteed to have to walk home.

One of the other Gateway Aviation pilots rented a room that turned out to be just above the screen of the cinema and slightly to the front of it. He told us that there was a small gap around the drainpipe of the bathroom sink, such that he could watch the films from above by lying on the floor, his head under the sink next to the toilet. He never invited us, as there was only room for one eye.

On Franklin Avenue, the main attraction was the Yellowknife Inn. The hotel was usually full. The rooms were comfortable, with hot and cold running water, double-glazed windows, and en-suite bathrooms but, of course, no television. As in most hotels, the carpets were made of nylon fibre, but the problem in Yellowknife was that because the air was so dry all year round, especially in winter, un-suspecting travelers would get a nasty shock, literally, every time they touched a metal door handle. It was easy to avoid the electric shock by grounding yourself—all you had to do was wear a small metal bracelet around your wrist and systematically discharge it using the back of your hand when you approached the knob—but it took a while for visitors and newcomers to get the hang of this.

On the ground floor of the Yellowknife Inn was a large dining room where guests dined by candlelight. A huge polar bear skin—a good 10 feet long—adorned one of the walls. In the next room was a bar and restaurant, very simple in style. This was where men got together: trappers, gold miners and other prospectors, civil servants, First Nations men, adventurers, miners, and the pilots of the five or six local airlines based in the bay. In a corner of the hotel, an Italian hairdresser had set up shop. The hotel was a whole world in itself, in the heart of the town.

Alcohol consumption was tightly regulated, to the extent of almost discouraging one from drinking. Naturally, we could not buy any alcohol at all, not even a glass of beer, on the Lord's Day. Not only were underage youngsters not allowed to drink, but we were not allowed to drink in their presence. A driver caught carrying an open beer crate in his car, even if all the bottles were still unopened, was liable to extremely harsh fines. Alcohol purchased from the liquor store had to be taken home via the most direct route, and the packaging had to remain untouched. I was once arrested driving an old second-hand car that I had just bought. The police searched the car and lifted all the carpets. One of the officers found three rusty beer caps under a seat. "Aha! You have been transporting alcohol and drinking it in your car! Follow me!" At the police station, it took me forever to get them to accept that, as a pilot, I only drank milk and orange juice. All these restrictions were the delight of taxi drivers, a number of whom illegally sold wine and beer to underage people or on Sundays.

Tom Doornbos, water carrier in Yellowknife, as shown on a 1966 postcard. Photo Fran Hurcomb.

It was on Franklin Avenue that I first met Tom Doornbos, Yellowknife's former water delivery man. He was almost 80 years old but walked fast and stood very upright. At the time, there were even postcards for sale that depicted him carrying a wooden yoke with a bucket of water hanging from each end. He baffled me one day by reciting French poetry. Tom died much later, formidably wealthy not because he had made a lot of money at 25 cents a bucket of water, but because he had lived like a pauper, spending virtually nothing. It was said that at the restaurant, instead of ordering a bowl of soup, he would ask for a bowl of hot water, which was free, and then pour the contents of the bottle of ketchup, placed on each table with the salt and pepper, into the hot water. He owned 13 building plots in the old town at the time of his death.

ʳeal men, the ᴍen who were _. ᴜothing, chased women, smoked a lot, and drank even more—in other words, the bush pilots, the miners, the construction workers, and the truck drivers—would get together two blocks away at the Gold Range Cafe bar. It was much bigger than the Yellowknife Inn saloon, yet

The Gold Range Hotel and Cafe. Photo Jewish Archives, Edmonton.

it was always difficult to find a free chair. That was where people talked caribou, moose, and beaver, or gold, silver, and copper ore. Pilots discussed engine failures, wing icing, and pontoons punctured on rocks.

The waitress, "Squeak," was an imposing woman on whose toes you had to be very careful not to tread. She would start off by going around to the tables of her favourite regulars, the pilots, with a large empty tray, where each of us had to deposit his knife. We all had a serious dagger on our belts to open oil cans, to pop the waterproof caps off the 45-gallon fuel barrels, and, above all, to cut, from the cockpit, the last rope attached to the strut and holding the plane when there was not enough room for takeoff and we had to shoot up at full throttle.

At the Gold Range, collecting the knives was a safety precaution: virtually every night, alcohol would fire up the patrons' hearts and minds, and brawls would break out. Fists would be swinging without anyone really knowing why. The only rule was: No standing up when throwing chairs, bottles, glasses, or ashtrays. Order was usually restored a few minutes later, but things did sometimes get a little out of hand, and the manager, with the help of Squeak and a few brawny men, would throw everyone out onto the curb in the dark in –40° F weather. Since most of the time the patrons were in shirt sleeves, the thirst to fight would quickly die down and everyone would sober up in no time. After that, we all would head back into the bar to order a new round and carry on with the serious discussions.

One winter evening I passed by the Gold Range and noticed a crowd gathered. A man was lying on the ground in his shirt, moaning a little but motionless. Most people were stepping over or walking around him, but two or three good Samaritans thought that the poor man would probably be better off spending the night somewhere else. Eventually a taxi driver offered to take him to Stanton Hospital (that was before it burned down). Several men bent to lift him up, but he was already partially frozen to the sidewalk, and a piece of his ear stayed behind.

Yellowknife was primarily known for its gold ore. When they were not at the bar, the men worked at the mines. Con Mine and Giant Mine, on the edge of the city, operated day and night. The third mine, Discovery, was located a little farther north.

The team rotations at Con and Giant, every eight hours, were the delight of taxi drivers, as Duncan Pryde once explained to me when he was driving taxis before becoming a Member of the Legislative Assembly. "When the siren sounds the team rotation in one mine or the other, the town goes into a frenzy and, for an hour, the drivers are completely overwhelmed. Once the husbands have left with the family car to go to the mine and spend eight hours underground, the wives and their admirers rush to each other's homes—by taxi, of course. A few hours later, before the siren rings again, everybody

Giant Mine, Yellowknife. The left branch (with a car) leads to the end of the one-thousand-mile gravel road from Edmonton, at a dead end some 30 miles farther north in the bush.

goes home, still in a taxi, and everyone is happy. After the siren, the whole dance starts again."

The mischievous Bob Olexin, a local taxi company owner who dabbled in many ventures and knew everyone, was the conductor, masterfully directing his team of drivers. Between mine shift changes, during his taxi trips with prospectors, he was known for trying to extract as much information as possible on claims and hot prospects, mineral deposits, and quartz veins containing specks of gold.

Long tunnels had been dug under the three mines, to a depth of several hundred feet, along the quartz veins that sometimes extended under Great Slave Lake. The gold was invisible, even under a magnifying glass. Sometimes a microscopic grain would sparkle in the sun, but most of the time it was a speck of iron pyrite ("fool's gold"). The gold ore around Yellowknife was among the richest in North America, but the government had to subsidize some of the gold mines due to the huge operating costs, and several small mines, lost in the rocks 50 to 100 miles from Yellowknife, had to shut down. All the machinery had to be airlifted by floatplanes and winched across the rocks, tons at a time. As for the ore, if opening a road proved impossible, it had to be flown to town by floatplanes. Over the years I carried dozens of tons of ore in small bags, wondering every time if I should not simply fly off with my load and head to sunny beaches lined with coconut trees, to lie on the fine sand surrounded by charming, half-naked young women wearing flower necklaces.

In 1954, Tony Gregson, one of the men working at Discovery Mine, had the same fantasy. Rather than just dreaming about it like the rest of us, however, he put his plan into action—the sign of a strong character and proof of undeniable boldness. Tony decided to steal ingots, or gold bars, rather than bags of concentrated ore, which made things easier. He quit the mine on a Friday and was flown to Yellowknife on Max Ward's

Discovery Mine. Photo Discovery Mine.

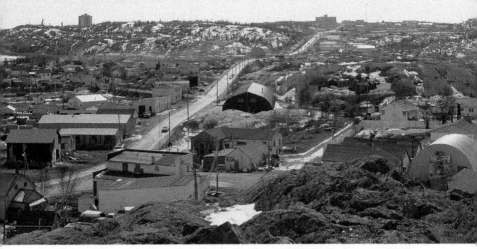

The continuation of Franklin Avenue, linking downtown (Yellowknife Inn) to the Old Town (float base).

Otter on floats, which also carried the mail bags that contained the gold bars. During the flight, Tony discreetly opened the mail bag, replaced two gold bars with two bars of lead, and closed the mail bag again. Nobody noticed until Monday, by which time Tony had chartered a Beaver to Hay River and taken a bus south. Unfortunately for him, three years later he was caught in Australia for having boarded a ship without a ticket.

Not all gold heists occurred in Yellowknife. The robbery of the century took place on March 1, 1966, a little farther east: an Air Canada truck that Ken Leishman and three partners had stolen at Winnipeg Airport was waiting for the plane from Red Lake, northern Ontario, which was loaded with gold from the local mine. The plane landed and the police, always ready to serve, set their machine guns down and kindly helped with the loading of the truck. Ken and his partners, in Air Canada coveralls, happily traded jokes with them, and soon the truck was full and the seals were in place. The men warmly thanked the police for their help, signed the receipts, and quietly disappeared with the truck. They abandoned it shortly thereafter but forgot to clean off their fingerprints and were behind bars within three weeks.

The Yellowknife gold did not always disappear. One summer a truck carrying several tons of gold bullion broke down at the side of the gravel road from Yellowknife to Edmonton and remained stuck there for 24 hours. The truck driver, a good man, did not utter a word to his friends, and the next day, when he came back to repair his truck, the gold was still there.

Exploration for new mining sites went on every summer. In June the ice would melt in the bay and the planes would switch from skis to floats. In early July the intense shuttling of gold diggers and other prospectors, back and forth from the town to the land, would start again. The sun barely set; it grazed the horizon and promptly rose again. Pilots worked 24 hours a day, seven days a week. We would try to catch a nap of 20 minutes here and there, perhaps 45 minutes during a stopover or while on a flight, when a mechanic was refueling or when we could hand over control to a passenger. We lived off sandwiches, smoked fish, and pieces of dried caribou meat. Sometimes, when we returned to base for a few hours after a week or two in the forest and the tundra, we would have time for a shirt change, a shave, and occasionally even some sleep. But soon the phone would ring and we would have to head out again.

Prospectors around Yellowknife spoke little and remained extremely discreet. Sometimes private individuals would rent a plane, at their own expense, and ask the pilot to drop them off on a lake 100, 200, or 500 miles north or east of Yellowknife. They would be picked up a few weeks or months later, provided they had not been forgotten, and would come back loaded with rock samples, their eyes glimmering with hope. They dressed like tramps, spent fortunes on drilling equipment and air travel, occasionally found a bit of gold or silver, and would sell their claims to mining companies after having rented them from the

Picking up a prospector forgotten for two weeks.

"All aboard!" Two uranium prospectors happy to go home.

government for a pittance during the exploration phase. Then they would start looking again somewhere else. They spent 5, 10, or 20 years looking for ore, digging up the rock with dynamite.

That was how, in 1944, Fred Giauque, one of the old prospectors, discovered the deposit that led to the 1950 construction of Discovery Mine, on the edge of Giauque Lake, not far north of Yellowknife. Max Ward brought the first ingots to Yellowknife by floatplane, and I took the last ones out in an Otter on floats in 1969. In the meantime, I flew several times with Fred Giauque, who carried on looking for gold veins.

The author at 27 by one of the Otters in Yellowknife.

But most of these tough men were employed by mining companies that rented planes for them, provided them with drilling equipment and explosives, housed and fed them, and dispatched them throughout the Northwest Territories. For example, I often transported drillers, prospectors, and geologists from Precambrian Mining Services Limited (PMSL) and Titan Drilling, men like Pat Parker, Shorty Brown, Bill Knutzen, Earl Curry, Smoky Hornby, and Dave Nickerson.

Flights with prospectors were always conducted under a cloak of mystery. When one of them asked for a plane, you had to worm the information necessary for the flight out of them.

"I'd like a Beaver for tomorrow morning. Takeoff at 4 a.m."

"How much gasoline?" The question is important because you had to choose between fuel or load; you could not get both.

"Prepare the plane for a 400-mile flight."

"Each way?"

"No, round trip."

"Where are we going?"

"I'll show you on the map once we're in the air."

"Okay, see you tomorrow."

The load was a perpetual problem: in a small Cessna 180, for example, a prospector would always try to cram in a load that would fit a lot more easily in the larger Beaver, much to the despair of the pilot, who spent his time pulling his hair out. Prospectors always had to bring at least eight days' worth of supplies, a tent, two or three rifles, pikes and pickaxes, gas-powered drills and other pneumatic equipment, detonators, and one or two cases of dynamite. Once, on the small landing strip at Fort Simpson, I had left the prospectors to load the plane, a Beaver on skis. When I came back, they had put their snowmobile right across the cabin because it did not fit length-wise. It stuck out two feet on either side, holding the aircraft doors wide open.

"What is this?" I said. "You can't be serious! Look at this contraption. It will never get off the ground with the two doors open at a right angle!"

For a moment I thought of simply removing the doors to reduce the drag, but I still did not believe it would fly, so we left the snowmobile behind.

Loading was easier on the water: we would fill the floatplane until it was about to sink, then try to take off. An overloaded float-plane simply could not get off the water, which was not very serious. Some birds had the same problem when they had eaten too much. Often, taking off with a floatplane making a lot of noise, I would see pelicans, geese, or wild ducks pedaling furiously on the water in front of us, trying to escape before the plane. They would frantically flap their wings, their muscles tense and their necks long, without being able to get airborne. Eventually they would dive below the surface as the floatplane caught up with them.

Other birds occasionally had problems with their landings, espe-cially on a smooth water surface flat as a mirror. I once saw a young seagull on final approach on a calm body of water, undercarriage down, 10 degrees of flaps ... adding a little power to further reduce the impact ... But it had misjudged its height, stalled about two feet above the surface, and nosed over into clear water right on its back before getting up, highly embarrassed and blushing with shame.

In the line of birds learning to fly, I must add the story of a baby crow that, not yet having understood that it should take off and land into the wind, arrived far too quickly downwind on the ground and cartwheeled on landing.

Anyway, one morning I was flying old Fred Giauque, who was returning to his island. It was an easy flight, barely one hour long. All his life he had been looking for ore, but a few days earlier he had discovered cobalt. We landed near a high and narrow rocky islet. I

Prospectors' camp 300 miles northeast of Yellowknife.

wondered how he had gotten there and by what incredible stroke of luck he had stumbled upon this vein, so far from any town, in the middle of the forest. But the cobalt was there, and he wanted to show it to me. Behind that rock? Over here? Nothing. Yet ... he had definitely seen that cobalt. And he knew this island like the back of his hand. It was positively this one.

For two hours we looked for the stones that supposedly bore traces of explosive. The man became worried, even afraid. He was overcome with anxiety. Surely he had not dreamt it? We carried on searching.

At last, come evening, he found the vein behind a rock. It was high-concentration cobalt. He broke off pieces feverishly. Jubilant, he gave me samples and patted me on the shoulder. The vein was narrow but sank deep underground. Maybe enough for a mine.

All Fred had to do was rent the plots of land on the island around the vein from the government and plant stakes to delimit his claims. He would then sell the land to a mining company at a very high price. Of course, I could have rushed to the government office before him and rented the land myself. But pilots did not do that: it

At the camp of prospector Fred Giauque with a Cessna 206.

was an unwritten law among us. Likewise, a pilot would never say where he had dropped off prospectors. He would pin the location on the wall map in his company's office, writing only a number on the small label attached. The details were recorded in a book under lock and key. On the map, pilots also marked the location of the few fuel barrels they dropped off by a lake for emergencies whenever the opportunity arose, without specifying what was there for fear that another pilot running out of fuel might use their reserve.

Gradually, especially farther north and east of Yellowknife, every pilot became familiar with the subsoil resources. It was easy to make friends with the prospectors we dropped off and picked up: they were solitary men, often withdrawn and silent but happy to discuss business with someone working with them. We helped them load and unload their gear. We also collected rock samples with them and, together, examined them before takeoff, feeling their weight and stroking them. There were traces of copper in that one. In this quartz, perhaps a few milligrams of invisible gold. You could see a trickle of silver mixed with lead in this vein. The secret was safe with the pilot.

Later, after analyzing the samples, the prospector would return to drop off some gear and a few men. Perhaps a week later, a well-dressed gentleman, probably a geologist, would be dropped off to examine the site. The plane would then head back loaded with ore. We always worked in absolute secrecy. Then, typically the following summer, the pilot would have to transport heavier gear, particularly diesel drills and hundreds of feet of steel pipes. That was when it was time to buy shares, because nobody knew yet. But rumours would soon start to spread, the frenzy would begin, and prices would rise. It was a way to make a fortune. John, one of my colleagues in Yellowknife, made $7,000 in two weeks one year. He had witnessed the discovery of a copper vein and bought a few shares. It helped make ends meet.

Once I spent a day on the tundra with a geologist who had gone to examine the terrain and carefully study the rock cores extracted from the boreholes. He started opening up to me, explaining how some clever scammers occasionally managed to benefit even more from these mineral discoveries and make a lot of money quickly and effortlessly, which was exactly what I was interested in. According

Prospectors' camp near the Arctic coast.

to the geologist, once you had dug a hole in the tundra and come across a quartz vein containing gold, you would start off by issuing and holding shares that were still "penny stock," worth nothing. Then you would announce the discovery of gold so the price of the shares would shoot up. Later, in the following season or summer, you would return to the same place and dig a second hole, a little farther away but very carefully inclined toward the original vein. Surprise, surprise, you would hit gold again. Share prices would rise even more. Then you would drill yet another hole at a third point, still slightly inclined in the right direction, and you would find even more gold. Prices would soar. Every time, the gold content would be officially verified by a laboratory, and the geologist would show an enthusiastic crowd the exact location, on a detailed geological map, where each borehole had been drilled and the depth of the ore. All this was very official and serious, and prices would shoot up. You would then sell your shares and go dig more holes somewhere else to start over.

All this was more profitable and fun than working a 9 to 5 job, and better at getting the adrenaline going.

3. Picking up Trappers and School Kids in Fort Smith

Fort Smith, May 1966.

The supply barge from the south traveled down the Slave River as far as Fort Fitzgerald (formerly known as Smith's Landing; eight residents at last count), upstream of the four impassable rapids now bypassed by a 15-mile portage to Fort Smith.

The most famous rapid is the "Rapids of the Drowned," where five men perished in 1786. They were part of the Cuthbert Grant expedition, which had set out to establish a trading post on Great Slave Lake. A little farther south, on Lake Athabasca, the winter had been harsh and they hadn't managed to catch enough fish or game, so they had few supplies with them. The explorers traveled in 25-foot canoes; the guides had smaller ones.

Hearing the roar of the rapids, Grant sent a small canoe along the riverbank to see if they were passable: the guides were to fire two gunshots to signal that it was safe. The rapids turned out to be very dangerous, and the guides, firing no shots, sat on a rock and smoked their pipes as they waited for their colleagues, who would have to pass the rapids on foot, towing their canoes with long ropes

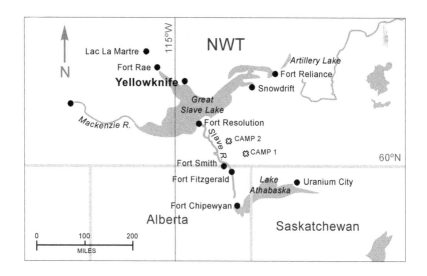

from the riverbank. But the guides were hungry, and when they saw wild ducks on a quiet stretch of water at the foot of the rapids, they couldn't resist shooting them. Hearing the agreed signal, the explorers promptly pushed their canoes into the water, only for two of them to crash into the rocks and capsize in the whirlpool.

The Pelican Rapids of the Slave River at Fort Smith.

The author changing an engine at Fort Smith airport.

The "Fitzgerald" of Fort Fitzgerald, at the southern end of the portage, was a Mountie at Fort McPherson, near Inuvik. On December 21, 1910, he set out by sled with three colleagues to reach Dawson City, 450 miles away. They spent nine days trying to find their way through the Richardson Mountains before turning back. The last note they wrote was dated February 5, 1911. The remains of the "Lost Patrol" were found in March, and this story became Yukon legend, along with the tale of the "Mad Trapper of Rat River," who was eventually caught and shot in February 1932, despite turning his snowshoes front to back to fool his pursuers.

As for the "Smith" of Fort Smith, at the northern end of the portage, that was Donald Smith, an extraordinary man. Born in Scotland, he became administrator of the Northwest Territories in 1870 when they included what are now the provinces of Alberta and Saskatchewan, and much of northern Manitoba, Ontario, and Quebec. He was appointed president of the Bank of Montreal in 1887, helped create the trans-Canada Canadian Pacific Railway, became governor of the Hudson's Bay Company and chancellor of McGill University in 1889, and founded the major Montreal hospital, the Royal Victoria, opened in 1893.

From the small town of Fort Smith (population 2,000), it was an easy journey on the Slave River to Great Slave Lake, and then to the Arctic coast down the Mackenzie River.

Every spring, the people of Fort Smith bet on the date when the ice in the river would break up. One morning, the stick of dynamite placed in an old 45-gallon barrel on the river ice by the edge of the town, connected to the shore by a wire attached to a detonator, would explode, warning all the inhabitants that the ice had given way.

When that long snake of ice disappeared, and the Slave River carried only a few blocks of ice, the town came to life. At night, beer from the supply barge once again flowed from the taps of the saloon, the main bar at the local hotel, where First Nations trappers and gold miners told of their hunting adventures and gold nuggets.

In the late '60s, the North was booming because of enormous mineral and natural gas potential. There were no roads, and people could only travel by small planes on floats or skis. Local private airlines started in many communities with Cessna 180s, 185s, and 206s, as well as De Havilland Beavers and Single Otters (these are single-engine Otters, but they were usually called Single Otters or just Otters to differentiate them from the Twin Otters). Larger carriers from the South established their own bases in the bigger settlements. Competition was fierce, and each carrier bragged about flying "bigger loads in worse weather."

Gateway Aviation had a floatplane base at Fort Smith. The

The dock boy at Fort Smith trying to recover the top half of the engine cowling which was dropped by the mechanic and carried away by the Slave River.

competition was Gordy Pascal (Northward Aviation), along with a few private floatplanes like those owned by Bob Gauchie (Northern Mountain), who made headlines around the world in 1967 when my colleague Ron Sheardown found him in the tundra with his Beaver on skis, after he'd endured 58 days of winter. Bob subsequently started Buffalo Airways, which Joe McBryan later bought and turned into the world's largest DC-3 and DC-4 airline, based in Yellowknife and flying throughout the Arctic and often beyond.

One year I was working at Gateway's Fort Smith base, one of two young pilots, about 25 years old, flying out of the base with the assistance of a mechanic and a boy at the docks. The manager, Paul Slager, handled sales and paperwork. Pilots were paid three cents per mile on the small airplanes like the Cessna 180, measured in a straight line, four cents on the bigger ones, and five cents on the ones with 10 passengers, like the Otter and the Beech 18. We also had a small base pay, but this meant we had to fly in all weather conditions.

When the ice went out of the river, we saw two young First Nations people on the opposite bank, lighting a fire. They'd been caught out by the thaw and couldn't make their way back. We went to pick them up by boat, and they told us their story: "25 miles northwest of here, Joe Mabillon needs a plane to get home. He has six dogs and a sled."

Back at the small Gateway Aviation cabin on the river, I told my colleague Joe McBryan about the situation. Joe was a cheerful lad from the village. "Why don't you go?" he said to me. "I'll take the next flight."

I jumped into the Cessna 180 on floats, CF-JWK, and promptly took off.

There were lakes absolutely everywhere. Where was the trapper? On this one maybe? I landed—no one. I glided on the step around the edge of the lake, the water spraying gently on either side of the floats. Nothing. I took off again. The old trapper should be around here ... "Hang on, is this it?" I landed again. It was just an old piece of fabric on a rock near the water, a piece of tent. No dogs, no trapper. The remains of a camp, no doubt, perhaps ravaged by wolves or a hungry bear in the spring? "Hello?" No reply. I glided to the centre of the lake, stopped the plane, climbed up on the wing, and fired a gunshot in the air. Only the echo replied. I took off again.

"Fort Smith, JWK, do you have any further details on the trapper's position?"

"Negative," Joe McBryan replied.

I tried another lake: same story. Still nothing.

While the aircraft was speedily gliding over the water on the step of the pontoons, it suddenly took a nosedive. The tail rose, the aircraft hovered for a moment and then fell back heavily into the water. I was 1,500 feet from shore, and the plane had just grounded in the mud.

Neither the oar nor the engine could get it to move. I called Fort Smith, no answer. It's pretty lonely in the middle of a lake! I jumped into the water, sinking and slipping in the mud. Using the oar as a lever, I dug around the plane for over an hour. Finally the aircraft moved a little, pivoted, and escaped the trap.

I was off, flying now along a thin stream scattered with waterfalls, almost between the trees, looking for a clue. Two miles farther, I spotted a canoe on the ground, upside down under the spruce trees. A few minutes later, there was my trapper by the edge of a clearing, lighting a fire near his sled that the dogs had pulled on the mud. He was setting up camp for the night.

Trapper Billy Berhens packing up his beaver hides to go home (Fort Smith).

"Fort Smith, from JWK: trapper found. Should be back tomorrow evening."

It had taken three hours of flying to find him.

Later I went to pick up another trapper, Billy Berhens, a man with a face worn by the wind, sun, and snow. He was a force of nature, pure muscle. Joe McBryan had dropped him off by a lake two months earlier, on skis. When I landed, he was taking down his large khaki tent with the roof pierced by the stove's chimney. He slept on a mattress on the floor, between half a dozen guns and a pile of beaver pelts. More pelts were drying in the sun in front of his tent, stretched with intricate peripheral lacing at the centre of a loop made from a branch folded back on itself. He was bringing back over a hundred pelts, worth enough for him to live off the sales for a year.

Billy's nine dogs were chained to nearby trees, their howling and barking deafening—they had heard the plane and wanted to go back to town. Billy threw them a bucket of fish and hauled his canoe up into a tree, out of the reach of bears.

We left the dogs and loaded the pelts, his sleeping bag, axes, about 20 traps, and two rifles. The plane was too heavy; we edged through a narrow gorge, dropped back into the water, bounced up again and narrowly missed a spruce tree, struggling to gain altitude.

"See that cabin over there?" Billy pointed. "That's my second camp. Let's go check it out."

The bears had been there: the ceiling was ripped open, the door torn off ... the whole place was a shambles. Outside, up on piles 10 feet off the ground, supposedly out of the bears' reach, a large rolled-up tent, tightly fastened with ropes, hung in tatters, shredded. Billy was not happy: "I'd love to know how the bears managed to get up there."

We set off back to Fort Smith.

"I'm going to need you to take some boards to the second camp for me. I have to rebuild my cabin. After that, you can go back to my first camp and bring the dogs home. Watch it, they're strong. Best if I went with you."

We loaded the plane, the floats now covered with the boards fastened with ropes—no way this thing would fly! At full throttle we set off down the Slave River. Water splattered on the boards, covering the floats and flooding the windshield. I wrestled with the aircraft as it dragged along in the water . . .

"Sorry, Billy, the plane is too heavy, I can't take you. You're going to have to get off!"

I took off with only the boards. If the front rope broke, the boards, held from the rear, would fan out and act as a giant air brake, and the plane would fall out of the sky. I remembered the sound advice of my aerobatics instructor in a Stampe, an open-cabin biplane. Pointing at the parachute handle on my chest, he explained its use: "If you

Boards on a Cessna 180 to repair a trapper's cabin damaged by bears.

fall off the plane when we fly upside down and start going down too fast towards the ground, pull the red handle. It's a hand brake and will slow you down."

The plane unhurriedly rose above the spruce trees while I was keeping an eye on the rope holding the boards. There was the lake, and the cabin. I dropped off the boards and headed back for the dogs. They were raging! Yanking on their chains, they leapt around their trees. I wrapped a chain around my belly, tied it to the neck of one of the animals, and unleashed it from its tree. The others were howling. The first one dashed toward the plane, dragging me between the spruce branches. He leapt on the rock, jumped up on the float, and slipped right into the water. I had to pull 75 pounds of muscle out of there and haul it up into the plane. The dog shook himself off, flooding the cockpit, and started licking the windows. Eight more to go ...

At the end of the season, the dogs are even happier to go home (Fort Smith) than trapper Pi Kennedy.

The dogs, bundled haphazardly into the cabin, were shaking themselves off one by one. In their haste, they'd all fallen into the water. The cabin was dripping, and you couldn't see a thing with all the condensation on the windows. I took off, holding the side window ajar so I could look out. The animals were restless, licking my neck, sitting in the co-pilot seat. When we landed, there was a mad scramble and all the dogs disappeared.

Billy told me not to worry: they'd come back. "It's the same thing every time. When they get back from the bush, it takes two days for the dogs to be normal again."

The men too, actually: 48 hours of women and alcohol, and they're back to their old selves.

The trappers had all returned from the winter season. Now some were heading out again for the summer. Their pilot, upon their return, would leave a note on the company's calendar and pin a label to the large wall map. Many of the thousands of lakes in the region were not represented, and most that were had no name; only the pins told us where the men were. On the label was a date, the number of dogs, and the weight of the equipment they had with them so we would know which plane to use to bring them home.

A trapper, in the Fort Smith area, shot the bear which was stealing his fish.

Practising water-bombing on a rock in Yellowknife with an Otter. I once dropped one ton of water on an unsuspecting fellow paddling his canoe behind the rock.

One day our little waterfront office by the docks was left empty for a while. A kid walked in, marveled at the map, and conscientiously removed the coloured pins and their labels, one by one. Dozens of trappers and prospectors, scattered across thousands of square miles, had just lost their identities.

We got all the pilots together. Generally, only the pilot who'd dropped off a trapper or prospector on a rock would be able to find him. But try remembering where you left a customer three weeks ago: every pilot landed on a dozen lakes and rivers a day, and dropped off or picked up men all over the place. For eight days we tried to retrace the flights wiped off the map. We went around to the bar, interviewing friends, and we combed the forest. It seems we found everyone in the end; no one complained about having lost a friend or relative.

Aside from trappers and prospectors, we would also ferry oil exploration teams that set off dynamite along seismic lines; teams from a small local hydroelectric dam that needed maintenance; men from the Water Resources Department, who regularly monitored river flows; government workers from Indian and Northern Affairs;

and men or women who were visiting First Nation families in their camps, bringing them food, tools, or sometimes a little gas. And we would help fight fires.

During the summer of 1966, the weather was dry in Fort Smith, and thousands of hectares of forest were burning. Twin-engine Canadair floatplanes had spent days and weeks dropping phenomenal amounts of water around the fires. An opening in the fuselage allowed for the cargo hold to fill with water as the planes skimmed over a lake: they would land and glide on the water for about 10 seconds before taking off again, dropping their load over the fire and coming back for more. Often a small observation plane, the "bird-dog," would organize the ballet. The risks were high and the loaded planes had to be flown slowly.

Forest fires were always a wonderful source of income for float-plane pilots, who were paid by the mile and flew the firefighters and all their gear to the edge of each fire, with regular subsequent trips to bring additional men, gear, and food. Once fires near dwellings were under control, all the men and their gear had to be taken out of there, adding more miles of flying. Naturally, gossipmongers liked to say that, in the summer, pilots kept the cockpit window open and had a tendency to recklessly flick out their cigarette butts. Bush pilots retorted that the men on the ground were also receiving very attractive wages, and they were fed for several weeks by the Forestry Department. The pilots suggested that the fires could have been caused by First Nations men who smoked when they went hunting or didn't put out their camp fires properly. However, firefighting in the forest was harsh, tiring, dangerous work, and all these stories of fires set by acts of negligence on the ground or in the air were nothing more than malicious gossip and slander.

The seats were stripped out of the Beavers and Otters on floats so they could transport the firemen and their gear. Shovels, pickaxes, tents, food supplies, motor pumps, and pipes were piled up on the floor of the planes, and the First Nations men lay flat on top of the gear, just below the ceiling. Not exactly legal, but everyone turned a blind eye as long as there was no damage and nobody got hurt; the fires had to be put out somehow.

On my way back from a drop near a fire, I spotted three small smoke columns. A team was quickly put together. I dropped everyone

Chasing the buffaloes to a corral for vaccination against anthrax, Fort Smith area.

off in two trips and carried on with a Forestry manager to a third fire. We docked and unpacked the gear, unrolled the pipes, and started the pump. Three hours later, blackened from head to toe, eyes watering, half suffocated, I returned to the plane, sinking into the ash: this last fire was under control.

We took off to return to Fort Smith, flying over fires burning across a 200-mile radius. The turbulence was brutal and the plane difficult to control. The high-voltage line connecting the dam to the Pine Point mine cut right through the heart of the fire. The aluminium pylons, originally installed by helicopter, were melting and twisting, the insulators were cracking, and the mine was plunged into darkness.

Thousands of buffaloes fled the fire. Heavy, massive, black, their heads buried under a thick mane, they escaped the fire but were still vulnerable to anthrax. The previous year, hundreds of them had been shot from helicopters and the carcasses burned to prevent spread of the disease. That seemed to have curbed the outbreak, but now the animals had to be vaccinated. They were rounded up by airplanes. Grazing the trees, turning and twirling over the panicked buffaloes racing through the forest, we pushed two or three thousand of them toward a huge corral. Once they were caught, veterinarians let them out one by one, giving them their injection on the way. The operation went on for over a week.

Fast-forward to September. Classes were starting again soon, and the Indigenous children had to be taken to school by floatplane. Every 100 miles we landed near a camp or village, picked up two or three kids, and took them into town 10 at a time.

Often, when the plane docked near a camp, the parents would hesitate, debating what to do. The children had been with them through the summer, living off the land in tents, and the parents were reluctant to let them go. The kids didn't want to go either, especially the boys, who would hide in the woods when they heard the plane. They wanted to stay to help set traps and prepare the sleds for the winter. So we collected mostly girls for school, 10- to 18-year-olds in their Sunday best, with high heels, white gloves, and handbags. The boys were harder to find. One of them was in the bush fighting a fire, so the Department of Education sent a helicopter to pick him up and bring him to the floatplane.

Once the plane was full, I'd return to town and then head back for another 300- to 600-mile circuit of school pick-ups in the forest.

The operation went on for several days; all available planes were

Classroom in Snowdrift.

commandeered. Meanwhile, along the Arctic coast and on the islands near the pole, we'd pick up Inuit children to take them to school.[4] The buffaloes were vaccinated, the high-voltage line repaired, the forest fires put out, and the children were in school. The long night of winter was near, and the air was getting colder. Another month and the forest would be covered in snow, the lakes and rivers frozen. Trappers were getting their dogs ready, polishing their guns, and cleaning their traps. First Nations men were ready. The great winter adventure was about to begin again.

---

[4] The removal of First Nations and Inuit children from their communities and from their families to "educate" them in the south turned out to be a traumatic experience for tens of thousands of them, their parents, and their descendants. The children were forced into a totally different culture, living in residential schools where they were not allowed to use their own language, often ill-treated and, at times, abused. During the summer, they returned to traditional environments and a way of life which they perceived as primitive, causing conflicts within their own families. The federal government eventually tried to mitigate the damage and established a Truth and Reconciliation Commission in 2008.

4. Gold, Dead Bodies, and Airplane Crashes on the Nahanni River

Fort Simpson, June 1966, Cessna 206 on floats.

"You're going to Fort Liard? Right on time! We've got mail that's been waiting for over a month."

We picked up the five or six letters and took off from Fort Simpson on the Mackenzie River, west of Great Slave Lake.

The Water Resources Department, run from Fort Smith by Dave Fowler and represented on this trip by my two passengers Woody and Flash, was doing a floatplane tour in the northern Rocky Mountains, more commonly known as the Mackenzie Mountains, to measure river levels and flows. This painstaking work had to be done regularly throughout the Arctic to collect information for potential hydroelectric projects. It also allowed

Downtown Fort Simpson.

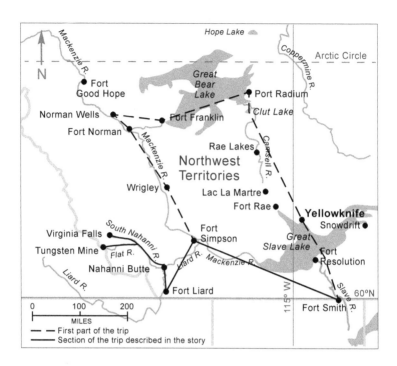

shipping companies to determine the maximum tonnage for barges going down the Mackenzie River to the Arctic coast, based on the current and depth of the water.

Our Cessna 206, CF-UEZ, was filled to the brim with over 800 pounds of gear: a rubber boat, an outboard motor, a fuel tank, two toolboxes, a winch, two anchors, sleeping bags, and food supplies. With three men on board and full tanks, the floatplane was most certainly overloaded—not a big deal for a single-engine aircraft, but you had to be aware of it.

Over eight days we had already traveled the whole northwest of Canada, from Fort Smith, south of Great Slave Lake, to Camsell River on the way to Great Bear Lake, then to Port Radium and Fort Franklin, respectively east and west of Great Bear Lake, and finally up the Mackenzie River, along the Mackenzie Mountains, to Fort Simpson in the south.

Fort Liard, a little farther south, had a Hudson's Bay Company trading post on the Liard River, a Royal Canadian Mounted Police cabin with two Mounties keeping the peace in the village, and a small chapel, next to which lived the priest. The nurse was also a social worker and lived on the edge of the village, not far from a couple of schoolteachers. The bulk of the population was First Nations families living off trapping, hunting, and fishing.

I went to say hello to Father Marie, a Parisian who had been living there for 10 years. Showing me around, he explained, "They have log houses, but they prefer living in tents in the summer."

When we were there in June, it was still broad daylight at 11 o'clock at night. The families sat in front of their tents, some tanning hides, others smoking fish. Altogether, the village was 1,000 feet long by 150 feet wide. A small path along the river connected all the houses to one another.

"The winters are harsh," said Father Marie. "For one or two months the temperature fluctuates between –20° F and –50° F. But things are getting better. A few years ago we'd hardly see more than one boat in the summer and three planes in the winter. Now we get mail almost every month. We even receive surprise visits. A while back a helicopter landed in front of the church—it had run out of gas. The pilot was a young Frenchman who'd just moved here and

Fort Liard, on the Liard River.

was completely lost. He flew along the river until he came across our hamlet."

I was about to undertake two spectacular flights from Fort Liard: one up the Flat River, and the other up the Nahanni, of which the Flat River is a tributary. These two rivers were home to most of the terrible stories going around the Northwest Territories. Back in Fort Smith, at base camp, one of my fellow pilots had warned me by showing me an article in *Weekend Magazine* about the Flat River: in late September 1958, five prospectors had been dropped off by a Wardair Otter at McMillan Lake. This is a very small lake near the source of the Flat River. The pilot was to come back for them five months later, in early March 1959, but the arrangements were somewhat vague. According to Max Ward, the president of Wardair, based in Yellowknife, who testified at the July 1959 investigation into the incident, all these arrangements had been made and changed several times at the bar, often late at night, and nothing was really definitive.

In the mountains, waiting to be picked up, the five men hunted

At Fort Smith, loading a Cessna 185 with gear for the Water Resources Department.

Brad Billings, with the Water Resources Department, adjusting his transit in Snowdrift.

a little and killed a few caribou. The dried meat would allow them to survive without any problem. However, in early January 1959, a federal conservation officer from Yellowknife showed up in a Pacific Western Airlines Otter on skis and seized half the caribou meat as a "sample." With him was Gus Kraus, a local trapper who lived in a cabin along the Nahanni River, not far from Nahanni Butte, and who knew the area well. A few days later, the same officer and Gus returned to McMillan Lake, this time accompanied by a Mountie who swiftly confiscated the rest of the caribou. By early March the five men had run out of supplies but expected to be picked up any day by the Wardair plane that never arrived.

On May 7, 1959, Chuck and Jimmy McAvoy, two Yellowknife pilots flying in the area for their own company, Ptarmigan Airways, came over in a Cessna 180 on skis, following the recommendations of the original Wardair pilot, who was surprised not to have seen his passengers in town for over seven months. On McMillan Lake, which was still frozen, they spotted an SOS sign made out of spruce tree branches and found two emaciated men, one of them severely traumatized. A third prospector had blown himself up with dynamite not far from there. The last two had tried to walk home, never to be seen again.

Coincidentally, tungsten had just been discovered nearby, and the conclusion of this whole episode was that there was enough tungsten there to open a mine. It was built in 1961 and began operations in 1962.

As for the Nahanni itself, a surprising number of horror stories surrounded it. The river had a reputation for not returning its pilots. Back in Fort Smith, when I told the good Mrs. Lacombe, my landlady, that I was heading to the Nahanni, she worried about my certain death and, more prosaically, about losing the regular income from her tenant. I was fond of Mrs. Lacombe; she was very kind and always cheerful. She was also rather plump, and whenever she sat down, she would first tuck her belly under the table and then lay her ample bosom on top. She had recently had a lot of pain in her side, and the doctor had given her medication for her very sick heart. It didn't seem to be getting any better, so she went back to him, but was seen by his replacement.

"My poor lady," he told her, "your heart is fine. You broke two ribs, probably rolling on your elbow in your sleep."

She stopped her heart medication, paid great attention to her ribs, and a week later was feeling much better.

"Be careful," she warned me. "Beware of the Nahanni: no plane has returned from there. An old man lives by the river and protects the gold mine he discovered by shooting down anyone who ventures there."

She told me the legend of the Nahanni trapper who lived along the river with his wife and son in a small wooden cabin. A few years earlier, the trapper had paddled his canoe down to Nahanni Butte, where five or six First Nations families had settled, gesturing like a madman and holding up a heavy stalactite of solid gold. "Gold, gold everywhere!" he proclaimed. "There's a whole cave full of it!" The news spread throughout the Northwest Territories, and prospectors rushed in from all over. But the mountain had shaken and the cave had closed up, trapping the gold within.

On another occasion, Mrs. Lacombe added, it was the trapper's wife who made a discovery. One day, as she wandered leisurely through the mountains, she stumbled upon a wide crevice with steep sides. A stunning light was emanating from it. Not believing what she was seeing, she leaned over the edge: the inside was covered in diamonds—huge, sparkling diamonds lining both walls of the crevice. But the bottom was full of clear water and, not knowing how to swim, the trapper's wife didn't dare to venture in. She ran back to the cabin to alert her husband. They returned together, but the earth had again shaken, the crevice had closed, and the diamonds had disappeared forever.

Mrs. Lacombe knew other stories, too, like the one about the famous Nahanni trapper who went for a night on the town in Nahanni Butte. He met a young First Nations girl he liked, but he must have let it slip when he got home, because he promptly received a bullet in his skull—which, according to Mrs. Lacombe, was still lodged there. In the end, he graciously forgave his wife for the gunshot wound, and she, in turn, forgave him for his escapades, and they returned to living peacefully by the Nahanni River. Then again, with Gus and his wife living in this small cabin, completely isolated with their 15-year-old son, they had little choice but to make peace.

Just to be sure I knew what I was getting myself into, one of my fellow pilots in Fort Smith gave me some additional background information on the Nahanni valley. In 1959, an airplane had crashed well upstream in bad weather; the pilot, Dan, and a passenger with a

A day in paradise; flying a Cessna 206 over the boreal forest north of Yellowknife.

Nahanni Butte, on the Nahanni River.

broken leg had taken several weeks to make their way out on a raft of spruce trees. During the same year, another pilot, Joe, had come down the Flat River and then the Nahanni on a raft. More recently, in September 1962, Ptarmigan Airways had lost a Cessna 185 that was unable to turn around in the Nahanni valley during bad weather. The pilot, Ken, was killed along with his three passengers, including the president of the charter airline.

I started to think that perhaps my company had taken advantage of my innocence and ignorance to send me on these two suicidal flights to the Flat River and the Nahanni. But now that I'd accepted the Water Resources flight and was already in Fort Liard, I didn't have much choice but to carry on.

For my first flight over the Flat River, the Mountie met me by the plane at two in the morning, as planned. I must have shown some signs of hesitation about going up the lower Nahanni and then the Flat River, and told him of the deadly risks we were running, based on what I had been told in Fort Smith.

The Mountie was eager not to lose his flight and tried to ease my concerns. He had indeed heard about the Nahanni man and his family. "It must have been Gus Kraus they told you about," he said. "But he's a trapper. I don't think he ever discovered any gold, and certainly no diamonds. I assure you that he doesn't shoot down passing aircraft."

I felt more comfortable, and off we went. Soon we were flying over "Dead Man's Valley," where the headless corpses of two prospectors, the McLeod brothers, were found in 1908. The mountains were getting taller and taller all around, their peaks covered in eternal snow. The river was rough, and the air in the valley pretty violent for my little floatplane. There was Gus's cabin, in a more open area of the valley. We landed as best we could among the boulders and the gravel banks, but the floatplane got caught in the eddies and lost balance: it swivelled and see-sawed, rocking from side to side. I hit the gas hard and did everything I could to regain control of the plane ... At last we docked on a pebble beach. It took four strong ropes to secure it against the current.

Gus's cabin was dark. Built with logs, it sat near a pond of hot water on a section of the river aptly named Hot Springs. The setting was all so reminiscent of Greek legends, Olympian gods, and tales of the Pythia. Gus and his family had always lived there, fishing and trapping, leading a simple life. They probably had no idea just how many legends circulated about them, and it would have been rude to enquire about their gold and diamonds.

The Mountie had a chat with them and found everything was in order. The main reason for our visit was the family dog: the mandatory rabies shot was administered to the tired old hound without much protest from the animal. And off we went, doing a U-turn in the eddies so we could take off downstream, toward where the valley widened.

It was now five in the morning, and we continued our trip a little farther up the Nahanni, then turned onto the Flat River. We had another two hours of flying deep in the mountains, between rock faces, over glaciers and seracs. The mountain was flooded with light, and all the snow was dazzling in the sun.

The Flat River became increasingly narrow as we got closer to its source, and the mine couldn't be far away. We flew along the side of the valley. The pass that we had to cross would likely be a downdraft zone, and it was better to fly through it diagonally so we

With the Water Resources men on Point Lake, at the head of the Coppermine River.

would be able to make a U-turn if the turbulence was too strong. A little farther along, on the mountainside, was the Tungsten Mine. Huge trucks were at work, slowly winding their way up the road. We flew over the camp, just above the houses, to signal our arrival. It was seven o'clock in the morning. Coffee should be ready.

McMillan Lake, a place of sad memories of the five forgotten prospectors, provided a place to land. It was short, and the rarefied air at that altitude gave us considerable ground speed, so the sudden braking of the floats on the water sent the plane diving. There was a risk it would flip over, but I had kept the nose up in anticipation.

The ore, concentrated at the mine site, was freighted westward to the Yukon on a long and difficult gravel road to the small town of Watson Lake. A team was finishing the construction of a 3,500-foot dirt track that would allow a DC-3 to land. The men were proud of their work and showed me around.

By the evening, my Mountie was done recording the identity of the hundred or so men working at the mine. Here, too, everything seemed to be in order. It was time to head back, so we got ready to take off from the small lake. We made the aircraft as light as possible by pumping the floats and leaving behind the small empty fuel drums that we no longer needed. The altitude almost doubled the takeoff distance, and the heat of the day made things worse by further reducing the air density. We took off by the skin of our teeth, 20 or 30 feet before the rocky shore, and struggled through the pass, skimming the rocks and a few scraggy trees. Two hours later we landed just outside Nahanni Butte, refueled, and were back in Fort Liard by midnight.

Meanwhile, Woody and Flash had been working on the Liard River near the village. They weren't quite done, so the next day I took off on my own to visit a prehistoric camp 10 miles northwest of Fort Liard on Fishermen Lake. The terraced ground revealed the different levels of the lake throughout the ages. An American student was leading a team of First Nations men on an excavation that was tremendously prolific. They scraped the ground with brushes, collecting bone arrowheads, carved flint, and pieces of charcoal. These remains were between 7,000 and 10,000 years old. Some tribes, making their way down from Asia through the Bering Strait, had stopped along the way and settled by the lake, while others carried on down south. The successive layers showed that fishermen had lived there for thousands of years, adapting to the water levels from terrace to terrace.

When I returned to Fort Liard, my teammates had completed their measurements, so we left that same evening, making our way to Nahanni Butte.

The village manager, Dick Turner, was relatively famous because of his books on the area, *Nahanni* and *Wings of the North*. The village of 79 inhabitants was very clean, and well-kept lawns surrounded the nice log huts. One of the First Nations families had a radio and was blasting it from a window for the others to enjoy. John Talbot, who loved to show off his new electric organ, was the teacher at the attractive local school.

The wife of trapper John Bruker invited us for dinner. To build his house, John had traveled miles away to find fir trunks nearly 15 inches in diameter—something quite rare for the region. He'd transported them on the river himself, then carved, dried, and adjusted them. He'd filled the cracks between the logs with mud and moss.

Now, here he came, pulling his canoe to the shore. He was built like a tank, walked like a gorilla, and spoke loudly. He punched the door open with a wide grin on his face, beaming: "Oy, woman, bring

Virginia Falls on the Nahanni River. I often landed with the Water Resources men on the smooth area above the falls. A colleague who took over from me crashed and killed all aboard. Photo by Darren Roberts.

us some food!" He swore like a trooper and burst out laughing. Two dozen cartridges hung from his shoulder strap, and as he threw a huge revolver down on the table, he laughed uproariously.

"I just surprised a young moose swimming across the river. I caught up to it with my canoe and tied its horns together, got its front legs in a lasso as it struggled frantically, then dragged it to the shore and immobilized it, with its legs all tied up, just outside the village."

"Anybody want some meat?" John had shouted out to his neighbours, announcing his feat. "I have 500 pounds of it. But if you want to eat it, you got to kill it first!"

The next day, Woody, Flash and I traveled back up the Nahanni, stopping in to see Gus Kraus, who'd never had so many visits. My Water Resources passengers wanted to measure the level of the river in front of his cabin. A little later we flew past the mouth of the Flat River but this time carried on straight up the Nahanni, eventually reaching Virginia Falls. The waterfall was nearly 300 feet high, twice the height of Niagara Falls. A huge rock cone, Mason's Rock, stood at the foot of the waterfall, right in the middle of the flow, causing the water to spray up in a mist that sparkled in the sun. The view was spectacular as we approached the waterfall, facing the wall of water above the curls of droplets. The bright hues of the almost complete rainbow stood out against the dark background of spruce trees and rocks.

Upstream of the waterfall, one or two miles away, the upper Nahanni valley was wide and the river very calm. A cable ran across the river to hold back the inflatable dinghy used to measure the current and river depth from one bank to the other. I had to land between the waterfall and the cable, and then make sure the engine didn't stall once we were on the water upstream of the waterfall.

On the right bank, to our left as we landed upstream over the waterfall, a path wound its way through the rocks. Every year, Albert Faille, an old adventurer who had spent his whole life searching for gold along the valley and who lived off the few nuggets he had found, would travel up the river and climb along the waterfall, carrying his canoe on his back. I once went to visit him in his cabin in Fort Simpson and had a long chat with him. He was 79 at the time and a legend in the North; the Nahanni was his river.

At this point, Flash discovered he had forgotten the flowmeter. A hydrographer without his flowmeter is like a soldier without a rifle, or a rider without a horse, so I headed back to Fort Liard, returning four hours later. It reminded me of the story of Samuel Hearne: in 1770, he set out on foot from Fort Prince of Wales, on the west

coast of Hudson Bay, crossed Canada from east to west up to Great Slave Lake, then veered north to reach the Arctic coast in search of copper in the tundra near the mouth of the Coppermine River. He walked through the forest for a few months.

Albert Faille, the man of the Nahanni River.

One day he damaged his sextant. "Never mind," he thought, "I'll go back to Fort Prince of Wales to get another one." He left shortly afterward and eventually returned to Fort Prince of Wales in 1772, after a 5,000-mile trek on foot through the forest and tundra up to the Arctic coast.

On my return, we safely docked the plane just upstream from the falls and inflated the dinghy. The outboard motor helped fight the current. We moved slowly along the cable, and at regular intervals Flash lowered the flowmeter to different depths, using the winch that rested on the side of the dinghy.

Suddenly, a screw from the winch punctured the side of the boat. The air escaped, the left side deflated, and the dinghy began to tilt. First there was panic on board: the water was quite cold this high in the mountains, and the fast current was taking us rapidly to the falls. Once we had the engine roaring, we all burst out laughing and frantically raced to the shore.

After patching the dinghy, we completed the measurements and headed back to the plane. A landslide on a nearby mountainside offered a glimpse of the permafrost. The ground is permanently frozen throughout the North to a depth of a few feet. Only with a jackhammer and dynamite could one dig into this mix of ice and

With the Water Resources Department at the Flat River to measure its flow and depth.

The author waiting for lunch at the west end of Point Lake with the Water Resources Department.

stone, which was hard as concrete. Locals were kindly asked to die in the summer, since only then could they be buried.

Just downstream from the cable, I opened the throttle, heading downstream. The plane obediently followed the river, took a turn on one float, and we were in the air 600 feet before the waterfall.

In the winter, the Water Resources men would sometimes come back in ski planes. In January 1962, a Yukon Air Services Beaver on skis got its tail caught in the cable hanging across the river during takeoff and ended its flight in the spruce trees a little farther upstream after lifting off without its fin. The pilot and passengers were picked up within a few days.[5]

We flew down the Nahanni, and when we reached the mouth of the Flat River, we followed it upstream, as I'd done the day before with the Mountie, but only for about 10 miles. The Flat River was narrow, turbulent, and shallow, and we got stuck on a pebble beach for over an hour before managing to pull out again. With the measurements taken, and following a really athletic takeoff that gave me quite a fright, we rose in spirals in the valley, using the upslope

[5] **Denny McCartney** described the six-week recovery of the plane during February and March 1962 in his book *Picking up the Pieces* (Victoria, BC: Trafford Publishing, 2002).

wind with every round to help lift us up. There was no way we could venture down the narrow canyons here. It brought back emotional memories of many slope flights with gliders, once upon a time.

The Flat River and the Nahanni returned their men to Fort Smith this time. But two summers later, in April 1969, with another brand new Cessna 206 on floats, the Water Resources Department wanted to take new measurements in these valleys. I was based farther north, in Yellowknife, at the time, so my company sent young Danny from Fort Smith, with two passengers: Dale, who was newly engaged, and Ian. Danny had just gotten married three weeks earlier. They were all killed.

To Mrs. Lacombe, I was a ghost. She welcomed me with particularly great enthusiasm: I'd arrived just in time to pay her next month's rent.

With the Water Resources men on the Hood River near the Arctic coast.
Photo Don Bradley, National Geographic, 1968.

5. The Most Atrocious Flight: Latitude 80° North in the dark at 60 below

Yellowknife, February 1969, –40° F, single-engine Otter on skis.

To the east, the stars were fading one by one, and soon the sun cast its first welcome ray of light toward us. I took an astro-compass sighting on the sun and reset the gyro: we were on course, heading straight north.

Three hours had elapsed since we left Yellowknife, and my passengers were dozing in their sleeping bags as we gently swayed under the stars. Bob Warnock, on my right, was also asleep. He had 7,000 hours of flight time in the North. Having permanently lost his licence a few months earlier, after being diagnosed with leukemia, he no longer

Bob Warnock, pilot and station manager for Gateway Aviation in Yellowknife.

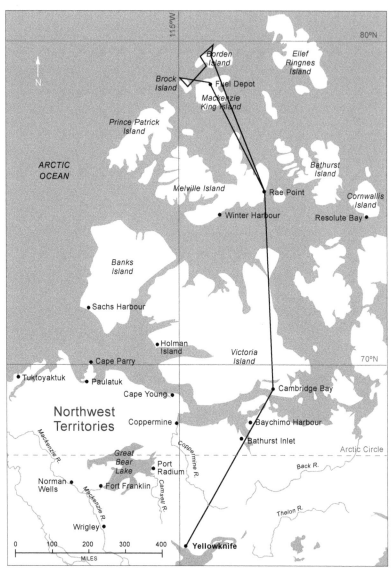

officially flew but was my co-pilot for this trip. It was good to have someone who could share the anguish I had been building up over the last few days at the thought of this really dicey expedition. The flight was absolute madness, in –60° F, in near total darkness, and into unexplored and hostile territory.

Pierre Maréchal, head of the Elf Petroleum/ Petropar team, was accompanied by Jean Millet from France, who was selling explosives, and Dick from Texas, who was selling seismic equipment. Elf had obtained permits to explore huge territories in the High Arctic, where there was hope of one day being able to exploit

Resetting the gyro compass (left corner) to South at noon in February, at latitude 80° N.

formidable oil reserves that seemed to extend across a basin bigger than the one in Texas. Icebreakers could not get through, and the oil would freeze in a pipeline. If they ever managed to extract this famous oil, it would probably be done with the help of nuclear submarines that would land gently on the ocean floor, under the icefields, and fill their tanks at giant taps before making their way to Europe, swinging north around the top of Greenland.

The plan right now was for me to take Pierre, Jean, and Dick to the desolate and miserable island of Borden, at latitude 80° N, on February 21, the day the top of the sun would be visible for a few moments at noon. Thanks to their slide rules and astronomy tables, my passengers had established that we would have a few minutes of light at noon before fading back into the night. How wonderful!

Now was the time to check the place out, because the exploration season would be short. In the middle of summer the melted snow was unable to drain because of the permafrost, and the Arctic islands turned into vast quagmires that were impossible to traverse, even on foot, so the crews could only work there in winter.

We crossed the Arctic Circle smoothly and without even feeling the bump. Two hours later we flew over the Arctic coast. On the other side of a stretch of Arctic Ocean, near the south coast of Victoria Island, we landed near the small community of Cambridge Bay, home to a few hundred Inuit and European adventurers, and refueled.

It was one o'clock in the afternoon, −40° F, and the sun was already about to set, which made continuing the flight even tougher. The oil company's base camp at Rae Point, on the east side of Melville Island, was a farther 600 miles north. That would take another five hours of flying in the dark with our old Otter, CF-OVN. Once at the base, we would spend the next few days taking long exploratory flights farther north in the coldest time of winter, under the stars.

I went to the Department of Transport office at the Cambridge Bay airport to check the weather. After several calls by radio-telephone and messages in Morse code, they eventually told me that the ceiling at the Rae Point camp was 500 feet and visibility was one mile. In Mould Bay, 300 miles west of the camp, visibility was zero. In Resolute Bay, 300 miles to the east, visibility was also zero. The entire northern Arctic was plunged into darkness, snow, and fog. It was already dark around us.

None of this weather information bothered Bob, who was ready to continue. "Let's move on," he said to me. "It should be fine."

I was worried about Bob, a wonderful fellow whom I admired greatly, but who was no longer afraid of anything.

To me, it was not fine at all. The idea of flying north for five hours over the ice pack at night, with no landmarks and no magnetic compass, in visibilities ranging from zero to one mile, and with un-determined or very low ceilings, definitely didn't sound appealing to me, notwithstanding my youthful enthusiasm and dedication to the cause. We would leave the next day.

Cambridge Bay around noon in February. The Arctic Ocean is in front, and the tundra in the back.

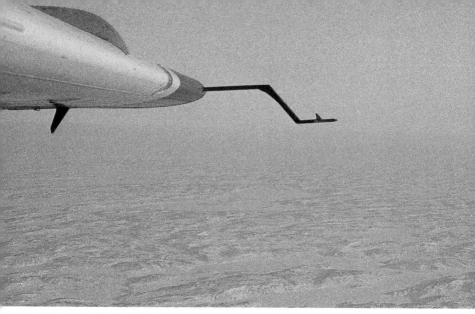
Midday over Victoria Island.

By 8 a.m. we were up in the air. It was still dark, but the forecast at the Cambridge Bay airport promised good weather. In other words, dim and dark grey light, with visibility limited by fine ice crystals suspended in the air, and no hope of seeing any relief on the snow, as there were no shadows. Heading straight north, we slowly made our way across endless territories, flat from one horizon to the other and uniformly grey before dawn. We were navigating with a C4 compass specially designed for polar flights. Theoretically, it could maintain its heading for several hours. Our traditional gyrocompass could not keep a direction at these latitudes for more than 20 or 30 minutes because of friction due to the cold and, most importantly, because of the famous "Coriolis Force," which makes everything turn to the right in the northern hemisphere. Coriolis had haunted my mechanics classes at university. I never liked him.

"You can't miss Rae Point," Bob had told me. "It's just straight ahead. Simply follow the meridian."

I was so stressed that I didn't appreciate his sense of humour, especially since the straight line was getting harder and harder to follow as we no longer had any landmarks on this grey and indefinite, flat snowscape. From time to time we would see patches of ice cleared by the wind, but there was no way to know if this was a small piece of the ice pack or one of the thousands of lakes that punctuated the tundra: we would have had to land and taste the ice for salt content. I thought of my passengers' courage, their crazy ambition: it was now –50° F outside, and if we got lost and ran out of fuel, or if a valve were to break or a cylinder fly off—as happened once in a while with the Otter's big radial engine—we would likely die of cold long before we could be found, assuming we survived a night landing on the tundra or the ice pack.

My passengers embodied the audacity of the first men who conquered the Far West. Dick impressed me the most. Just the day before he had been in Texas, and his strange outfit was a patchwork of cowboy and Inuit styles. He had come to sell Pierre a new type of machine, the Vibroseis, made in Texas. These were large hydraulic cylinders mounted on caterpillar tracks that vibrate on the earth's surface and create shock waves, which bounce off deep ground layers and allow mapping of the underground rock formations. The device had never been tried on ice. Jean, on the other hand, wanted to sell Pierre his dynamite: nothing like the good old-fashioned methods. Pierre was willing to try anything, but could the new machines be moved and operated on extremely chaotic ice? They had decided to take a look at the area to find out what they were dealing with, and this was the purpose of our flight.

I thought the whole idea was totally crazy. We had eight days of supplies onboard, plus three or four guns that wouldn't actually be of much use since nothing lived here, and each of us had brought two huge Arctic duvets, "guaranteed to keep you alive in a cold of minus 40° F"—though the tag did not specify for how long.

Everyone was scanning the ground, trying to spot any irregularity that could serve as a reference point. Something looked like a shoreline. We would go take a closer look, but no, it was just a ripple on the snow. At times I thought I could recognize a lake, but it was just a frozen plateau. The flight was getting increasingly frustrating and stressful. I decided that if I were a geologist, I'd go to Tahiti to look for oil!

By now it was almost dark again. Since there was nothing left to see outside, I became

Vibroseis equipment for seismic surveys.

The airstrip at Rae Point on Melville Island during early afternoon in February. Note the Arctic Ocean up front, then land with the airstrip, and the ocean again beyond the strip.

mesmerized by the C4 compass, rigorously keeping a heading of 360 degrees to follow the meridian, as Bob had suggested.

We had left Cambridge Bay almost five hours earlier, so we should soon catch the signal from the small radio beacon at the base camp on Melville Island. Every five minutes I tried to tune the radio compass, but only background noise crackled in the headset. If the beacon didn't work, we would never find the camp. I was starting to hate crude oil and the geologists looking for it.

A moment later, Bob looked at me in surprise. I suddenly had a huge smile on my face and was blissfully relaxed into my seat. He must have thought, "Dominique has gone mad; it must be the stress."

I could no longer hide my relief and burst out with joyful laughter, pointing at the dial of the radio compass: we were picking up the Morse code signal from the Rae Point radio beacon, and the radio compass needle was pointing straight ahead.

Half an hour later we spotted a narrow strip, cleared of snow and marked by lights, on which we landed. We had crossed the southern shoreline of Melville Island without even realizing it, because the coast was flat and invisible under the snow.

About 20 men lived at the camp in one long barrack between the kitchen and the offices, close to two large bladders of diesel fuel. This organization of Panarctic Oil's base camp into a single building was most surprising: in the event of a fire, everyone would have to bail out into the polar night in their slippers and pyjamas, onto the frozen tundra, with nowhere else to go.

The *Hecla* and *Griper*, Winter Harbour, Melville Island, December 1819.

We were about 60 miles east of Winter Harbour, a little farther along the south shore of Melville Island, near the western end of a 750-mile-long east-west passage, which is often clear of ice toward the end of the summer, and which directly connects Baffin Bay and Lancaster Sound, on the Greenland side, to McClure Strait and the Beaufort Sea north of Alaska. Winter Harbour was where William

Navigating by the moon in February in the middle of the day, at latitude 80° N.

Landing along the shoreline to check the ice (background) around noon, at latitude 80° N and –55° F.

Parry, while searching for the Northwest Passage, had been trapped by the ice on September 17, 1819, and spent 11 months with his two ships, the *Hecla* and the *Griper*. The men had covered both ships with tarpaulins to keep out the cold, surrounded the hulls with mountains of snow for insulation, and used wolf skins as blankets. To maintain the troops' morale, Parry had organized theatre performances and managed the publication of two journals. He was barely 30 years old.

They were released by the ice on August 1, 1820, and Parry returned triumphantly to England without having lost a single man. His lieutenant was the young James Clark Ross, 20-year old nephew of John Ross who had turned around the previous summer because he thought he had seen a line of mountains, which he named the Croker Mountains, blocking the entrance to this east-west passage through the Arctic islands. One can only imagine how awkward it must have been for young James Clark Ross to tell his uncle John that his Croker Mountains were just a crock of his imagination.

In February 1969, it was –60° F at the base camp on Melville Island, and nothing was working: the rubber boots protecting my caribou-leg mukluks were so brittle that they snapped after the first few steps. The flexible clips on the engine tent broke. The plug-in electric heaters, used to prevent the engine from freezing solid, had partially seized and were creaking while barely turning, at least initially. They were placed next to the large battery in the tail section, to the front of the engine next to the cylinders, and under the large oil tank to prevent it from freezing solid during long stopovers. Even the insulation of the electrical cables was breaking. The flight instruments were half frozen, the large three-blade propeller was stuck in fully fine pitch, the flaps were jammed halfway out because of the cold, and the skis only worked in fits and starts, so we often landed with a ski on one side and a wheel on the other. The control cables had shrunk so much from the cold and were now so tight that the aircraft was really hard to manoeuvre and I was always afraid that something would snap.

The next morning, thanks to all the electric heaters distributed around it, the Otter was defrosted and warmed up in barely an hour. We took off in the pitch-dark at 7 a.m. and flew north for 11 hours over the last islands at the top of the world, over the ice pack, and back to base. The plan was to refuel from 45-gallon barrels on the way back to base camp, at an isolated fuel depot on the small, flat island of Mackenzie King, assuming we could find the island and the depot. Our only navigation system was the famous C4 compass, if it continued holding its direction.

I turned off the heater to save fuel. It was –50° F in the cabin, and my passengers were curled up in their sleeping bags. One of them took out a bottle of whiskey and laughed as he passed it around. When the bottle reached the cockpit, I thought to myself that my passengers were very gracious to remember me: they must have assumed that I needed a sip of alcohol to give me courage, and I appreciated this kind gesture. But the whiskey was in a solid state. It had turned into an ice block. It was my passengers' polite way of pointing out that it was really cold inside the plane.

In fact, the frost on the windshield caused by my own breath was setting so quickly that I regularly had to clean the glass with a cloth soaked in antifreeze. The problem was that the antifreeze was methyl alcohol, and the vapours were making my head spin each time I wiped the windshield. I was slowly getting drunk. This was indeed one way to reduce the tension, but it was all pretty pointless anyhow, since the frost quickly built up again. I eventually gave up, as the obscured windshield wasn't actually a problem. It was still so dark outside that there was nothing to see. The weather was fine but the

Checking the ocean ice at noon in February, latitude 80° N and –55° F.

moon had set; we could only see the stars above, and nothing below.

After four hours of stressful flying, at 11 a.m., we reached the south coast of Borden Island. My passengers wanted to see if they could get across the ice with a convoy of machines, derricks, and mobile huts in order to start drilling, and they asked me to land. The ice was totally chaotic, and I was surprised they would even ask. The request was totally ridiculous.

We continued along the shoreline, and they came back to the cockpit on a couple of occasions, insisting that we land. I became a little annoyed: "We cannot land, and we are not landing. Don't even think about it!"

This is exactly how people get killed: the passengers are paying for the flight and expect the pilot to do what they want—otherwise they complain to the company, and the pilot is fired.

We flew around for a while at very low altitudes so they could look at the ice and try, in the dark, to figure out what the surface was like. Then I spotted a moraine of large rocks near the shore, with a slim, snow-covered ridge that seemed to be about one mile long. We did two or three reconnaissance circuits to evaluate the risk of landing, and I decided to go for it. I think I was so drained that I simply wanted to end the flight, and it didn't matter how many pieces the airplane might break into during the process. I also wanted to prove to them that I was right after all: "I told you: we should never have tried to land there." The strip was very narrow, irregular, and slightly twisted, and we could not see the relief because there were no shadows. The rocks were barely covered by a layer of snow, which would probably be too thin to prevent the skis from scraping.

The landing went surprisingly smoothly, however, and we stopped in line with the ridge without hitting anything. I was stunned, not having expected such success, but at least we were back on the ground and I could relax for a while. It was –65° F.

I thought all these people were irresponsible, decided I didn't like them anymore, and refused to join them in their leisurely walk across the countryside. My argument was that I needed to remain in the cockpit to keep an eye on the engine: if it ran slowly for too long and stalled, we'd never be able to leave because the battery, at the back of the fuselage, was likely completely frozen by now.

Walking slowly on the very chaotic ice, one man returned to the plane. In the Arctic, one has to move gently to avoid freezing one's lungs by breathing too fast.

"Quick, hand me a gun, there are fresh bear tracks."

The bear never showed up. He had probably been disturbed in his sleep, taken a quick look around, and gone back to bed in a hole under a pile of snow on the ice pack.

To turn around for takeoff on the narrow ridge, I needed my passengers' help. We were all pushing and pulling, but it was a nightmare working in the wash of the propeller. The plane got stuck, then moved a little, and finally aligned with the ridge in the opposite direction.

In the meantime, Bob had gone to see what we had landed on and how we were going to take off again. He came back shaking his head. "We'll never be able to take off. There's a step right across the ridge, about three feet high!"

I didn't care, and I didn't want to hear about it. We had managed to land, so we would be able to take off. I didn't even ask Bob how far away this step was or which way it was facing. Would we hit it head-on during takeoff and tear off the undercarriage, or fall over its edge before being airborne and drop down heavily a little bit farther along?

I pushed the throttle into over-boost, well past the red line, jerked the Otter off the ground as soon as I could with a quick extension of the flaps and a hard pull on the elevator, peeled off to the right down the side of the moraine toward the ice pack until we had enough speed to fly, and off we went again without any trouble.

We continued northward at low altitude, exploring the still impassable ice pack. According to the map, we were now at latitude 80° N, it was exactly noon, and the view was magnificent. Far to the south, exactly on a bearing of 180°, the tip of the sun appeared for a moment above the horizon and cast a brief ray of light. I quickly reset the C4 compass.

My passengers wanted to test the ice again and asked me to land directly on the ice pack. I felt like telling them that it was the same as the ice they had tested an hour ago, and the plane would simply explode on impact if we tried to land on this solid chaos. But I couldn't take the stress anymore. "They want to land?" I thought. "Fine with me. I'll show them why it's totally irresponsible. Let's land, and see if I care."

The sun had disappeared below the horizon after a few minutes, so it was dark again. Somehow I spotted an ice fissure, frozen over

The oil exploration camp at Rae Point on Melville Island, midday in February.

into a smooth surface, but it was dangerous. There was no way to tell if the new ice in the crack had formed recently, in which case we would most likely fall through, or if it was already thick enough to land on. I should have first flown over the smooth surface of the new ice to test it, bouncing hard on it several times and circling back to see if water had risen through the cracks—which would indicate that the ice was too thin for a landing. But I was physically and mentally drained and no longer concerned: we would land anyhow. If the ice held, great; if not, that would be a shame, but so be it.

On approach, I was expecting Bob to shout, "You can't land before testing the ice!" He probably didn't care any more than I did.

We landed. The ice held, and I stayed put to keep an eye on the engine again while my passengers examined the ice pack around us. From the cockpit, it seemed so chaotic that I couldn't imagine how one could get through there with a caterpillar convoy, but that was my passengers' problem.

We took off again half an hour later and headed southwest to Brock Island. We missed it altogether, turned back, and finally found the shoreline. And my passengers, one more time, insisted on landing. It was turning into a routine, and my sense of distress and anxiety was somewhat mitigated. We landed on a rock ledge covered with a little snow, similar to the one we had used on Borden Island. I remained in the cockpit to monitor the engine while my passengers got out to examine the ice. Even a dogsled could not sneak between the blocks of ice knocked over onto one another.

Bob went to examine the ridge that we had used as a landing strip and came back shaking his head, just as he had done a few hours earlier: "This is crazy. We're going to end up crashing if we keep playing this game!"

The situation must have been serious for Bob to talk like that. Since he had been told that his life was coming to an end, nothing could scare him anymore. I was so exhausted that I no longer cared myself. But I vowed that I would never agree to do a similar flight again. In fact, the chief pilot later confessed that he had asked me directly because he didn't think any of the other Yellowknife pilots would accept the assignment.

We eventually took off without breaking anything and continued our flight south to Mackenzie King Island, where we found the fuel

Noon in February, latitude 80° N. The engine was running for 11 hours non-stop, even during refueling.

depot in the middle of the tundra after a long and tense search. I slowly taxied the Otter toward the hundreds of 45-gallon barrels, but Bob, as always, was more intrepid than me: "You should be able to just climb over the barrels. It'll make refueling easier."

Normally I would never have dared to try hoisting my big Otter on skis over 45-gallon barrels of fuel. I knew that the barrels might collapse, and sparks could set the whole lot on fire, but by this point I no longer cared and thought this was a great idea. It did turn out to be easy. The barrels were mostly under the snow anyhow.

The chamois skin we used to filter the fuel in the wash of the propeller was frozen and not letting anything flow through, and I had to shake it regularly to break the ice. In one hour we barely managed to put 150 gallons of fuel in the tanks, and the small hand pump eventually packed in. It was 3 p.m. and high time to head back, for it was getting really dark.

When we returned to the base camp of Rae Point on Melville Island, guided by its weak radio beacon, it was pitch-dark. The engine had been running for nearly 11 hours straight, and this flight had exhausted me to the point that I had lost all ability to think clearly. We landed in the wrong direction, with a 20 mph tailwind. Fortunately, the landing strip was long!

The next day we headed south while it was still dark. Within five hours we were back in Cambridge Bay. We refueled in 20 minutes, and five hours later we could see the north shore of Great Slave Lake. The weather was great, the sun was a full disc of a nice orange colour, a little above the horizon, and the temperature was so balmy that we were sweating in our thermal clothes. Yellowknife was –15° F, 50 degrees warmer than Borden Island.

I was beaming, radiant, in an astonishing state of bliss. I felt triumphant, invincible. I unbuttoned my down parka and strolled into town to the bar, smiling at everyone as though drugged.

Jean sold Pierre his dynamite and seismographs; they would be flown to Brock Island. As for Dick, he'd never imagined that it could get so cold and that the ice pack would be so chaotic. He returned glumly to his native Texas to warm his toes and fingertips.

6. Mayday: Load Shift after Takeoff

Yellowknife, August 1967, Single Otter on floats.

The Canadian North had been ablaze for several weeks. Thousands of hectares of dry spruce trees had burned in the Mackenzie Mountains, along the Mackenzie River, on both sides of the Slave River, and farther north between Great Slave Lake and Great Bear Lake. Even the tundra was on fire. There had been no rain for two months, and a series of thunderstorms had sparked raging fires throughout the Northwest Territories. The sun had almost disappeared behind the smoke, and visibility was so reduced that many planes, unable to navigate, remained grounded. A floatplane had just crashed on Great Slave Lake, exploding on the surface as it attempted a blind landing in thick smoke.

I had landed close to Rae Lakes, a small First Nations settlement lost in the forest some 150 miles northwest of Great Slave Lake, to pick up 10 men who had just put out a fire that had been burning uncontrollably right outside the village.

On my last trip I crammed the last few men into my floatplane, along with pumps, hoses, shovels, and tents, but I had to leave crates of food behind in the forest for fear that my Otter would sink. The plane was so overloaded that Ministry of Transport inspectors would

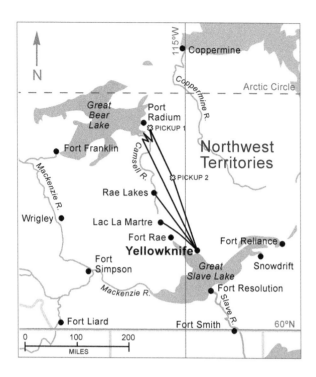

rub their hands in glee if they got wind of it and were waiting for me on arrival. I had been given a warning the year before for flying dangerously overweight.

And so, on the edge of the small lake, in this forest in the Northwest Territories that was managed by the federal government in Ottawa and therefore belonged to all Canadians and particularly to the First Nations populations, I left these food crates originally intended for the Rae Lakes men who were fighting the fire. Not addressing anyone in particular, I announced that I would come back for them one day, but I was not sure that anyone heard me. The quiet life in Rae Lakes could now resume, and in the forest the food crates waited to be picked up.

Back in Yellowknife, Father Amouroux, a Frenchman from the Alps who had spent his life among the First Nations people, was about to leave for Rae Lakes to replace Father Duchaussois, who had just built a chapel there. Father Amouroux—"Yath'ikawouia," as the First Nations people called him, which means "the man who preaches and brings back supplies"—loaded the Otter with barrels of fuel for outboard motors, then piled in crates of food, two-by-fours, sheets of plywood, and mountains of varied items for the First Nations families, including a bag of mail and a case of milk powder for a baby.

The school bell at Lac La Martre.

The floatplane was heavily loaded and the rear of the floats sank into the water. After what seemed like a never-ending takeoff from Yellowknife Bay, we dragged along at low altitude in the smoke, above the spruce trees and the rocks. An hour later we landed at Rae Lakes, docked, and started unloading the plane. The whole population was there: the children on the dock, the men a little farther away, and the women, shy, far behind the others, carrying their babies on their backs.

I disembarked my passengers and all their gear, and promptly took off again to go and collect the crates of food that I had left behind the previous day, just over the hill, near the fire. You could clearly see the spruce-branch litter and tent sites where the men had lived for nearly two weeks while they fought the fire. But next to a mountain of empty cans, not a single box of food was left. Instead,

Fetching water in Lac La Martre.

a bear's head was impaled on a stake, looking at me. I perceived this as a personal insult, a way of mocking me, and I thought it was unfair because I was just doing my job. I later found out that this was, in fact, a traditional rite, a form of cultural or religious symbolism, a gesture of respect for nature. I promptly took off back to Rae Lakes.

Obviously, I was not happy. "Does anyone know what happened to all the crates of food?"

There was much commotion on the dock as they all chatted amongst themselves. Of course, nobody knew.

"There were a dozen crates full of cans. Where are they?"

Second round of consultation. Eventually someone suggested, "You should ask Peter Arrowmaker."

"Where is he?"

Peter, who was on the dock next to me, introduced himself.

"Where are the crates?"

"I don't know."

I was starting to get annoyed. Father Amouroux, smiling, crouching peacefully on the dock, was smoking his pipe without saying a word. I questioned Peter again. "Did you take the crates from the abandoned camp?"

"Yes, I brought some back," he replied.

"Did anyone else also take crates?"

"I don't know."

As usual, nobody knew anything about anything, and their faces remained imperturbable. One thing was certain, Peter had gone by canoe to the abandoned camp to collect the food crates left behind, which he then most certainly distributed in the village.

Bringing supplies to Rae Lakes with a Beaver.

Unloading firefighting gear near Fort Smith.

I turned to Father Amouroux. "They should really return those crates to Forestry."

But the priest, more indigenous than the Indigenous People, eternally smiling and drawing on his pipe, raised his arms in a sign of helplessness. "You can see that no one knows where they are!"

"You must be joking. Peter went to pick them up last night or this morning, and no one knows where they are?"

The priest took offense at the severity of my comments. "First of all, Peter did nothing wrong."

He chatted with Peter in the Dene language. The whole village listened. Finally the father translated for me: "Peter took the crates because he was told to bring them back to the village. It was Isadore, the chief's nephew, who asked him to do so." The father added with a big smile: "You see, it's not Peter's fault. He simply brought back the crates as he was asked." The whole audience approved and nodded their heads.

I had to admit that there was a certain logic to this reasoning: in a First Nations forest, the government had provided crates of supplies specifically for the men of Rae Lakes who were fighting the fire, and when those crates were left behind, the chief's nephew told

Peter to bring them back to the village and distribute the contents to everyone rather than leave them in the forest. All this was very straightforward and perfectly logical.

Father Amouroux continued. "Peter, would you have taken these boxes if Isadore had not asked you to bring them back to the village?"

Peter looked offended. "Absolutely not, of course not."

The priest turned to me, delighted. "I told you so."

For the First Nations people there was never a problem in the first place, and the matter was resolved. However, with my European mind, I thought I should ask Isadore by what right he had considered that these food crates belonged to the people of Rae Lakes, and how he had the nerve to ask someone to bring them back to the village.

"Where is Isadore?"

The villagers consulted one another. Then a child translated into English for me: "He flew back to Yellowknife yesterday in your plane."

Without Isadore, I could never get to the bottom of this story, and it was my fault for having taken him back to town in the first place. Once in Yellowknife, Isadore would be nowhere to be found and there would be no point looking for him. The case was therefore effectively closed, and everyone was happy.

I was about to jump into my floatplane when Georgina called me. She was 20 years old, with long, jet-black hair held back by a red headband, almond eyes sparkling with mischief, tanned skin, the gait of a dancer, and the character of an Italian woman, which was surprising among the First Nations, who are traditionally so reserved and shy. I knew her well, having often met her in her community of Fort Franklin, west of Great Bear Lake, and at the Arctic Circle Lodge, a luxurious camp for American fishermen northeast of the lake, where she worked for several summers. She stood apart from the

Fort Franklin.

Arctic Circle Lodge, Great Bear Lake.

rest of the women and carried a baby on her back. She had tremendous charm, knew it, had everyone wrapped around her finger. She would probably one day be elected Miss Northwest Territories. It was certainly for her baby that I had brought a case of milk powder.

Georgina came toward me. "Dominique, not all the men who fought the fire have been paid. Where are their cheques? My father and my brother haven't been paid."

"I'll ask Forestry in Yellowknife and bring the cheques back on my next trip."

"And also tell those fools that the forest is still burning over the hill and that they had better come back to get some men. What idiots!" She burst out laughing, her fists on her hips, and everyone smiled at her insolence.

Father Duchaussois, Chief Andrew Gon, and five or six other men hopped on board and we took off. Once we were back in

Georgina Mantla, of Fort Franklin, at Arctic Circle Lodge.

Yellowknife, all I had to do was tell George Hudson, the head of Forestry, that his food crates had vanished. As for the missing cheques, it would take another eight days: the offices had been looted and all the cheques had been stolen. That was hardly surprising in this frontier town, inhabited by miners from all over the world who spent eight hours a day far underground in the two gold mines. One of the police cars had recently been blown up with a couple of sticks of dynamite. A few months earlier, a man had come back to town holding his belly in both hands: after fighting over a woman, he had lost a kidney, part of his liver, and half of his stomach to an explosive bullet used for hunting moose, caribou, and muskox. He managed to reach a house, where someone called the hospital and asked for him to be picked up, as he seemed to have difficulty walking. More recently, a fellow had been shot dead by the police in the middle of the street in Yellowknife. The simple looting of a government office, therefore, made no waves and was given no attention whatsoever in the local paper.

My day had just begun, and I now had to leave for Lac La Martre, 125 miles northwest of Great Slave Lake, to pick up a ton and a half of fresh fish. The whitefish were in tubs made of plastic that was rigid but not quite rigid enough. They were stacked three high, and I passed two ropes around the back of the load to prevent them from slipping at takeoff. Everything was going well until, during the climb, one of the lower tubs collapsed under the weight, then another, and another. The fish started sliding back toward the tail section, into the space where the radios and survival equipment were stored. The centre of gravity was soon beyond limits, and the aircraft, now completely out of balance, became nearly impossible to control.

I pushed the yoke forward all the way to get the aircraft's nose horizontal, set the trim to full "nose down" position, dropped a bit of flap to lower the nose a little more, and reduced the engine thrust to coax the aircraft to pitch downward while trying to maintain enough altitude to reach Yellowknife. There was nothing else I could do, but the plane was still flying with a nose-up attitude. I felt that it was on the verge of stalling—and if it did, it was likely to immediately start a spin toward the small islands and rocks along the shores of Great Slave Lake. The fish would be thrown around, and there would be no hope of recovery.

Bringing supplies to Lac La Martre.

I sent a Mayday, and the Yellowknife tower wished me good luck. There was nothing else they could do. I called my company, Gateway Aviation, and told them to clear the docks so I could arrive there straightaway and at high speed before the plane tipped back into the water—assuming I made it back at all.

The situation on board eventually stabilized, and there was no further collapse of the plastic tubs. The plane was losing altitude but very slowly, so I felt more confident I would reach the floatplane base. In the end, I arrived from a distance, parallel to the docks, and slid across the water at high speed to prevent the overloaded back end pulling the Otter into the lake tail first. The whole ground crew caught the plane as it passed the dock at great velocity and tied it up. Although the tail did partially sink, the ropes were strong and the back of the aircraft did not go down any farther.

I took off again in the early afternoon, this time with a Cessna 206, to fly to a camp 300 miles north, near Great Bear Lake and the Arctic Circle, close to the treeline. My company had forgotten two prospectors who should have been picked up about 10 days earlier.

I landed near their camp but there was no one there. They had left a note dated three or four days earlier: "Our plane seven days late; no more grub; leaving on foot for Silver Bay Mine, on Camsell River; if you head that way, we'll send flares for pick up." The message was signed by Frank Smith and Joe Lafleur.

I flew very slowly, zigzagging along their presumed route, but—try to find two men in the forest! Eventually I spotted a tiny white cloud above the stunted spruce trees. I recognized it as the smoke that lingers a few seconds following the firing of a red flare. The flare itself I had not seen. The men had to be there, so I landed on a small nearby lake to wait for them to come to me. Half an hour later they emerged from the forest, glad to have been found, and we left for Yellowknife.

After two hours of flight, well into the evening, I was starting to worry about our landing in Yellowknife as it would certainly be dark. Night landings were strictly prohibited due to the high risk when you could see neither the water nor the rocks.

Just then a red flare rose into the air and burst—far below and ahead of us. Again? The flare was clearly visible now that it was dark, but my passengers were dozing away and had not noticed it. For a moment I thought of pretending I had not seen it either: I was tired and really concerned about this landing in the dark in Yellowknife. Still, this was probably a case of distress, so we landed.

The flare had been set off by a prospector who had just spent a month or two alone in his cabin and wanted to get back into town. This additional twilight landing and the half-hour delay it would

Looking for two forgotten prospectors trying to rejoin civilization on foot.

Resupplying prospectors north of Yellowknife. Note the food cache up the tree against the bears.

cause to our landing in Yellowknife really upset me, especially since the prospector was meant to be picked up two weeks later and had no pressing issue.

We carried on to Yellowknife, where we landed very discreetly in the dark at the far side of the bay. I needed my pilot's salary and could not risk losing my licence. In the meantime, I had called the manager of the floatplane base by high-frequency radio to let him know that I had three men on board who were hungry and thirsty, and in urgent need of civilization—that is, tobacco, alcohol, and women, and not necessarily in that order. When we arrived at the dock, Neil Murphy was waiting for my passengers with three burgers, three portions of fries, three Cokes, and three packs of cigarettes. He then poured each of them a large glass of whiskey to reconcile them with life. As for women, it was up to the passengers to find them. The company offered no help on that front.

The fires were out, and the Forestry Department had done a good job. The men from Rae Lakes had worked hard and earned a good living; there was even food for a feast in the community, including cans of pineapple, strawberries, and whipped cream. The pilots had flown a great quantity of miles to and from the fires, the whole operation had been a terrific success, and everybody was happy. In addition, I had survived the brutal shift of a full load of fish, which very nearly spun my aircraft out of control and caused my premature death, and then I had "rescued" three trappers who were now celebrating in the bar their return to civilization. Another great day!

I was very tired, so I headed home to get a few hours of sleep at the company's house, smiling at the thought of bubbly Georgina.

During the summer, getting any rest was really difficult. Pilots flew non-stop in June and July, every day all day, because there was no night and only civil servants could tell the difference between one day of the week and another.

This chronic lack of sleep was dangerous. My colleague John Daykin was returning from a flight one day in an Otter on floats. The helpers at the docks let the 10 passengers off and unloaded their luggage, but John was still in the cockpit. When I went to see why he was not getting off, I found him sound asleep, a few minutes after turning off the engine, his head resting on the wheel. Another time, Bob Warnock came back, also with a fully loaded Otter. He got out of the cockpit and walked to the office, but stopped at the door to rest his back on the frame for a moment. A few seconds later he was snoring steadily and quietly, upright, leaning on the doorpost, everyone carefully walking past him so as not to wake him.

I, too, once fell asleep on arrival. After two or three days of uninterrupted flying—as often happened in summer when you had to refuel, load the plane, take off, fly, land, unload, refuel, and

Resupplying another prospector.

start the whole process again—I became keenly aware that I was on the verge of collapsing at the wheel of my Otter and might not make it to the lake where I had to drop off two or three men with their gear and food in front of a prospectors' camp. I was fighting sleep as hard as I could, but realized

Lunch at a prospector's camp: fried potatoes and onions, and fresh lake trout.

I was about to break down, risking the lives of everyone on board. I first opened the window, then tuned the radio to create an increasingly loud whistle in my headset, and finally pulled out my dagger to sharply prick my thigh. I just managed to reach the edge of the lake, executed the flare-out, and switched off the engine as soon as the plane started to slide on the water. At that moment I must have collapsed on the wheel, since I have no recollection of what happened next. I woke up one or two hours later in front of the camp, still sitting in the cockpit with my head down. The men at the camp explained to me that they had noticed us stopped on the water a mile or two away and had come to get us with a motorboat. They found me collapsed in the cockpit but still looking alive, and dragged us across the water to the camp. They emptied the plane without waking me up, and when I finally emerged they served me a six-egg omelette and made me drink half a dozen large cups of strong coffee so I could head back to the base to get on with my work and fly other planes.

The days were long, at least in the summer, but we had the whole winter to hibernate and catch up on our sleep.

7. Sinking with a Floatplane in the Arctic Ocean

Yellowknife, July 1966, Cessna 185 on floats.

At the Gateway Aviation office, I received a high-frequency radio call from the manager of Great Slave Lodge, a luxury log hotel on the north shore of Great Slave Lake, which hosted American fishermen every summer.

"It's a doctor from Chicago, his young wife, and a salesman," the lodge told me. "They want to spend the day in the Arctic fishing char."

"Okay, I'll take care of it," I replied.

At the end of the day I took off in the Cessna 185, CF-OMF, and headed for the lodge where I would refuel and overnight.

With a full load of fuel in the wings and three 10-gallon kegs on board, we had nine hours of autonomy, more than enough to reach the Arctic coast and then a small fuel depot on the way back, about an hour north of the lodge on a small island in the tundra, where I had dropped off two 10-gallon kegs during an earlier flight, just in case.

Five o'clock in the morning. The first takeoff in front of the

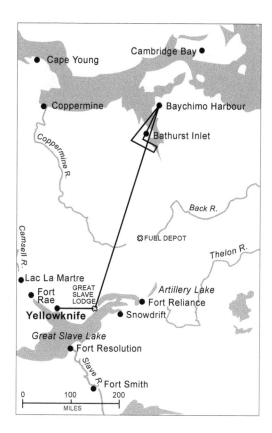

lodge was a total fiasco: we made an awful lot of noise and sprayed a considerable amount of water, but three or four miles later we were still stuck on the glassy water and the engine needles were already in the red. We had to return to the lodge.

"Sorry!" I told my passengers. "We're grossly overloaded and the plane can't get on the step. We'll have to lighten the load."

I dropped off one of the fuel barrels. Those 10 gallons amounted to almost an hour's worth of fuel—we had just given up over 100 miles of flying. I hoped we would have enough fuel to reach the depot on the way back.

The second attempt at takeoff was a great success. Half an hour later, heading northeast, we crossed the treeline. Ahead of us was

Without a working magnetic compass so close to the North Pole, and without reliable maps, navigation in the summer is challenging. In the winter, it is awful.

tundra as far as the eye could see, immense, desolate, flat all the way to the horizon, dotted with thousands of small lakes that made navigation difficult. In winter, when all the lakes and rivers were frozen and covered with snow, in the dark, and without a working magnetic compass so close to the magnetic north, navigation was nearly impossible. Many a pilot had got lost in the tundra, especially during the winter months.

Adding to the challenge, the white and blue maps—with no indication of relief—showed only the largest lakes, which were often unrecognizable because their shape was frequently wrong. They had probably been drawn from aerial photographs taken when the lakes were still partially frozen.

Soon the shrubs disappeared and only wild grass dotted with a few grey rocks covered the Arctic plateau. Then the grass became increasingly scarce. So close to the magnetic north, the compass oscillated slowly in its globe without giving any reliable direction. I was navigating with the gyrocompass, which had to be manually adjusted as accurately as possible every 45 minutes, at least, by lining it up with a clearly identified landmark of known orientation, such as a river segment or the edge of a lake.

I had radioed a Flight Notification to the Yellowknife control tower shortly after takeoff. "Yellowknife from CF-OMF, takeoff from Great Slave Lodge, flying to Baychimo Harbour, direct. Back in two days. Four on board."

"Roger, OMF. Baychimo, two days."

If we were not back 24 hours after the scheduled date, a search would begin. No living creature, human or animal, lived on the tundra, except for a few small groups of muskoxen, and thousands of caribou in herds during the migrations between the Arctic coast and the boreal forest.

The air was calm, the plane smooth and docile. The passengers were asleep. It was hard to know exactly where we were, but our course should be fine according to the direction of the sun, so I dozed off. Such was the job of the bush pilot in the Arctic in summer: 200 hours, or more, of actual flying per month; on the go 24 hours a day, seven days a week. You had to sleep quickly and intensely at every stopover, if only for half an hour. Or you could nap in flight if a mechanic or passenger could take over part of the flight. Indeed, I would often ask the passenger sitting next to me to take

Typical map of the Northwest Territories in the late sixties. The black and red lines converge at the Water Resources shack at the mouth of the Perry River, not far from an Inuit summer camp (photo p.199). A short distance to the west along the coast, I noted, in black pen, a small Hudson's Bay trading post, a possible refuge in case of emergency.

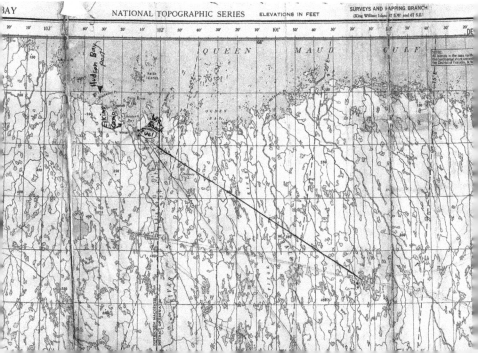

Noon over the tundra at 40 below. In the winter, navigation without the use of a magnetic compass is extremely stressful.

the controls so I could sleep for a while. Three minutes of training were enough, that's how simple airplanes are to fly. The only problem was to maintain the correct direction, so I would ask the passenger taking over to please wake me up if the sun in the cockpit moved to another angle.

After perhaps 10 minutes I woke up and looked around. To our left, far to the west, a dark line on the horizon was the first sign that a front was slowly heading our way, a warning that the weather could seriously deteriorate. But we would be back home tomorrow by the end of the day.

We reached the Arctic coast, which gave me a chance to get my bearings. We were flying over a fjord. Large swells crashed against the rocks. The coast was ragged, inhospitable. We finally spotted the small bay with the sleeping village of Baychimo Harbour on the far side. The wind had maintained its direction; the little harbour was still sheltered, and we landed. The 15 or 20 Inuit from the settlement had already come out of their tents and the few cabins and were running toward the tiny dock.

The water was muddy, and you could not see the bottom. We approached, gently rolling in the waves. The Inuit, with their dark skin and almond eyes, stood still, observing us, silent but evidently intrigued. The men were in front, in a semicircle. Behind them the women, in their long parkas, carried their babies directly on their backs, skin to skin. All their parkas had hoods rimmed with wolverine fur, which prevented the frost produced by their breath from crystallising on the fur in winter. Wolverines are

A young Inuit mother and her baby. Photo Bob Warnock.

ferocious animals. They have been known to chew off their own leg when caught in a wolf trap, and they've completely ravaged camps on the tundra that were temporarily left unoccupied.

Abruptly, the plane came to a halt. We were stranded on a sandbank. The Inuit all smiled at once. They knew it was very shallow there and had been wondering how we would get through. Now that the plane had beached, as they had expected, everything was back to normal, and they were amused by this anticipated

Baychimo Harbour. At the mouth of the small river stand the three buildings of the Hudson's Bay trading post.

though uncertain outcome. In the Arctic, you could never be sure of anything, and the Inuit found amusement in any event that surprised them. To be fair, they had neither radio, television, or cinemas to entertain themselves, and our arrival was most intriguing.

I got down onto the float and threw a long rope toward the people on shore, but the plane was not moving. Five hundred feet away, a seal popped its head out of the water to examine this unusual sight.

"Would you mind getting a canoe to pick up my passengers?" I called to the onlookers.

One of the men pushed a small wooden boat into the water. The boat had probably been transported from Great Slave Lake down the Mackenzie River by barge for some 1,000 miles to Inuvik and Tuktoyaktuk, near the Alaska border, and then another 1,000 miles along the Arctic coast. With the load lightened, the plane could float again, and I taxied over to the rudimentary dock.

The only white man in the village, Duncan Pryde, was a Scot who would later become a Member of the Legislative Assembly for the Northwest Territories and make the cover of *Time* magazine. He ran the tiny Hudson's Bay Company trading post, which bought seal and caribou skins from the Inuit and sold them guns, blankets, and some food. I was surprised he had not come to greet us.

Baychimo Harbour. My Cessna 185 provides the entertainment of the year.

I asked an Inuk, "Is the store manager not around?"

"I don't know."

The Inuk did not know because he had not entered the store recently to check. He had seen Duncan leave in a canoe the day before, but the manager might have returned surreptitiously.

Duncan Pryde catching a char near Bathurst Inlet.

"Has the manager left?"

"Yes."

"A while ago?"

"Yesterday."

"Where is he?"

"I don't know." How could one know where, in the Arctic, was a man who had left by canoe?

"Where did he say he was going?"

"Cambridge Bay." This was a community on Victoria Island, 100 miles northeast.

"When will he be back?"

"I don't know."

"When did he say he'd be back?"

"Tomorrow."

By now, my fishermen passengers had mutated into Martians, covered in green mosquito nets and loaded with cameras. The younger man chose a fishing rod and cast the hook near the plane, at a depth of three or four feet.

The Inuk, still impassive, looked at him, surprised. They may have thought that the white man knew something they did not.

The fisherman then turned around and addressed a splendid old man in English: "Are there any fish here?"

"I don't know."

"Will I be able to catch any in this bay?"

"Maybe."

"And that meat drying on a line over there, is it not fish?"

Baychimo Harbour trading post for the Hudson's Bay Company.

"Yes."

"Where was it caught?"

"I don't know."

Meanwhile, I refueled with the help of two young Inuit men, using the two 10-gallon kegs I had brought in the plane, a funnel, a chamois skin, and a bucket. It was not easy to balance on the wing as the aircraft pitched and rolled. I felt sorry for my tourists: there were probably no fish in the muddy, shallow bay, and certainly not near the dock. I got off the wing.

"Would you have a canoe to take my three passengers char fishing?"

"I don't know."

Again, I had not phrased the question properly.

"Do you have a canoe?"

"Yes, this one."

"Could you push it into the water, test the engine, and take my passengers fishing?"

"Yes."

Off they went, in a swarm of fishing rods and strange utensils "made in U.S.A."

Refuelling of the plane was now complete. It was in situations like this that one appreciated the value of fuel, and I regretted the 10-gallon keg we'd had to leave behind at the start of the journey. We should be able to just make it to the small fuel depot on our way back, provided we could fly there directly, and assuming that the weather did not deteriorate and force us to make detours. And also provided that the wind did not blow directly from the southwest, and the bay remained sufficiently sheltered for us to take off.

Escorted by little kids, Jerry, Alan, Jim, and Ike, round as marbles and always smiling, I took a walk into the village. Each tent was occupied by a family—father, mother, children, grandparents—who slept tightly together on seal and caribou skins. The wolfdogs were chained up in teams, and each animal dug a hole in the ground in which it curled up into a ball. They would go at each other's throats if not kept far enough apart.

In the last tent lived an elderly couple, who introduced themselves as Lucie Anagiak and John Ohenak. Lucie was small, skinny, and wrinkled. John was slim, tall, and even more wrinkled. They were both smiling, and looked happy and totally at peace after a good but very hard life. Lucie's long dress covered woolen trousers; caribou mukluks kept her feet warm. John was back from fishing and docked his canoe on the beach. His nine dogs were standing, yanking on their chains and howling. He threw each of them two large chars,

Arctic char at Baychimo Harbour.

Inuit woman scraping a seal skin with an *ulu* at Baychimo Harbour.

some of which were still jiggling after a short journey at the bottom of the boat, and which the dogs killed with a single bite and swallowed head first. Calm returned. Without saying a word, John invited me for dinner at his home. Few people spoke any English.

Squatting in front of the tent, John smoked his pipe, calm and content. His wife was skinning a seal with a copper scraper, an *ulu* set in a muskox-horn handle. The copper was collected along the coast in its natural state; it simply had to be hammered to make arrowheads or knife blades.

Lucie picked up an empty chipped metal cup on the ground, a few feet from her tent, and scooped a pile of old tea leaves out of it with her forefinger. She handed the cup to me with a smile and proudly poured me a hot cup of tea she had just made by adding a few leaves to a teapot that was already full of them, on a small gasoline burner. The fish of the day was too fresh, but she had raw and fermented fish in reserve. It was more tender, had greater flavour, and tasted fine on a piece of stale bread that she took out from under a sealskin. I marveled at the calm of this country, and the gentle, kind disposition of this quiet people.

At 10 o'clock in the evening I was still waiting for my fishermen. We should have been long gone, for the front was moving from the west and would soon block our way. This would make our high-frequency radio communications even more precarious because of static from the thunderclouds.

At last they arrived with their Inuk guide. They had spent 12 hours at sea, moving along the coast, and were returning empty-handed. On the way back their guide had made a pit stop to pick up the 30 or 40 big Arctic char that were struggling in the nets he left there all summer. This allowed him to feed his dogs and family every day without too much effort.

I got them loaded on the plane again. We skipped over the waves, violently bounced off a crest, and were in the air. Meanwhile, a family of seals basked in the sun on a rock before the storm.

Midnight. We headed southwest, cut across the Arctic coast, and continued inland, flying at 5,000 feet, but the ceiling was dropping. It was getting darker and darker. The sales rep turned on the light to continue reading his novel. The young woman was asleep.

Next to me, the old doctor Wishnick, a gynecologist from Chicago and a private pilot, pointed at the horizon: "That's not very inviting."

"Oh well, we should be able to get through." It was a way of saying "I've seen worse," an attempt to reassure myself, but I was beginning to worry.

To maintain their passengers' trust, pilots constantly had to convey a serious but relaxed air, calm and confident, with the right hand casually resting on the wheel and the left index finger on the map. But it was difficult to smile when you had knots growing tighter in your stomach.

John Ohenak at Baychimo Harbour.

Fifteen hundred feet. The ceiling was still dropping. It was almost dark.

"Would you mind turning off the light, please?"

Behind me, the representative made his answer clear: "No. I still have a chapter to read."

I turned out the light myself, and the young representative started sulking.

Three hundred feet. We were gliding over the endless, almost flat, rocky tundra at close to 120 miles per hour. It was starting to snow. I unreeled the high-frequency antenna and called Yellowknife, far to the south. No answer.

My right-hand neighbour, the doctor, was curious about the flight. "Have you made contact with Yellowknife?"

"Not yet, but the weather should be fine over there."

I smiled at my adventurous co-pilot. He was satisfied. Tomorrow night he would be back in Chicago.

One hundred and fifty feet. It was getting really dark. Navigation was tricky because visibility, in light drizzle and wet snow, was about one mile—enough to see things coming, but we really had to be careful. Fortunately, the ground was flat, and there was little risk of hitting a church steeple or getting tangled up in telephone wires. I slowed down and extended the flaps to 20 degrees. We should be able to manage, but the flight was getting very tense and tiring.

Altitude: 60 feet. Things were serious. The plane zigzagged between the light reliefs. It was hard to see much, and the conditions were becoming increasingly dangerous.

I finally gave up, and we made a U-turn back toward the north-east. It was prudent to gain a little altitude, and I was soon flying on instruments in the lower stratus. Five minutes later, at an altitude of 250 feet above the tundra, we emerged from the clouds. The windshield was covered in light ice and snow.

I tried again to get through the front 30 miles farther south, pushing the plane under the stratus right above the ground, but it was solid, unwavering. I had reeled up the trailing HF antenna long ago so it would not snare the ground.

To avoid a cluster of rocks I made a very quick turn, and the gyrocompass flipped and lost its reference. Now we had no way to determine our direction, as the magnetic compass did not work at all.

The tundra near the Arctic coast, east of Great Bear Lake.

We shortly ended up above a shallow basin, between the stratus and the rocks, from which there was no escape. We flew around in circles for 10 minutes, one wing grazing the tundra, the other scratching the bottom of the clouds. There was no place to land, and I wished I were somewhere else.

I tried to be comforting to the passengers, and to reassure myself. "Are you feeling cold?"

"No, thanks, I'm fine."

"We're going to have to head back north, we can't get through."

"All right."

Fortunately, these were good-natured fishermen. The problem was getting out of the little basin—and, assuming we could sneak out, determining which direction was north or northeast. We had almost two hours' worth of fuel left, but I was so tired after weeks of flying day and night with virtually no rest that I lacked the courage to keep going in circles like this under such awful conditions. I could have ascended into the clouds, but I did not know which direction to go. We were caught between a rock and a cloud.

We finally managed to slip out through a shallow opening. We passed a long, thin stretch of water, and I thought we would land immediately, but the lake was less than three feet deep and dotted with rocks. Even if we could land without any damage to the plane, it would be impossible to take off again.

The surface of the lake was a little lower than the surrounding ground, so, just under the clouds, we were now flying at nearly 200 feet. This was a lot less stressful, and I could finally take a quick look at the map. I identified the lake and, using the long lakeshore as an indication of our direction, I reset the gyrocompass: with 65 degrees of heading error, we were 25 miles west of our route, set to fade into oblivion somewhere in the tundra.

I couldn't stop here, so we had to continue flying in this awful weather. The hardest part was to continue chatting away with the passengers, maintaining a broad smile. "You look quite relaxed," a passenger had once remarked while we were flying over the tundra with very little visibility, my stomach in knots from flying so low for so long without being sure of the direction of our flight. I felt like telling him, "It's just for show, man. I am actually terrorized, and I don't know what to do."

Looking for seals in Bathurst inlet; note the sledge and caribou hides.

Trying to find a way through, near Bathurst Inlet.

We reached the coast and ascended to 3,000 feet. Everything was easy now that we knew where we were and, above all, in which direction we were flying. Thirty miles farther, we approached what geographers call "Bathurst Inlet." Judging by the map, you would think it was the capital of the Arctic. There seemed to be a port, an aeronautic base marked with a small blue anchor, and a radio station. I looked for the town, it had to be there, behind the hill ... And there it was. We had arrived.

I woke my people up. "We're going to stop here overnight."

They looked out, surprised but happy. They were probably glad to arrive somewhere, intrigued by the appearance of the place, disappointed by its obvious coldness. There was neither a port nor a dock, and the coast was desolate. All that stood there were six Inuit tents and three plywood shacks. Never before had a human settlement seemed so welcoming to me.

We landed at the mouth of the river because the sea was too rough. The river was muddy, dotted with sandbanks. If we hit one of them, the plane would flip over.

The gods were definitely in our favour and we landed safely. I suddenly felt much better. The locals must have been fast asleep, since no one came to greet us. To be fair, it was 3 a.m. Still, the Inuit

Inuit in Baychimo Harbour.

did not have any set schedule for waking and sleeping, at least not during the summer, so it was surprising no one was around. We docked nose up on a small rocky beach.

"Wait here. I'll go see where we can spend the night."

The first tent was empty. I went in and instantly rushed out. Seal and caribou skins had been rotting in there for months, along with fish remains. The smell was pungent. The next place, a plywood cabin covered with a tent cloth, was in the same state. Three times I filled my lungs before diving in to explore for a moment, then ran out: old cans of food, animal skins, and fish leftovers had all been abandoned there, strewn across the tent.

The front was catching up with us: light rain was starting to fall, and the cold seeped into my bones. It would be impossible to sleep in these tents, let alone put my passengers up in them. The three

Bathurst Inlet, where my floatplane sank.

small plywood shacks were boarded up. In the remains of a church, a lonely and sad pedal organ awaited the return of the faithful. A few keys produced a kind of death rattle. I played "O Canada."

"The village is abandoned. The cabins are uninhabitable. The best thing for you is to remain in the plane. I'll sleep on the floor in the church."

The tide was high. If I dragged the plane over the

Inuit woman. Photo Bob Warnock.

rocks tail first, I risked puncturing the floats and finding the plane high and dry once the sea had receded. I therefore decided to moor it a few feet from the coast, facing the mainland, held by two nylon ropes. With three people on board to keep an eye on things, it should be safe.

"If the wind rises any more, or if the plane starts bumping against the rocks, wake me up."

"Okay. Goodnight."

It was 3:30 a.m. At 5 a.m, the young representative came to wake me up. He was cold. I took the door of the church off its hinges to serve as a makeshift mattress, and he lay down on it.

Nine o'clock. This time the doctor came over.

"I think the weather is improving. Maybe we could take off."

By now it was really cold, the stratus clouds were hugging the coast, and layers of fog covered the sea. Quite a joker, this doctor. No way could we even think of flying in this weather, with low stratus clouds hanging on the small hills all around.

"It might be a little early," I told the doctor, "but we could always have breakfast."

If he only knew how exhausted I was, he would not have woken me up. But the passenger pays for the flight, so he or she is always right. We started walking toward the plane.

"You know, I think the floats took in some water during the night," he told me on the way.

Floatplane pilots spent almost as much time pumping water from their floats as they did flying their plane, but I thought it could not be too serious after just five hours.

The wind had shifted to the north, and the cool air from the ice pack was really waking me up.

Over the dune, I saw the plane. I stopped, dumbfounded, and my jaw dropped in amazement. The plane had sunk! Only the tips of the pontoons, the cabin, and the engine cowling were above the surface. The two ropes holding it to the shoreline were taut. The tail, the back of the fuselage, and most of the pontoons were underwater. I had a feeling my passengers would have a lot of adventures to tell their friends in Chicago—assuming they ever got back.

Staring at this amazing sight, I asked the doctor, "What happened?"

"Shortly after you left, we heard water dripping into the floats. Then, two or three hours later, it seemed to run faster and it felt like we were sinking a little."

"And you didn't come to wake me up?"

"Yes, of course. But there were so many mosquitoes that I rushed back to the plane. Then it carried on sinking, faster and faster, and all of a sudden it tipped backward, sank, and stabilized on the bottom."

After the representative had left, the doctor and his wife had settled in the front of the plane, which was still dry. Ultimately, as one of my instructor friends liked to say, "the only thing which really matters in life is remaining in good health." Indeed, we were all in good health, at least so far.

I helped the young woman off the airplane and rushed in to grab everything I could salvage. Some of the radios and electrical gear in the fuselage behind the cabin were partially underwater. However, the double-barrel rifle, the cartridges, and the Emergency Location Transmitter (ELT) were fine, as was the large box of supplies: everything was sealed in waterproof packaging. We set ourselves up on the rocks.

"Do you think the plane will be able to fly again?"

"Well, I don't know. We'll try to get it out of there, but in any case, someone will soon come and get us." I thought about the situation a little more and asked, "Would you mind helping me pull the plane out of the water?"

Bathurst Inlet, on the Arctic coast. Note that the pontoons of my Cessna 185 are entirely underwater, except for the front tip. Painting by Hélène Girard from sketches and photos by the author.

With the engine running, and my passengers pulling on the ropes, I tried to move the plane up the rock and pebble beach to get the pontoons above water so I could pump them out and get the plane floating again, but nothing worked. I switched off the ignition and set my passengers up in the church, on my sleeping bag. Had there been something to burn, we would gladly have made a fire. It was cold in this part of the world: 39° F on average in July.

We had salvaged from the plane the big char they were triumphantly taking back to the United States—which they had bought for a dollar from their Inuit guide who was going to feed it to his dogs. An old Indigenous man near Great Slave Lake had once taught me how to open and gut a fish. It was an art that could not be improvised.

"Would you like some?"

"No, thank you."

It was fresh, but admittedly not very appetizing: the poor creature had spent 12 hours wrapped in newspaper without being gutted. It was very tasty though, and this would certainly be the last meal we would be having in the next several days.

My passengers had a lot of fun watching me gobble up their raw fish. I was deliberately clowning about to cheer them up. Morale had been high from the start.

"Do you really think we'll get out of here?"

"Damn right! Tomorrow night at the latest."

I explained to them that within a few hours the company would start to worry. It would send out planes to look for us and, thanks to our distress beacon, which would reach anything that flew within about 50 miles, finding us would be child's play.

In reality, no one would start to wonder where we were until the next day or the day after that. It would be another 24 hours before someone got seriously worried. After that, the planes sent out to search for us would come up against the same front that had stopped us and would turn back with their minds at rest: "They're trapped by the bad weather and will return with the sunshine." Later, when the good weather would arrive and we were still missing, the search would intensify. As for the Emergency Location Transmitter, it actually had a range of only 20 or 30 miles, and operated for only about 20 hours. Even then, only search aircraft equipped with a special direction finder operating on the VHF distress frequency would pick up the signal, and those direction finders were only mounted on large civil and military rescue aircraft. Search and Rescue would look for us along our 600-mile route, covering an increasingly wider strip. Bathurst Inlet was far from our direct course. Within eight days, someone would certainly find us, and I was not worried—nothing like a week's holiday: sleep, late mornings, daydreaming, listening to the waves, and more sleep.

I finished my fish while my passengers heartily dug into the box of supplies. They had probably never been camping before and were having a ball: they made tea and soup on the tiny gasoline stove, ate big biscuits packed with vitamins, and joked around. With four of us, thanks to these biscuits, horrible dried meat, sugar cubes, and cans of food, we would have no trouble lasting eight days. By some wonderful stroke of luck, we were at the mouth of a river, and the water—albeit muddy—was fresh and therefore drinkable.

At 11 a.m., the sky was still overcast and the ceiling very low.

Bathurst Inlet.

The enthusiastic manual of the emergency transmitter would cheer up even the most discouraged castaway. In two days I would start turning on the transmitter for one or two hours at a time, at the times stated in the instructions to save the batteries.

"Can you call someone with this device?"

"No, it just emits a distress signal for planes. You'll see, we won't even need to use it. But first I'll call with the radios on board."

I returned to the plane. The radios, in the fuselage behind the cabin, were dipped in salt water. Without turning on the power for fear of causing a short circuit, I spoke into the microphone. The doctor, who had followed me, heard me talking about latitude, longitude, and "sunken airplane." The word "Mayday" came up regularly. He was satisfied. I wore the headset on my ears—under the pretext that it was more sensitive than the cabin speaker—and that way he could not hear the total silence of the radio. A real circus act.

"Did you manage to get in touch with anyone?"

"No, but the message must have reached somewhere and will be relayed."

The other user guide, from the survival kit, was like a Robinson Crusoe story. It was just as enthusiastic as the ELT manual: "Above all, keep a cool head." In the Arctic, that's the easy part.

"Set up camp." Many drawings showed how to shield oneself from the wind and the rain: one only needed to cut tree branches. We had the axe but not the trees.

"Make a fire." It was easy: all you had to do was build a pyramid of dead wood. If you had no matches, you could rub two pieces of wood together, using a shoelace and a branch bent into an arc. Unfortunately, again, there was no wood, dead or otherwise.

One could also write SOS in the snow. There was no snow either, but in a month or two there would certainly be lots of it.

The "traps" section was the most exciting. Using more shoelaces and arched branches, you could cobble together the most effective traps. The manual warned that eating too much rabbit was bad for the digestive system. This wasn't really a concern, though, since there were no rabbits around. Just a few rare lemmings or small ground-squirrels. Funny how there was always something missing.

Yes, eight days of vacation, 10 or 15, perhaps, if we were lucky; it was unhoped-for luxury.

My passengers were getting organized in the church, and I headed back to the plane. The back half of the floats was underwater so I couldn't pump the water out. To lighten the load and try to raise

Downtown Bathurst Inlet.

the plane a bit on the water, I retrieved the two empty fuel barrels from the cabin and used them to drain the wing tanks. For over two hours I hugged the 10-gallon keg with my right arm, holding it under the wing while pressing the drain valve with my left thumb. I would collect a small trickle of fuel, which I then had to empty into a rusty 45-gallon drum full of sand and seawater lying nearby. I was in and out of the water all the time, so I remained naked from the waist down.

An hour later, exhausted and frozen, I emptied the fuel from the second wing tank into the 45-gallon drum, leaving just two or three gallons to allow the engine to run. I pumped the floats one more time, just in case. Then, at full throttle, I tried to hoist the aircraft out of the water again. The plane did not move.

It was now 10 p.m. I put on my trousers, headed back to the church, where everybody was sleeping, and swallowed a dozen sugar cubes. Then, totally naked, I began working under the floats, digging a trench to move the aircraft forward. The sea was rising. I had to dive under the floatplane, push a rock aside, remove a pebble, come back up to breathe, go down again, dig some more, breathe again, dive again, and repeat. I used an old rifle as a lever.

Again, the engine roared. The propeller sprayed up columns of water; the plane rocked from side to side, hesitated a little. Victory. We had gained a couple of inches. Nothing like it to cheer up a pilot. If I could just get the airplane higher, I could pump out the water from the next compartment.

It was time to prepare tomorrow's breakfast: in other words, catch fish. I swam out to stretch the small net across the river, anchoring it with a rock. Pushed downstream by the current, I was walking along the beach back to the plane when I came to a sudden halt: a nice cabin, the door ajar, seemed to invite visitors. The inside was empty but clean. A wooden table, a bench ... and three beds! Well, three bunks, one of which was even graced with an old mattress. There were no sheets or blankets, but all this luxury was unexpected.

Running like a kid who had just unwrapped a tricycle at Christmas, I rushed toward the church ... No, my brave fishermen would take offence at my nudity. After a quick detour by the plane to collect my trousers, I ran to share the good news with my passengers, who were fast asleep.

"Come and see, a castle, a palace ..."

They laughed, and we started moving our treasures.

"What are you doing?"

"Oh, I'm working on the plane."

"Any progress?"

"Getting there, getting there."

"Can we help you?"

"No, thank you."

"When can we head back?"

"Maybe tomorrow." I was starting to talk like the Inuit: nothing was ever certain.

"How about dinner?"

"Good idea. Make yourselves some soup, I'm going back to the plane."

I sucked on a tea bag. If the cold got too brutal I would light a fuel fire, but for now every drop was precious. The survival biscuits were not bad after all.

Midnight. I kept digging under the plane, but soon my fingers were bleeding and I had to give up. The rocks under the floats were immovable. I came out of the water, put on a damp sweater, and sat on a rock, meditating. Something was making my head itch. I ran my hand through my hair. Nothing. Well, we were definitely going to be here for a while. There, it was itching again. I ran my hand through my hair and caught ... a bird. A little sparrow, startled, whom I was holding prisoner. It was very warm.

"Are you lost too?"

It must have been starving and happily gobbled up my biscuit leftovers. For a moment I mused about eating it, for, apart from the lemmings, if there were any, it was probably the only living game within several hundred miles.

"Go on, we're all castaways. Let's not eat each other up."

I opened my hand, but the bird did not move. Then, a while later, it leapt away without a chirp, rose very high into the sky, and disappeared toward the north. My floatplane looked so sad, tilted and miserable!

For hours I fought vertigo, sleep, the urge to give up and let the cold take over. I wandered between the tents, my teeth chattering, in search of an idea. I tried a variety of empty canister combinations,

Baychimo Harbour.

under the fuselage or the floats, to get the plane out. Nothing worked.

The light bulb went on when I saw the corner of a rusty 10-gallon keg, half buried in the ground. I pulled it out and cleaned it up. I found another keg near a cabin. Added to the two empty kegs from the plane, these barrels should provide enough buoyancy to lift the back of the aircraft to the surface.

It was 2 a.m. Two and a half hours later I had set up a system of ropes underwater to force the four barrels under the fuselage and the pontoons. Our plane began to rise. I was intoxicated by this success. The fin was now completely out of the water. Then the horizontal stabilizer emerged. Soon the whole fuselage was lifted, and the water drained out through a small panel I had unscrewed under the tail section.

What a beautiful sight! The plane rose up proudly. The tops of the floats were now completely out of the water and, swimming around them, I could pump each compartment, one after the other. Perhaps 50 gallons of water came out. *Hang on, little pump, don't give up on me.*

Six o'clock in the morning. The seats were back in place, the cabin cleaned. Gallon by gallon, I slowly poured the fuel back into the wings. Every time I had to fill the bucket with fuel, walk barefoot across the rocks and into the water, and climb onto the float, then onto the engine hood, then onto the wing to pour the fuel into the tanks with a funnel and through a chamois skin, all without spilling the bucket. Twenty times I repeated the maneuver.

I went to collect the fish net: it was empty. The plane was now dry; I removed the barrels attached to the back of the floats. My

Bathurst Inlet.

passengers were sound asleep in their cabin, which was almost warm. The box of supplies lay on the ground, half empty. It was my fault; I had promised them that our stay at this miserable place would be short. A tin of corned beef was hanging out among some dirty papers. The young woman had found it too fatty, so she had thrown it away. Little did she know that she had narrowly escaped some serious weight loss!

"Is the plane ready?"

"Absolutely, ma'am."

"So, we're leaving?"

"Whenever you like."

I would have liked to sleep for an hour or two, but the most urgent step was to inform the outside world of the state of our health. The floats looked good, but we had best hurry and take off promptly before they filled up again.

"How did you manage to get the plane out?"

"I floated it back up with empty fuel kegs and was able to pump the water out of the pontoons. It took longer than expected."

To the southwest, the sky was still pitch-black, and the weather was still just as worrying. We probably had enough fuel to reach the small fuel depot on the tiny island 200 miles to the south—provided we could fly direct, in a straight line. However, if we had to struggle under the low stratus clouds and make long detours that would extend our route, we risked running out of fuel and having to try to land on the tundra with a floatplane.

The horizon was overcast, and I no longer had the courage to fight the clouds, with the added handicap of having to fly in a straight line for lack of fuel. I could not take it anymore. I was exhausted, cold, and miserable; the task was too hard; and I simply gave up. We headed northeast, toward Baychimo Harbour and its friendly Inuit. One hour later we were among the good people we had met two days earlier.

This time we avoided the sandbank and reached the dock without any problems. The Inuit welcomed us back. I set up my passengers at the Hudson's Bay Company post. What a comfortable little store! If someone had filled the water tank, we could even have washed our hands. And the place was so warm, too, thanks to the oil stove! We were in a very good mood, and my passengers all lay down—one on a bed, the other on the floor, and the third on a couch.

I wrestled with the store's radio set, an old transmitter in a corner. I spent half an hour calling, giving our latitude, longitude, and aircraft registration, and asking for fuel. No reply. I tried all possible combinations of frequencies and buttons, but the speaker remained silent. There were three or four unmarked frequency crystals for calling, selected by a large knob, but their transmission frequencies were

The author refueling a Cessna 206 with a 10-gallon keg.

The Hudson's Bay Company trading post, Baychimo Harbour.

not indicated and the receiver was variable, like the receiver on an old radio set, so I did not know where to set it to listen for a reply.

A crowd of curious Inuit gradually invaded the room, listening to my messages. No one spoke, and when I turned around, they all smiled kindly. I lay down on a pile of sealskins, wrapped myself in them, and fell asleep, knocked out by fatigue.

Five hours later, John Daykin, manager of our Yellowknife base, woke me up, frantically shaking me. One of our distress messages had been picked up by a Hudson's Bay Company station, relayed from one radio set to another throughout the Arctic, then south all the way to Yellowknife, where someone had called my company. John was already up in the air looking for us, loaded with fuel; he had two observers on board, one of whom was a mechanic. The radio message, relayed through Yellowknife, reached him just as he thought he had found us: he had spotted a float drifting on a lake, with a twisted plane carcass on the rocks. As he later learned, that was from an old accident. This time, we were going home for real.

Before waking me up, John and his two helpers had refueled our plane and pulled it out of the water ... again, because it had sunk along the dock—in two feet of water this time, which made it a whole lot easier to rescue. It was the start of the summer season, and the floats, which had spent the winter in the hangar, had been fitted back on to replace the skis without anyone checking that they were waterproof. There must have been a small leak somewhere. One can never think of everything!

We headed back to the lodge on Great Slave Lake for breakfast, chatting and telling stories. My passengers took showers and picked up their luggage, and I flew them back to Yellowknife. The rest of their group had already left. Luckily, a DC-3 with passengers for another lodge had landed at noon and was headed south again, connecting with the regular plane to Winnipeg and then Chicago.

I told my company that I needed 18 hours of peace to sleep; if they called me for a flight, I'd quit.

A few weeks later, John Daykin, seeing me arrive at the floatplane base, stood up from his desk, came to open the door, stood to attention, and gave me a military salute. "Sir, it is an honour for me to welcome such a hero."

As I stood there, stunned, he laughed and handed me a letter. The good Dr. Wishnick had written such an enthusiastic letter to the company that it made us smile: "Never in my life have I ever seen such a tenacious, ingenious, persistent, resilient and fantastic young man, be it in the army or in the civilian world ..."

Well, the tribute was nice to read, and it offered some compensation for the cold baths and sleepless nights.

8. In the Frozen Darkness of the Arctic Islands

Yellowknife, December 1968,
−40° F, Otter on wheels and skis.

Bob Warnock, the manager of the Yellowknife base and a remarkable pilot, came over to me, grinning from ear to ear. He looked like he was about to make a good joke. "Departure tomorrow morning," he said, "for eight days in the north of Victoria Island with CF-OVN, the Otter on wheels and skis."

I was used to those jokes. "Sure, why not? And why wait till tomorrow? I might as well leave right now."

Winter in Yellowknife was harsh. In mid-December it was dark at 2 p.m., the wind blew sometimes at 10 or even 20 knots, making life miserable, and the local temperature was typically around −30° F, not accounting for the wind factor. I doubted we would be flying much before Christmas. I hated Bob's occasional announcements of idiotic flights: my heart and breathing stopped each time for a second, my blood pressure went through the roof, and it was bad for my physical and mental health. Not at all amused, I shrugged my shoulders and returned to my newspaper.

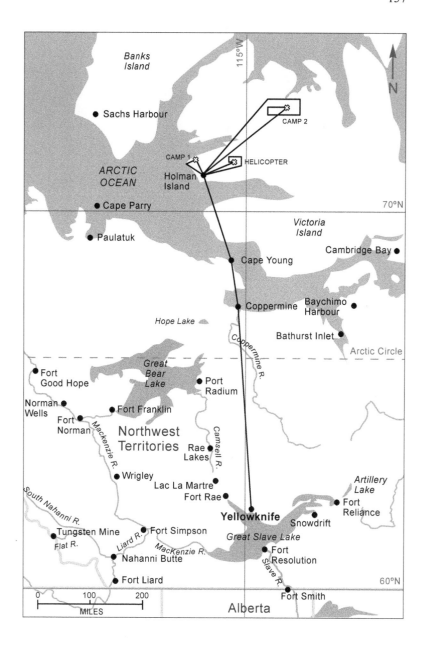

But Bob insisted. "I'm not kidding, you know!"

A kind of terror must have shown on my face, and I felt I was turning pale. Still, I tried to convince myself that he was pulling my leg. It would be pure madness to go near the pole in late December, when the frozen tundra was covered in snow and one could not see any relief. Even at noon the sun was very low on the horizon, or below it at higher latitudes, and the sky was usually so overcast that it was practically dark. As everything was greyish and there were no shadows, the pilot had no way to estimate his height above the ground. In addition, it was impossible to recognize lakes under the ice and snow, so maps were of no help. Not only did the pilot not know where he was, but he also could not be sure which direction he was flying—this close to the magnetic pole, the compass leaned pathetically in its small globe, indicating completely random headings. To make these flights even more challenging, fine ice crystals suspended in the atmosphere reduced visibility.

Bob was smiling at my anguished look and burst out laughing. However, if there were truly a customer who wanted to go north at this time of year, it was no laughing matter. I thought of asking him why he wasn't taking the flight himself, if he found the idea so amusing. But he had become the manager and did not fly anymore since being diagnosed with leukemia.

A Gateway Aviation Otter on wheel-skis in front of the company base in Yellowknife.

De-icing an Otter in Yellowknife.

Then he dealt the final blow: "You have to take Joe Flemming of Arctic Enterprises, with Graham Adams and Stan, two of his prospectors, a snowmobile, a sled, two or three 45-gallon fuel drums, and all the gear they need for their camp. You'll be heading somewhere near the 73rd parallel north. It shouldn't be any problem. You'll have an almost-full moon to help you navigate."

With Bob, there was never a problem: "Hakuna Matata" as they say in Tanzania. I wondered how he had managed to survive so many years of flying in the North with that mindset.

This flight was insane, but it had to be done since the customer was very real, and I needed the money to go back to college the following year.

To make things worse, pilots were paid only if the flight was actually completed, and they were paid by the mile along the direct route requested by the customer. Detours did not count, nor did four- or five-hour flights at the end of which you did not reach the destination or were unable to land. So after preparing the plane, loading the cargo, and taking off, you had to go all the way, even if it meant making stops of a few hours—or sometimes a few days—to wait for the weather to improve.

It took me half an hour to recover from the shock, two hours to gather all the maps of the region, and 10 hours to prepare the plane

Coppermine, on the Arctic coast.

and load the gear. After a few hours of restless sleep, I took off on skis from Great Slave Lake at 9 a.m., one hour before sunrise, to head to the Arctic coast, where the sun would be below the horizon and the sky would be even darker.

During the first couple of hours, navigation was relatively easy for someone used to flying in the Arctic in winter, as, even in the dull grey landscape with minimal light, the frozen lakes clearly stood out from the dark background of stunted spruce trees, which meant they could be identified on a map. These maps were often inaccurate and gave no indication of relief: the ground was shown in white, which was fitting at this time of the year, and the lakes, rivers, and Arctic Ocean were all a pretty light blue, which was supposed to represent the colour of water in the summer. But in winter, once you crossed the treeline and reached the tundra, the lakes and rivers completely disappeared under ice and snow, and that was when pilots started to get knots in their stomachs.

I finally got my bearings when we reached the Coppermine River and eventually picked up Morse code signals from the radio beacon in Coppermine, an Inuit village on the coast to which my automatic direction finder (ADF) was now guiding me. The end of the flight was easy, even though I could no longer see a thing, what with the fog banks, the drifting snow, and the low stratus clouds, all in darkness. At this latitude in December, the sun never peeped over the horizon. I decided enough was enough, at least for today, and we were going to stop here.

There was little snow on the ocean ice, so I decided to land the Otter on wheels rather than skis, and began to gently descend parallel to the shore in front of the village, which was sheltered by a large bay. The snowdrifts were frozen but small enough that the landing was not as rough as I had anticipated. We found locals who would put us up for the night, but I had to refuel first.

Joe Melukchuk was a devoted Inuit employee of the Hudson's Bay Company's small local trading post. He very kindly offered to help me transport the 45-gallon fuel drums that Gateway Aviation had dropped by barge on the beach during the previous summer to refuel their planes throughout the year. Joe's offer to help, and his snowmobile, was a godsend, and I gladly took him up on it.

The operation went on into the night. The hardest part was getting the fuel drums out of the snow and breaking, with an axe, the ice that had accumulated around them. Then we had to roll the drums across the snow to the sled so Joe could take them to the plane. The strong wind lashed at our faces as I bustled about beside

Downtown Coppermine.

the fuel drum, trying to operate the small hand pump and refuel the plane. Meanwhile, at the other end of the fuel hose, Joe was carefully pouring the precious liquid into a large funnel, through a chamois-skin filter, and into the plane's fuel tank.

"Maybe your cheek is frozen," Joe suddenly said to me with a smile. In the Arctic, nothing was ever certain, which was reflected in the way people spoke: statements often started with "Maybe ...," even when there was certainty. If Joe was suggesting that "maybe my cheek was frozen," this meant that maybe it was serious, and maybe I needed to act quickly.

I had not felt anything at all, but in a cabin along the shoreline I discovered a large patch of frozen, white flesh on one of my cheeks. Patches like that could be thawed by applying a bare hand to the spot, but if you waited too long the white skin turned black and fell off, leaving a hole in your cheek or where your nose used to be.

Once my cheek had regained its human colour, I went back to the plane. We then had to go fetch a third drum. We spent over an hour trying to wrestle it out of the ice with bars and axes. It was well and truly stuck.

"Maybe the barrel is frozen in the ice," explained Joe, still with a big smile on his face. Indeed, that was very likely—some would even say "certain."

I smiled back at him. "I think you're right."

Eventually we got the third drum out. It's lucky we did not need any more fuel: the remaining barrels were jammed solid among the rocks and the ice.

As we emptied the last drum into the aircraft's tanks, Joe opened up: "I think on Sunday I'll go caribou hunting with my sled. Very many caribous a day away from here. I'll give you a piece." Caribou meat was delicious. He then added, with a detached but hesitant look, "Maybe, when you come back through Coppermine, you could bring me a small bottle of whiskey. Just a little one, for Christmas."

I promised him his bottle, but in the end didn't get it to him until seven months later, in July, when I was back in the area with a floatplane. For Christmas, Joe would drink water. I then asked him if the weather would be good the next day.

"Maybe," he said to me with his eternal smile. He was very kind and told me what I wanted to hear, which would help me get some sleep. But later, when he took me back to his cabin on his snowmobile, he spent 20 minutes before he went in, checking that all his belongings were put away and securely fastened. He took special care to ensure his tent was folded up in a bundle as well as his seal and caribou skins. He then carefully placed a piece of tarpaulin over his snowmobile before going to check on his dogs. They were tied up with thin chains to stakes planted in the ground.

If he is checking everything so carefully, I thought to myself, it must be because bad weather is coming. He must have told me a white lie to keep me happy.

Sure enough, the blizzard set in during the night, and the next day there was no question of moving. Same thing the following day. By the third day at dawn—that is, at around 10 a.m., since the sun always remained below the horizon, even at noon, during the winter months—the storm was almost over. In just two hours, thanks to the blow pots, the engine had thawed enough for me to start it. Half an hour later it was warm enough to take off.

For the first 100 miles we were flying strictly on instruments in low clouds of ice crystals. At last we started picking up the small Cape Young radio beacon, flew over the American Distant Early Warning (DEW) Line station built for radar detection of Russian bombers coming over the pole to attack, and then emerged from the clouds heading straight north over the frozen ocean.

By the time we arrived at Holman Island it was 3 p.m. and it had already been night for a while. We had made the whole flight from Cape Young at an altitude of just 1,000 feet and with less than two miles of visibility. In a place where everything was uniformly grey and you could not see the relief, that was not a lot of clearance over the ground, especially at night.

For 10 minutes we flew around in circles, looking

Warming up the engine of an Otter with blow pots in the tundra.

for somewhere to land, but everything was grey or black, and I had no desire to land on the ocean due to the large snow drifts and ice ridges. The only place left to land was right in the middle of the Inuit village, between the tents and the plywood cabins that lined each side of a single main avenue leading to the church square. Fortunately, a light bulb shone in front of each house, and we landed as easily as we might have on the runway of a large airfield.

I kept the engine slowly running for a few more minutes to let it cool gently before turning it off, and the people of the village came to greet us. In the dark we could make out the faces of perhaps a hundred Inuit children. The men were a little farther behind, and the women farther still, carrying their babies on their backs, inside their parkas. The few white people in the hamlet also came to welcome us. The administrator, Wayne Born, took us to his house for coffee. He was particularly proud of the polar bear hide adorning one of the walls.

I apologized for having landed in the centre of his village between two rows of houses: "The light bulbs in front of the cabins served as runway lights."

"You did well," he replied. "That's our landing strip. Everyone lands there." By "everyone," he meant the three or four crazy bush pilots like me who would visit over the 10 months of winter. "But you need to buzz the community first to get the kids off the street before landing!"

We headed from the administrator's home to go pay old Bill Joss a visit. The heart of Holman Island, the hub of the small hamlet, the community centre, was Bill's house. That was the radio station: Bill received and transmitted all messages on high frequency and acted as a gateway to the outside world—when the radio worked, that is. Bill's house was also where the village celebrated the arrival of a plane. We had arrived on Holman Island ready to pay the traditional landing fee: a few pounds of potatoes, carrots, and oranges, and, above all, a good bottle or two. And so, after about an hour, perhaps 50 people were crammed in Bill's small living room. The Inuit sat on the floor and everyone smiled pleasantly, just looking around.

Bill reigned over the Hudson's Bay Company's trading post. But the main attraction was his indoor golf course, the only one in the Canadian Arctic. Between the kitchen and the living room, Bill

Holman Island. Airplanes land downtown, on the main street.

had cut out a hole in the floorboards and fitted it with a small net to collect the golf balls. On holidays, the carpet was rolled back to uncover the hole, and the games would begin. You had to be really careful when you swung the golf club not to hit the ceiling lamp or the plates drying above the stove. Bill was probably the only player ever to have managed to get the ball into the hole without breaking glasses or knocking down a pile of dishes.

I'd been there for an hour, and I figured my engine must have cooled down enough to avoid the immediate evaporation of the gallon of fuel I was about to pour into the oil tank. This oil dilution would help with start-up the next day. I set up boards of plywood in front of the engine to shield it from the wind and the snow, and covered it with an engine tent. I then took out the heavy battery and carried it back to Bill's house on a sled he had lent me. I could have left it in the plane and kept it at a reasonable temperature with one or two small flameless catalytic stoves, covering it with a sleeping bag, but it was safer to store the battery somewhere warm. I knew from experience that the sleeping bag could melt or be scorched by the heat from the blow pots, or get eaten away by the acid from the battery and turn into lace, so that, when we took off the next day, we would find ourselves in a cloud of down.

With all that said and done, I was starting to feel the long day wearing me down. I went to find somewhere to sleep, since the administrator had not invited me to spend the night at his place, and there was no room at Bill's. In these cases, in Inuit or First Nations villages, I would usually go and knock on the door of the local nurse or schoolteacher. They were always glad to receive visitors and were usually very nice. Some of them were even *really* nice.

I was told that the teacher on Holman Island was Miss Myrtle Delany. As I was getting ready to go knock on her door with my sleeping bag under my arm, she arrived at Bill's house with Joe Flemming, the head of the expedition. The nerve! Joe had taken advantage of my absence while I was preparing my plane for the night to go and set himself up at her place. I was furious. Teachers were supposed to welcome and comfort pilots, not passengers! I was told that she was also the nurse, so there was no point knocking on the door of the infirmary. Joe's two associates had disappeared, but I was so mad I didn't even think to ask where they had gone for the night and if I could join them. I asked Bill if I could sleep on the floor right there, at his place.

"Sure," he said, "no problem. You can lie down under the kitchen table."

That is where I spent the night: in my sleeping bag, right in the middle of the golf course.

A couple of years later, in Yellowknife, I was still hearing about

Downtown Holman Island.

old Bill. Word had it that he had come to town to marry a young Inuit girl from Holman Island. "And how old is the young lady?" asked the clerk of the court. "Sixteen years old," she replied. "Ah, miss, unfortunately in that case I cannot help you. You'll have to come back in a couple of years." I never heard the end of the story.

Anyhow, at 6 a.m. I sat up and banged my head on the underside of the table, which swiftly woke me up. I rolled up my sleeping bag and went to get everything ready for the flight. First the wings and the windshield had to be de-iced. This was a dangerous job because it required climbing on the wings, without slipping, to sweep away the ice. That took about an hour. I then had to set up the two small fuel burners under the engine tent and arrange aluminium stovepipes end to end over the blow pots to guide the heat—two or three pipes toward the radial engine's cylinders, and one or two more to the oil tank.

Once I could turn the propeller a little by hand, following an hour or two of warming, I could try starting it up after removing the engine tent, the plywood boards placed in front of the engine, the stovepipes, and the blow pots. When everything went well, it took two or three hours to defrost the plane and thaw the engine before trying to start it, and then a good half hour to warm it up before taking off. All this was obviously "pro bono" work, for we were paid by the mile.

Thus, on December 18 at 11 a.m. we began to pick up speed between the cabins, in front of which the light bulbs clearly demarcated the main street that had served as a landing strip. We had already tried to get to the base camp the day before, but had to turn back in the snow and the fog. Today, however, the weather was fine. The sun was below the horizon, but the moon lit up the uniformly grey landscape a little. I took a sighting on the moon with the astrocompass to reset our heading and maintained our course, even though I could not locate us on the map at all. We should arrive after three-quarters of an hour, but we were already lost.

I tried to follow the coast by flying very low, but it was flat, frozen, and hidden under a cover of snow. Following 10 minutes of quick zigzags, the shoreline, or what I thought was the shoreline, disappeared: I had been following a crack in the ice. We turned around in the dark and soon found the real shoreline, recognizable by a few grey rocks. Eventually we spotted the little white tent of base camp (you'd think they would have the brains to paint it orange!) and very cautiously landed on the tundra, unloaded the fuel drums and snowmobile, and returned to Holman Island in total darkness. The fine ice crystals suspended in the air did not help with the navigation.

I was now staying with Father Tardy and could lay my sleeping bag on the couch. When neither the teacher nor the nurse was available in an Indigenous village—they were sometimes there with their husbands—a great alternative was the presbytery. There was always room, even if it meant sleeping on a bench in the small wooden church. If the priest was traveling and his house was locked, there was still one last resort: the Royal Canadian Mounted Police (RCMP) station. The Mounted Police were very friendly but often did not have a great sense of humour, and evenings spent there were not as lively as elsewhere.

The most pleasant place to spend the night on Holman Island was actually the village cooperative. This was where exquisite artefacts of great value made by the Inuit were sold, such as beautiful serpentine sculptures, magnificent parkas, caribou boots and mittens lined with wolf fur, and exceptional lithographs, especially those of the old Kalvak. On another flight, several years later, I spent a few idyllic days there, in the room of the cooperative manager who was in Ottawa for the week. What a luxury compared to Bill's kitchen floor under the table, and even to the good father's couch!

At Father Tardy's place I met Guy Causse, a French veteran from the war in Algeria who was now an Alouette helicopter pilot-instructor. He and a Japanese helicopter pilot had been hired a little earlier by Joe Flemming to stake some claims in the area. Joe had arranged for two Alouettes to be flown in on a Hercules to Cambridge Bay, and then the two helicopters followed an Otter on skis, like mine, to Holman Island. Once they reached their base camp, Guy and the Japanese pilot, who had never seen the Arctic before, let alone flown near the pole during winter, decided that it would be wiser to stay on the ground. It was a sound decision, since they had no way of following a course or finding their bearings. In fact, Ron Sheardown, the pilot who found Bob Gauchie in the tundra after two months of winter (Chapter 3), and who rescued me in Coppermine after my engine smoked and sputtered for a while

Resupplying a prospector's camp in the tundra.

until finally quitting altogether over the shoreline (Chapter 10), had spotted the two helicopters in Yellowknife and noticed that they were not even equipped with an ordinary gyrocompass. "This is foolish and hopeless," he thought. "They'll never be able to do the job." Ron had been staking his own claims in the same area northeast of Holman Island, and he was unhappy to see Joe Flemming trying his luck just around the corner.

One day, however, Joe Flemming's men were so insistent they go somewhere that the Japanese pilot took off with one of them, Smoky Hornby, a prospector from Yellowknife. After three miles the helicopter hit a snow-covered hill in the dark. The pilot and his passenger were rescued just in time, as they were starting to freeze to death, by a couple of Ron Sheardown's own prospectors—Eddy Mercredi and Zek (Isadore) McDonald. "Two fantastic fellows," according to Ron. They called Ron in Yellowknife with the camp's high-frequency radio, and at four the next morning, in total darkness, Ron took off from Yellowknife with his turbo Beaver to recover Joe Flemming's Japanese pilot and Smoky Hornby and bring them back to town.

Guy had then tried to make another flight by himself, got lost, eventually ran out of fuel, landed on the tundra, and waited until an Inuk passed by on a dogsled. Guy stuck out his thumb and hitchhiked back to Holman Island. Naturally, he asked me if I would take him to try to find his helicopter, which was especially difficult as he had no idea where he had landed. We nevertheless ended up spotting it, alone in the snow, about 20 miles from the village. We landed and refilled its tanks. As it was too late to get it flying that night, I took Guy back to Father Tardy's place and the next day dropped him off by his helicopter again, then flew around in circles until he had taken off so he could follow me. Unfortunately, he was flying much slower than I was, and despite all my zigzagging to try to slow down, we eventually lost each other. He still managed to get back to Holman Island and was so happy that he offered me a free helicopter ride over the village.

That evening, rumour spread in the village that the pastor, Terry Buckel, was going to show a film in the small Protestant chapel. The locals were terribly thrilled. This annoyed Father Tardy, who soon announced that he himself would be showing a film in the hall of the small church. The crowd was large: there must have been about a hundred Inuit, children and adults of all ages, sitting on the floor. It was a black-and-white film, projected on a sheet hung across the end of the room. The poor hero was in very bad shape and clearly close to dying of thirst and exhaustion: he was crawling on all fours in the middle of the desert under a blazing sun, his tongue hanging out. Just at that dramatic moment, a latecomer opened the door of the hall, a flurry of snow swept in, the cold air woke everyone up, and the poor fellow on all fours in the desert went swishing in all directions on the bedsheet. Then everything went back to normal, and our hero continued to drag himself in the sand. I forget how his story ended.

The last flight, the next day, was the most interesting one: 200 miles in each direction to pick up gear left at a now-abandoned camp at the northern end of Victoria Island. I took along an Inuk who had worked there to serve as a guide. We took off in the dark a little before 10 a.m., flew over the base camp, got lost, completely missed another camp where the helicopters had worked for a few days, found our bearings, got lost again for another two hours, and eventually reached a range of hills shrouded in fog. We flew around in circles for an hour, and my Inuit guide suddenly jumped up.

"This is it, it's right here!"

My guide had recognized a piece of cliff that he had scaled several times. The camp was indeed around there, but he could not

Midday over the tundra. The landmarks are few and far between.

tell where, for it was not visible from above and we could not descend any lower because of the ground fog and the grey hills, whose relief we could not see. It was far too risky. Too bad, after all this effort, but I gave up and we headed back to Holman. Two hours later we landed there without any difficulty. We had flown five difficult and tiring hours that day and returned to the village without having accomplished our mission, which for me meant another day of hard, stressful flying for no pay.

I went to knock on the teacher's door to let Joe know that we had not been able to bring his gear back from the north of Victoria Island, and I had a feeling it would not be possible until spring. He told me that, in that case, there was nothing more to do on Holman Island, and we would return to Yellowknife the next day. We had been on the move for over a week already.

The next day, loaded with letters and parcels for family and friends in the south—Christmas was fast approaching—we took off from Holman at 9 a.m., after an emotional goodbye from the locals. Ten minutes later the stars and the moon had disappeared; we must have been in the clouds. I was not too worried, for within half an hour I should be picking up the Cape Young radio beacon, and an hour later the one in Coppermine, on the Arctic coast, 100 miles farther south, toward which my ADF would guide me directly.

Two hours later we were indeed above the Coppermine radio beacon, still in the clouds and flying on instruments. We slowly descended in a spiral north of the station, over the frozen ocean to avoid the hills. The local radio operator from the small Department of Transport station gave me the weather: "Ceiling 300 feet and visibility half a mile in light snow and fog." We landed on the ice, bounced off the snowdrifts, and slowly approached the village.

Bryan, one of the men from the Department of Transport station who gave the weather and talked to pilots, came to greet us and smiled, shaking his head: "The last time you flew over Coppermine, just before you landed now, I couldn't see you, but when I heard you, I thought that you were really low and were going to hit the hills behind the village."

"I was worried too" I replied, "but it was my last round before final descent, and I wanted to make sure I would land on the ice of the bay in front of the village and not on the strips of rocks on either side."

Indeed, it was not very reasonable to have flown in such weather, especially when the sun was below the horizon, but poor Bill Joss's radio back in Holman Island had been down for three days, and we had no way of communicating with the outside world to get the

Resupplying a prospector with an Otter near Yellowknife. Note the boards in front of the engine during the stopover.

weather. In any case, when we realized that we were in the clouds shortly after taking off from Holman Island, it was already too late to turn back, for we would never have found the village.

Bryan communicated with his colleagues in the South in Morse code. He chatted while handling his key at tremendous speed, without ever needing to write anything down. He was amused and chuckling to himself, then burst out laughing: the person on the other end must have been quite a joker—all with dots and dashes of sound.

Five minutes later, once the jokes were over, Bryan announced: "In Yellowknife, clear skies, unlimited visibility."

I emptied a 45-gallon barrel of fuel into the plane, picked up my passengers, and we were off. I had to manage on my own, for Joe Melukchuk was not there; he must have been caribou hunting. It was 1 p.m. and therefore dark already.

We spent the first hour in the clouds, heading very roughly south, before eventually ascending through the layer of low clouds and carrying on under the stars. I had reset my gyrocompass on the ground before leaving, taking a sighting on the Coppermine coast, but it soon started precessing. At first I could verify our heading with Coppermine's radio beacon behind us. But as that signal weakened, I maintained our direction using the stars as a guide, and in particular what I thought must be a planet, a very bright spot ahead of us on the left. It was strange, for it was too far from the sun to have been Venus, and very white, almost blue, so it could not have been Mars. It must have been Jupiter, then, but I had never seen it so bright.

Twenty minutes later our course was still based on my planet, but the rest of the sky seemed to have changed. I checked the heading with the gyrocompass, but it had become dark and the instrument was hard to read, as were all the other dials. Strange! I increased the brightness of the dials and realized that our compass course had changed 40 degrees to the left since takeoff. It eventually dawned on me that the planet I had been following was not a planet at all: it was Echo 2, the huge balloon satellite that had been orbiting the Earth for three or four years! I rolled the plane to the right and we headed toward another corner of the sky, still in the night and above the clouds.

The lights on the dashboard kept dimming until they eventually failed: we had totally run out of electricity, most certainly because of an inoperative alternator, which was no longer charging the now empty battery. No radio, no ADF, no dashboard lighting, no position lights, not even a little power for the landing light. I felt pretty distressed, especially since we had not seen the ground for over two hours. We were flying in a pitch-black plane at night, invisible and unreachable, completely cut off from the world. As I had no desire to attempt a night landing in the fog over the forest, we carried on. From time to time I lit up the dashboard with matches: the flashlight at the bottom of my big bag of maps was completely frozen and totally useless. In the co-pilot seat, Joe Flemming was surely wondering what game I was playing and must have been thinking that bush pilots really are a crazy bunch. But he was discreet and refrained from asking embarrassing questions.

I carried on navigating by the stars, occasionally taking a quick look at the gyrocompass but without trusting it much because it had been precessing over the last two or three hours. Meanwhile, the sky was also turning, and our course, very roughly southward, was becoming more and more approximate. I had been counting on the Yellowknife radio beacon to guide us to our destination at the end of the journey, but without power we no longer had an ADF to catch the radio signal. I wondered where we would be able to land if we failed to sight the town and its airport, for it was surrounded by hundreds of miles of forests, rocks, and lakes, and the ground was completely covered with low clouds.

By the time I was starting to worry, because, by my calculations, we should have been approaching Yellowknife, we suddenly reached the end of the low stratus, and the frozen lakes were now clearly visible against the black forest. That was reassuring: if we could not find Yellowknife and ran out of gas, we would still be able to land on a lake on skis. I felt much better. The star-spangled sky was magnificent; it was just a shame that there was no

Inuit boy on Victoria Island.

Crossing the Arctic coast in an area where it is very clearly visible.

aurora borealis. I woke up Joe to show him a second satellite, more discreet than Echo 2 but still very noticeable.

A moment later I spotted a glow on the horizon, 30 degrees to the left. I could not see the town but it had to be Yellowknife, and I changed course directly toward it. The town was small, but the visibility was excellent and we could see the lights from about 25 miles away. When we flew over the aerodrome, all the lights were out; no one was waiting for us. I tried one runway, but it was right in the crosswind, so I tried another one. They were clearly visible, black in a white landscape. We stopped at the foot of the control tower and I went up to say hello.

The controllers stared at me, stunned: "But when did you land? We didn't hear you on the radio and didn't see your navigation or landing lights."

I explained to them that we had suffered a power failure, and they nodded their heads, dumbfounded.

"And you've just come from Coppermine? The weather's atrocious up there."

"It is! That's why we came here. Things are always better in Yellowknife."

The controllers then closed my Flight Notification, a kind of route plan in which you described your itinerary, detailing how many days you would be gone—eight days in this case—and how many passengers you were taking. A search would be launched if you were not back 24 hours after the date you indicated for your return.

All I had to do now was go down to the base to drop off my mileage sheet and tell Bob Warnock that we were back. I would then go celebrate this successful flight at the Gold Range Cafe—just in time for the evening brawl!

9. Crashing through the Ice

Yellowknife, November 1971, –20° F, Cessna 180 with wheels and skis.

The weather was bad that day, as always in the Canadian North at the start of winter: fog, snow, and low stratus. My young wife, Dominique, and I had been married for only a few months, and we had left Yellowknife that morning in a Cessna 180 fitted with wheels and skis to measure the depth of the ice on a lake near Fort Reliance, at the eastern end of Great Slave Lake, a little past Snowdrift.

I had met Dominique in Paris two years earlier, when she was fresh out of the Sorbonne and living with her family in the exclusive district of Neuilly, and it had taken me all this time to convince her to marry me and join me in Yellowknife to share the life of a bush pilot.

My wife Dominique in Cambridge Bay.

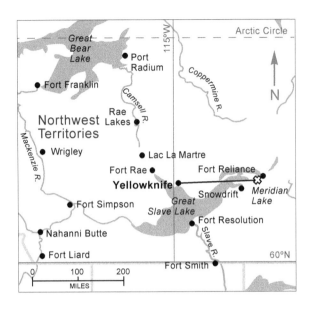

I worried as we flew above the cloud layer, for the weather report had forecast snow and bad weather for Yellowknife at sunset around 3 p.m., and we would have a hard time getting home before 4 p.m. Flying back on instruments at night in this plane, fitted only with a high-frequency radio and an automatic direction finder, did not sound the slightest bit appealing. But we were not there yet, so why worry.

After two hours of flight, as we approached our destination, the sky rapidly cleared and we were soon able to get our bearings. It was 11:30 a.m. when I notified the small weather station in Fort Reliance that we were going to land on Meridian Lake, 15 miles away.

Great Slave Lake was still open, but the small nearby lakes were frozen. On Meridian Lake, a thin layer of snow prevented us from seeing the ice, but not a crack, not a single trace of overflow suggested the slightest weakness, and the surface seemed uniformly solid to me. In fact, the manager of our base in Yellowknife had told me that the lake "should be frozen to the bottom." We did a reconnaissance and landed gently near the shore, in front of the three abandoned cabins of a camp where men from a mining exploration company had lived the previous summer. Our intention was to walk across the lake to see if the ice had the required 20-inch depth to allow a twin-engine Beech 18 on wheels to land and bring the supplies needed to reopen the camp for the winter.

We landed on the wheels, with the skis up, rolling quickly across the solid surface, and I started braking to stop the plane directly in front of the camp. Dominique, to my right, was busy reading the outside temperature on the plane's thermometer: −20° F.

The plane slowed down progressively, and I was thrilled that I had just impressed my new wife with the gentleness and elegance of this graceful landing. Then, from under the cabin of our plane, came a metallic noise, a continuous rattle, which intensified for a few seconds. This often happened when the back of the skis scraped increasingly hard against the ice during landing, as the tail of the aircraft lowered. But the noise was far more intense this time, and rapidly grew louder, culminating in a dull explosion. The landscape disappeared, and I could no longer see anything ahead of me.

Toward the end of the landing I had marveled at the beauty of this spectacle of ice, snow, hills, and spruce trees, and now it was gone: all I could see before me was grey. Stunned, no longer sure what was happening, I sat there for a few seconds, wondering where the beautiful landscape had disappeared to.

An air bubble rising from the engine cowl brought a glimmer of realization just as I noticed the small ripples on a sandy background

Trying to sneak through in November, 200 miles east of Yellowknife.

in front of me. The ice under the plane had broken, and I was looking through the windshield at the bottom of the lake. The engine had stopped, which I had not noticed as this had all happened so fast. The propeller was still, and it was now rather dark inside the cabin.

The aircraft had suddenly plunged forward through the ice, flipping on its nose to a 45-degree angle under water, its tail in the air, immobile for a moment. I looked to the left through the side window: the front parts of the wings, above us, were resting on the ice. The plane soon started rotating backwards, however, towards a more natural horizontal position, the fuselage and the tail coming down through the broken ice and into the water.

An extraordinary calm reigned. Neither Dominique nor I had time to be afraid or surprised, or even to understand that we had gone through the ice. After more than two hours of immense freedom, flying above the clouds and then in clear skies, laughing at the world, we were trapped, prisoners, fastened to our seats as we were being brutally pushed forward under the ice and into the water, in cathedral-like silence.

My first reaction was to try to open the door on my side, pushing it outward. But it was already resisting because of the pressure of the water. In the cabin, the water was rising slowly. We had to open this damn door *now*, before it became blocked completely by the water pressure as the cabin sank. Otherwise, we would have to go down with the plane and wait for the pressure inside and outside to balance. I got really mad, pushing against the door with all my weight and strength. It eventually opened slightly, and the cold water rushed into the cabin.

I shouted to Dominique: "Quick, get out on my side!" as she took off her mittens to try to undo her seatbelt, which was already underwater.

The water level in the cabin was rising quickly now that it was rushing in through the open door. I managed to get out of the plane just as Dominique, finally out of her seat, her head barely above the surface, was trying to move to the pilot's seat so she could also exit the plane. I braced myself against the door to keep it ajar and felt as though I was holding the door of a car open for an elegant woman. Dominique finally emerged and swam next to me in the small triangle of open water between the fuselage, the back of the wings, and the

Going through the ice in late November (30° F below) in front of a locked camp abandoned for the winter. Painting by Hélène Girard from an image reconstructed by Linda Mitsui from unusable photos, and from sketches by the author.

ice. We were weighed down by our thick clothes and fur-lined boots, but with a little help she managed to climb onto the fragile ice and I shouted to her to run to the cabins.

By now I had been in the water for quite a while, and my down jacket, woolen clothes, and fur-lined boots were completely soaked and dragging me deeper. I was leaning on the ice with my left hand. To lift myself up with both arms, I placed my right hand on the trailing edge of the wing, which was now resting flat on the ice, forgetting that the metal was at −20° F. My wet fingertips instantly froze when they touched the wing, with a little sizzle that reminded me of the sound of skin touching a red-hot stove. With a strong reflex I tore my hand away before it got so stuck that I would have to wait until it thawed in spring. I left only very small strips of skin behind, frozen to the cold aluminium.

Finally, after falling back into the water twice, I managed to get myself onto the ice. Now it was my turn to scurry across the fine snow. The outer layer of our clothes froze immediately. If we could not get into the cabins and warm up immediately, we were done for. In –20° weather, soaked, we would not survive 20 minutes.

As we neared the cabins, though, I thought to myself, "There is supposed to be a warden in this camp, but there is no smoke, and no footprints in the snow." The camp was deserted.

We headed to the third cabin, which I knew was the kitchen, where we should find matches. All my survival gear—my emergency location transmitter, sleeping bags, food cases, tool kits, smoke flares, red flares, signal mirrors, axe, snowshoes, tents, and matches in waterproof boxes—was at the bottom of the plane, under the ice. The matches I had in my pocket were wet and already frozen.

I first tried to force the cabin door open with my shoulder, but the padlock wouldn't budge. My clothes were stiff, frozen, and I could feel a layer of ice at the bottom of my boots. Dominique, on my orders, was pacing around the cabin so as not to lose her warmth, but she was already running out of breath and starting to slow down. The door would not give, and there was not a single tool outside to break it down.

Then Dominique spotted a crowbar, bent into a triangle and hanging from a tree. Probably a rudimentary gong to call the men for supper.

"Maybe you could use that?"

I yanked the rope off the tree, forced the corner of the bar into the door, and the padlock finally gave way. We rushed inside.

"Matches, quick, look for matches."

But there were none to be found. I turned on the tap of a small oil stove, but, of course, nothing happened. I also opened the taps of both gas stoves, but no gas came out. The bottles, stored outside, were most likely frozen.

"Keep circling the cabin, don't stop, never stop."

But Dominique was struggling to walk. I figured that in a few minutes she would stop and sit in the snow. And yet, she carried on walking, calmly, and I admired her courage, her tenacity. Not once did she complain or moan.

In a corner of the kitchen I finally discovered a small pack of paper matches, behind a tin can. But the oil was still not flowing, and the gas stove could not be coaxed into working. If only there were paper, or an axe to cut a leg off the kitchen table! Dominique called me. She was numb with cold, exhausted, and could no longer walk. I myself was ready to give up; my body was completely numb, I was having more and more difficulty moving and even thinking, and my fingers, curled up from the cold, were almost unusable.

I went out to get a barrel of airplane fuel, half buried under the snow. Without an axe I could not open it, and gave up after breaking a kitchen knife and twisting a can opener on it.

Our last hope was the other two cabins. I broke the padlock on the second, but found only a hodgepodge of snowshoes, metal camp beds, rock samples, and shovels.

I staggered toward the third cabin and snapped the padlock. Behind the door—a wood stove! I ripped a map off the wall. The paper was thick and cold. I crumpled it up and threw it into the stove, along with a few small pieces of wood that were lying on the ground, and some sawdust. I tried to pull out one of the little paper matches, but, with my fingers already half frozen and curled up, I didn't have the dexterity. Then all the matches suddenly came off, still stuck together. I struck them against the edge of the pack, the

A trapper's camp near Yellowknife.

matches all ignited at once, and I threw the flaming pack into the stove. This was our only chance.

The map caught fire, and soon I could close the stove lid.

Never has a fire seemed so benevolent to me, never has a flame felt so warm. I thought about the two young Indigenous men, Napoléon and Catholique, who had frozen to death very close to where we were after their canoe capsized on Great Slave Lake in October. They had reached an island, but their matches were wet, and they were found curled up near a fire they had not managed to light. The previous summer they had worked as guides for Roger Frison-Roche, and their pictures appeared in one of his books on northern Canada.

We had great difficulty undressing and needed to rip our clothes apart because of the sheath of ice. It took another several minutes for Dominique to warm up enough for her teeth to chatter and for her to shiver from the cold.

"That's a good sign," I said, laughing. "Life is coming back."

An hour later, standing naked beside our white-hot stove, we began to truly appreciate life and to find great humour in the situation. Our clothes were already almost dry, and we went out looking for our dinner. It was 3 p.m., and the sun was setting. The weather was splendid here, and our cabins under the snow, on the shore of this large frozen lake, seemed like a little piece of paradise. The air was fresh, wonderfully pure, and the silence absolute.

I went back to the kitchen. Everything was so easy now that we had warmed up and had time to think! The oil stove had not worked earlier because the tank, which was outside, was closed by a tap: all we had to do was open it. The same went for the gas bottles. It now seemed so simple and obvious!

We chose a can of mushroom soup and one of tuna. A real treat! Then we settled in for the night. It was still quite cold in our cabin: there was ice on the ground and on the walls. I started off by filling the holes with paper, then stapling plastic sheets to the walls for insulation. But all the heat was accumulating toward the ceiling, so we piled up about 15 foam rubber mattresses that raised us six feet above the ground. A tent canvas thrown over the pile of mattresses served as a sheet.

"Oh, dear princess and the pea, your bed is ready."

But Dominique spotted a large cardboard box under the bed.

"Oh no," she said. "No way!"

It was a case of dynamite.

I went outside to put it in the snow, far from the cabin and the fire, behind a tree.

We obviously had no blanket or sleeping bag, but it was nice and snug under our roof as long as the stove was working. Much to our delight, we had discovered a pile of wood nearby and had stocked up for the night. It was important not to let the fire go out, and we refilled the stove every hour for safety's sake. Morale was high. The sky was pitch-black, dotted with stars, illuminated by northern lights. And there was no sound, not even a whisper of wind, in the forest.

Around 10 a.m. the next day, the weather was still just as good when the sun rose. Dominique woke up.

"Do you hear that noise?"

I listened. Was it an airplane, or just the stove humming? I went to have a look outside. Soon one of the company's Beech 18s appeared above the hills and circled over the camp. We ran across the ice and I wrote on the snow on the lake with my feet:

All OK. Ice: one inch. Drop sleeping bags.

The plane moved away and flew back past us right above the ground. A small piece of paper fell out, slowly fluttering down.

Sorry, no sleeping bags on board. We'll be back as soon as we can. Much love. Paul.

A Gateway Aviation Beech 18 on skis at Grise Fiord. Photo Bob Warnock.

It was Paul Weston, one of my fellow pilots. He headed back to Yellowknife.

For breakfast, French toast. The bread was somewhat stale after being out for four months, but we softened it in the snow, coated it with flour, and toasted it in lard. Just like at the Ritz. I then went back to the plane, opened the top of the cabin with an axe (thinking of the poor mechanics who would have to fix the damage!), broke the ice that had formed in the cabin overnight, and, using a branch, recovered some of our gear that was underwater. Our down jackets and down trousers, as well as our sleeping bags, were solid ice—it would take two days for them to thaw and dry.

Just then I thought I heard bells chiming in the distance. I stood up and called Dominique. She was already outside, looking toward the other side of the lake. We could see a dog-team making its way slowly toward us, following the shoreline very closely. Nice, a visitor.

As they got closer, we could see it was a First Nations man with his dogsled.

"Hush," the man said softly.

The dogs instantly came to a halt and sat, waiting for the next command. He introduced himself: "Noël Drybone."

He had just set traps in the forest and left his wife and children at the camp, 40 miles away. He looked at the plane, of which only the top of the wings and the fuselage, as well as the tail, protruded from the ice.

"The ice isn't very strong yet," he said with a smile.

Yes, we had noticed.

He handed me a cigarette, and we offered him a cup of tea. He

A trapper's sled dog.

laughed at our makeshift bed and at all the traces in the snow around our cabin.

"That was a big wolf," he said, still smiling.

He then told us that he had come to see what was happening because he had heard our plane land the day before, but not take off again. He knew from experience, he added, that

Trapper on Great Slave Lake.

when planes landed near a camp, they always left after a while. Ours had not taken off, so he had come to see what was going on.

"My dogs are tired. I have to head back now. I'm going to Reliance. It's a two-hour journey and I'd like to get there before dark."

He turned his team of dogs around.

"I have a bit of moose meat. Would you like some?"

He handed me a small packet of frozen meat that he had picked up from the bottom of his sled. Then he left as he had arrived, silently sliding on the light snow. He had just come to say hello and bring us dinner. The sound of the bells slowly faded as the sled disappeared into the distance. The men of the North live calmly and quietly, and nothing ever seems to surprise them.

The company's twin-engine aircraft had not returned, and we settled in for a second night. It was still –20° outside, but we were nice and warm in our small cabin. During the night a wolf howled nearby, perhaps the same one who had wandered silently around the camp the previous night, leaving the tracks that our visitor had noticed. Its presence worried Dominique—we had left the door ajar for ventilation because of the stove. The next morning we again found its tracks around the cabin, disappearing into the forest a little farther on.

At about 10 a.m. the bells chimed: Noël was back.

"I just came from Fort Reliance. The ice is now thick enough along the shoreline for a sled: I can take you there if you want. Wrap up warm, it's a bit chilly."

That was one way to describe the situation! We quickly packed our bags and started tidying up the cabin.

But there was another development. It sounded like a distant helicopter. We went out to see, but there was nothing. Ten minutes later I heard the noise again.

"Well, Prinet, you must be hearing voices."

I went outside again to hear better and, sure enough, it was indeed a helicopter. A few minutes later a big, turbine-powered Bell 205 appeared. It had arrived in Yellowknife the day before from Calgary, almost 1,100 miles farther south.

Two mechanics from my company jumped out, smiling and cheerful: "Hi! We're here to pick up the plane."

The quick and efficient response of all these managers, pilots, and mechanics amazed me.

We walked toward the plane and broke the ice around it with an axe and a power saw. The helicopter

Bell 205.

took off, hovered above the plane as we fastened cables, then ripped out the Cessna, which was still fused to the ice, and put it down a little farther away, right at the edge of the lake.

Apart from the propeller blades, the tips of which were slightly bent, and the top of the cabin, which I had opened with an axe, the plane did not have a single scratch. The mechanics dismantled the panels under the fuselage, along with the lower spark plugs, to drain the water before it froze, and to prevent the fuselage and the engine from shattering.

"It's too late now to take the Cessna back to Yellowknife," said the helicopter pilot. "It'll be dark in two or three hours. I'll drop off the plane and your mechanics in Fort Reliance, near the weather station cabin, and I'll come back to pick you up in a bit."

The mechanics assured me that it would take no more than two

Oops! I am not the only one! A colleague through the ice with a Cessna 185 at Terra Mines, near Great Bear Lake.

days to dry out the whole plane and fix it, and it would soon be ready to spread its wings and fly back to Yellowknife. The helicopter took off with the two mechanics, my plane waddling along at the end of the cable.

Noël Drybone took Dominique for a sleigh ride, much to her delight. Then, with nothing more to do at the camp, he returned to where he had come from, without a sound. We were alone again, but not for long. The helicopter soon came back and took us to town.

Headfirst into the water ... in a hot bath this time!

Two days later the Cessna was as good as new—except for the open cabin roof—and returned to Yellowknife, flown by one of the mechanics.

They almost somersaulted into the cold water at takeoff. Because they did not have a heavy load, they had thought that they would take off within 1,500 feet on skis. They had drained the water from the plane after pulling it out of the lake with the helicopter, and they had drained it again when they arrived in Fort Reliance, but much of the water in the wings and the fuselage was already frozen by then, so, unbeknown to them, they must have been carrying an additional load of 500 pounds of ice when they tried to

Children at Snowdrift, a small First Nations community at the east end of Great Slave Lake, not far from where we crashed.

take off. As a result, the aircraft could not get airborne despite its speed. As they got farther from shore, the ice got thinner, and then they reached open water. It was impossible to stop the plane in time. As they later told me, they continued on the water for a while, water skiing, until they eventually managed to take off and bring home their new convertible model. Operating in the Arctic requires adaptation and imagination.

Ultimately, going through the ice is like falling off a horse: that is how one learns the job. The day after Dominique and I had returned to Yellowknife, I was out again, landing on frozen

My wife in Yellowknife, back to normal a few days after we had crashed through the ice.

lakes. In three or four days, the ice had thickened quite a bit. Nothing to it, as long as one waits until it is solid enough.

10. Crazy Flights in December

Yellowknife, December 1968, −40° F, Otter on skis.

We had been heading north for over an hour. The sun was already setting, far behind us to the left, beyond the frozen shores of Great Slave Lake. We were flying into the night, but the weather forecast promised clear skies. My passengers were Al Wilson and Brad Billings of the Water Resources Department in Fort Smith, whose mission was to spend a couple of weeks flying around the Canadian Arctic, digging holes through the ice to find out how much water was flowing in some rivers during the winter, and what its precise temperature might be.

Two hours later we reached the Arctic Circle at Port Radium, a mining area on the northeast shore of Great Bear Lake from which the uranium for the Hiroshima bomb had been extracted. When the radioactive material ran out, silver and a bit of gold were extracted from a new mine, Echo Bay. In fact, I had flown tons of bags of enriched silver ore south from Port Radium, tempted each time to continue south on to the Caribbean or the Bahamas for an early retirement.

At the mine, a small, one-way landing strip, which required fairly acrobatic landings, had been cleared on the mountainside. We

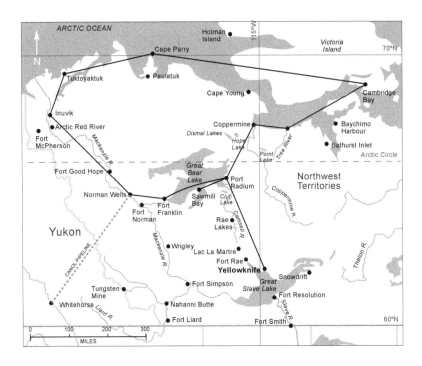

had planned to land there to spend the night, but as we approached I discovered that Port Radium was shrouded in fog.

My passengers were relaxed, for they had no idea that we were now facing a serious challenge. It was nearly dark and we did not have enough fuel to fly back to Yellowknife, a three-hour flight to the south. Theoretically, we should be able to reach Coppermine, 150 statute miles northeast on the Arctic coast, but we would have to land there in total darkness, trying our luck either on the frozen ocean in front of the Inuit village or on an unlit sandbank at the foot of the cliffs by the river mouth, which was not really an option. To make matters worse, the Arctic coast was rapidly becoming overcast, and the Coppermine radio station was reporting a blizzard with visibility of less than 300 feet in fog. We could not risk carrying on to Coppermine and having to land en route if we could not get through, as the ice on the lakes over which we would be flying was not yet thick enough to support the four or five tons of our heavily

loaded Otter, CF-WJB. I was transporting the two fellows from Water
Resources and all their gear, including a snowmobile, fuel drums,
and a large wooden sled.

I was thus feeling rather miserable, and I decided that, when you
think of it, pilots were paid not to fly planes, which anyone could do,
but to worry intensely while wearing a relaxed smile and not letting
on any of the anguish caused by the ghastly dramas that loomed
and, in most cases, accumulated quickly. To add to the hardship
of this dangerous and difficult work, bush pilots suffered shocking
injustice: the poor men were paid, depending on the airplane type,
3 to 5 cents per mile, measured in a straight line from the departure
point to the destination.

These pilots were truly saints, with remarkable dedication. They
worked frantically around the plane, loading and unloading impossible cargo, and looking tenderly after the passengers with motherly
self-sacrifice. They risked their lives with every flight to discover
new land or save the weak and the helpless, braving dreadful blizzards to rush to hospital the sick—who always waited for winter,
nighttime, and terrible weather to put a foot in the grave—or the
young women in labour with serious complications, who typically
wanted to have their babies in December or January. Finally, in
1967, a magnificent obelisk was erected in Yellowknife to the glory

Port Radium (Great Bear Lake) in July.

of bush pilots. It was the least the government could do.

Anyway, in December 1968 I was scratching my head, trying to find a solution to my landing problem in Port Radium, when something clicked in my terrified brain. I suddenly remembered the dirt landing strip in Sawmill Bay, about 60 miles west of Port Radium. This was an old military landing strip that had served for stopovers during World War II to refuel US planes—fighters and bombers en route to Alaska and the Russian Front. The landing strip had been deserted for 25

Monument to bush pilots, Yellowknife.

years and was lined with thousands of empty 45-gallon fuel barrels, but it was still used about ten times each summer to drop off American fishermen who spent eight days in one of the two or three lodges at the east end of Great Bear Lake.

We followed the shoreline toward this old earth strip, and I announced in a calm, confident, and therefore reassuring tone that we were making a diversion to Sawmill Bay because of the fog, and we would soon be arriving without any problem. Since they had never heard of this airstrip, Al and Brad asked no questions, probably for fear of coming across as ignorant of northern geography. Fortunately, the landing strip was clear of fog and we landed without difficulty, bouncing vigorously off the frozen snowdrifts. My passengers were certainly not impressed by my flying ability, but I didn't bother telling them about the snowdrifts and explaining why our very rough landing was not exclusively caused by my crass incompetence.

The terminal building of this once international airport was a 15- by 20-foot plywood cabin, particularly well ventilated since there was no door and the two small windows had long since been ripped off by bears. We cleared the snow and stretched out a large sheet of plastic to set up a semblance of a tent inside the cabin. It was already 4 p.m., and the sky was dotted with stars, the immense coloured draperies of the northern lights unfolding between them. It was −50° F outside and probably even colder inside the cabin, the walls of which were covered with long streaks of ice. No one slept much that night.

The next morning the air had warmed up a little: it was now only −40° F. In spite of the warmer temperature, a thin coat of frost on the edge of the hood of my parka was rubbing against my face. The sensation was very unpleasant, and the friction of these ice crystals on my cheeks would awaken even a corpse. We were on our feet before dawn, at 10:30 a.m. The Otter was firmly stuck in the fresh snow in front of our cabin, and we spent the next three hours with shovels in hand, trying to clear the plane in order to take off.

While my passengers were shovelling the snow around the Otter, I tried to warm up the oil tank and the engine itself, using two fuel stoves or blow pots set up at the bottom end of stovepipes going into the guts of the engine. One pipe led to the oil tank, the other to the cylinders. I installed the engine tent, letting the ends droop in the snow, and set up a round plywood board in front of the cylinders to shield them from the wind and preserve the heat from the stoves. It took over an hour for the oil to thaw enough to allow me to swing the propeller a little by hand. It helped that I had poured about a gallon of gasoline into the oil tank to dilute it after turning off the

Port Radium in August.

engine the night before and letting it cool down for a while. Between the fuel in the oil and the two heaters running at full blast under the engine, just in front of the fuel tanks at the front of the fuselage, I was expecting it all to catch fire at any moment and was ready to jump back and roll in the snow.

When it became possible to slightly move the propeller blades by hand, I had to remove the wooden board in front of the engine, pull out the engine tent, turn off and remove the two blow pots, dismantle the stovepipes, and jump into the cockpit to test the engine starter, which was connected to a frozen and therefore probably flat battery at the rear of the aircraft. This was a job for enthusiastic—and a little reckless—young men.

Once the engine had started—and if the oil pressure had risen within 30 seconds, if only just a little, to indicate that some oil was flowing—the proper heating of the engine could begin. Half an hour or 45 minutes later, the engine would eventually agree to run at full throttle. If it was not warm enough, it would cough and choke up, which could completely ruin the takeoff.

With the help of the snowmobile we had on board, we turned the plane around, and I finally took off at 2 p.m., alone and without cargo, when it was already getting dark. After about ten landings on

Sawmill Bay (Great Bear Lake). A chartered DC-6 brings in American fishermen and supplies for one week at Arctic Circle Lodge.

skis to level the snow and prepare a very rudimentary landing strip, I landed with full flaps and on wheels so I could stop the plane in less than 200 feet, at the start of the landing strip, ready to take off straight ahead the next morning. It was now night again. We reloaded the plane and went back to curl up in our sleeping bags and wait nearly 20 hours for there to be enough light to be able to take off.

At 11 a.m. the next day we were in the air, having overcome the standard issues: frozen engine, skis stuck in the snow, and frost on the wings, all at −40° F and in the dark. We had a little over an hour's worth of fuel left, just enough to get to Port Radium in a straight line and back to Sawmill Bay to wait for help if Port Radium was still overcast. Naturally, the fog from two days earlier was still there, but a small opening in the thick cover allowed us to land.

The mine, operated by about 50 men, was comfortable. We refueled with 45-gallon barrels and prepared the plane for the night. What a joy to sleep in a heated room!

The following day, while it was still dark, we took off from the small dirt strip on the hillside by the mine and continued to Coppermine on the Arctic coast, 150 miles to the northeast. Half an hour later, above the tundra, we were flying over Hope Lake. What appeared to be one of the largest copper deposits in North America had been discovered there in the spring of 1967. Large blocks of pure copper, some of them weighing several pounds, were scattered across the tundra.

"There must be three million tons of copper there, at least 100 times more copper than in Congo," a geologist had told me. "The concentration of the ore is exceptional: between 65 and 70 percent!"

Some 50 mining companies had immediately rushed to get hold of claims, 1,500-by-1,500-foot plots of land that they staked and leased from the government for a dollar a year on condition that they spent $100 per plot, each year, on drilling and related work. By 1968, some 10,000 square miles of tundra had been staked for mining.

The copper rush was pure madness, and the airlines that supplied the camps could no longer keep up. Prospector camps had been set up by the lakes (for access by float or ski planes) throughout the region during the two months of summer, and during the winter, convoys of half-tracks from Great Slave Lake brought drilling equipment 600 miles through the forest and over frozen rivers and lakes. The

The tundra in October.

convoys had arrived at Hope Lake at the end of the previous winter, and bulldozers had then cleared a 5,000-foot landing strip there, big enough for a daily Hercules that could carry up to 24 tons of freight. Another geologist had told me that "air traffic at Hope Lake was worse than around Chicago's O'Hare," one of the busiest airports in the world at the time.

One could only admire the audacity of these men who explored and mined the Arctic, investing hundreds of millions of dollars in the hope of extracting the oil and ore that would make their fortune. This was one of the fascinating sides of Canada: the country was being opened up by men who had the courage to break their ties with civilization, to give up their old habits and get out of the rut they felt stuck in, and to discover and develop a region with virtually unlimited but, until then, inaccessible resources. Some risked their lives, like bush pilots in the 1930s and 1940s, isolated gold diggers, and solitary prospectors. Others risked savings that they had spent a lifetime building up.

As far back as 1770, the Hudson's Bay Company had sent young Samuel Hearne from Fort Prince of Wales, on the west coast of Hudson Bay, to the Hope Lake region and to Coppermine, on the Arctic coast. Hearne was to explore the area where, since time immemorial, the Inuit had used pieces of natural copper collected on the tundra to forge tools, arrowheads, and harpoons or hooks. The expedition was a nightmare, and upon his return, Samuel Hearne had declared that "no white man could live up there." In his view, the copper could not be mined and was, in any case, impossible to transport.

Speaking of transportation to the north, the Arctic coast may one day be connected to Yellowknife by a gravel road. For the time being, this road from Yellowknife was advancing at a rate of three or four miles each year. Rocks had to be blown up with dynamite, lakes filled, bridges built, and gravel trucked in to protect the permafrost. The road was already about 10 miles long in 1968: in another 150 or 200 years it would surely reach the Arctic coast. In the meantime, a Danish company, J. Lauritzen of Copenhagen, was offering to ship the Hope Lake copper ore out of Coppermine and take it to Japan, sailing around Alaska.

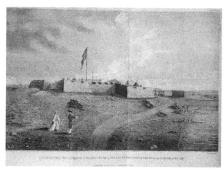

Fort Prince of Wales (west coast of Hudson Bay), 1771.

At the end of Hope Lake we spotted Ron Sheardown's Cessna 206 with wheels and skis. Ron was around 30, a pilot whose small blue eyes sparkled with mischief. He spent his life flying for mining companies. People were saying he was a multi-millionaire and more, but that had not stopped him from enjoying flying as much as he always had. One day in August 1966, he was cruising near Coppermine and saw my Cessna parked on a small beach in front of the village. Ron landed to say hello.

"Are you alright?" he asked.

"No, not at all," I told him. "My engine was smoking and back-firing for an hour and a half until it completely gave up on me just above the coast, and I glided down and landed on the ocean."

An intake pipe had punctured, and the cylinder was sucking in more fresh air than fuel fumes. To make matters worse, an exhaust

The north end of the Coppermine River to the Arctic Ocean as drawn by Samuel Hearne. Hope Lake is under the compass rose. Note "Bloody Falls" where the river widens, where Samuel Hearne mentions the "Northern Indians killed the Esquimaux."

pipe had lost a piece of its gasket, so the burning gases were ejected directly onto the top of the engine, which cremated the spark plug wires, destroying their insulation.

"How long have you been here?"

"Twenty-four hours. I landed yesterday from Yellowknife with an Inuit family: the father, the mother, and their four children."

Ron had his toolbox and spare parts for his aircraft on board. That same evening my engine was good as new.

"You can buy me a beer next time we see each other!" He left soon after and I was able to take off without any trouble.[6]

Now, with my two Water Resources fellows, I was happily flying over the frozen tundra around Hope Lake without worrying too much about where we were, lazily following the radio compass needle, which was pointing toward Coppermine's little radio beacon, when I suddenly realized the needle was pointing backward! The landscape was so uniformly flat and white that, without even noticing, we had crossed the Arctic coast, flown over Coppermine, and were now carrying on over the frozen ocean and the Arctic islands. A strong

---

[6] Ron did get his beer—more than 50 years later, when we were in our 80s. He even got a second one as interest payment.

Northward Aviation Beech 18 in front of Coppermine.

wind was sweeping the snow right above the ground and hiding all landmarks.

We turned around; there was the village. I chatted by radio for a few minutes with Bryan, the radio operator at the Department of Transport radio station, and we wished each other a Merry Christmas. Then I continued eastward along the coast. Given our ground speed and drift of 40 degrees, I figured the wind at 6,000 feet was blowing at about 75 miles per hour!

We then followed the Arctic coast, where the weather was starting to clear, to the mouth of the Tree River. The famous tree cannot have been very tall, for in the three years I had been flying in the region, I had yet to spot it. Anyhow, at the mouth of the Tree River we landed in the wild on relatively flat terrain covered by a few inches of snow. A moose was scratching at the snow nearby, unperturbed. Except perhaps for a few muskoxen, the moose was probably the only animal in the region; the caribou had wisely migrated south two or three months earlier.

For two days we measured the flow of the Tree River by lowering a probe to several depths underwater until it reached the bottom, using holes cut through the ice with a huge auger driven by a small two-stroke engine. In –40° F weather, your fingertips could easily freeze, and the probe itself would freeze instantly every time we brought it up to the surface, which made the whole exercise even more frustrating.

We also had to measure the water temperature. It was always 32° F, give or take one or two degrees—in rivers, the water flow is turbulent, and freezing occurs at slightly lower temperatures—but the government wanted to know precisely how cold the water was. I was delighted at the thought that my taxes were being spent so wisely on such important scientific research, and I wondered what would happen to the world if we did not know whether the water rapidly flowing under the ice of the Tree River in late December was at 30, 31, or 32 degrees; clearly, that made all the difference.

Once all these measurements had been completed from one side of the Tree River to the other, a topographic survey still had to be done. The general goal of our expedition, the first of its kind in the Arctic in winter, was to determine the flow of a few "typical" rivers at different times of the year.

At dawn on the third day, just before 11 a.m., we left our small aluminium cabin on the Tree River to get to the plane with our snow-mobile, pulling along the heavy Inuit sled onto which we had loaded

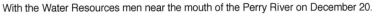

With the Water Resources men near the mouth of the Perry River on December 20.

Unloading a snowmobile and supplies for Water Resources on the Tree River.

all of our gear. I clung to the luggage on the sled, while Al and Brad sat on the snowmobile. As we rode across a huge sheet of bare and perfectly polished ice, they reduced the throttle for a second and the sled caught up with them, sliding sideways and even overtaking the snowmobile for a moment, which made us all burst out laughing. We entertained ourselves as best we could in the night and the cold.

The sun at noon was well below the horizon, but the sky was clear and we had no difficulty taking off in half darkness. Two hours later we landed in the pitch-dark night between the lights of the Cambridge Bay runway on Victoria Island. This was one of the main settlements in the Arctic: about 1,000 people lived there, both Inuit and European. The first wave of pre-Dorset Inuit had arrived 4,000 years earlier, followed by the Dorset about 2,500 years after that.

We had reached the easternmost point of our trip. From now on we would continue westward, practically following the Arctic coast until we got close to the border with Alaska. Al and Brad were going to record low tides all along the Arctic coast and change the paper in the recording devices. All this was clearly very important, and I was glad to be not only paying taxes but also risking my life and my passengers' lives to advance human knowledge.

The next stage was long for this time of year: we were going 500 miles west, mostly at night, to the American DEW Line radar station at Cape Parry. The weather was good and the flight went ahead without difficulty under the stars. Of course, visibility outside was poor because it was dark, and tiny ice crystals obscured our view of the ground, which was uniformly grey anyhow, so reading landmarks was challenging, to say the least. The magnetic compass was going around in circles without a care in the world, but all that became routine, and I simply stopped worrying about it. The most important thing was not to lose faith, hang tough, and keep flying.

The US radar base at Cape Parry lay at the end of a system of islands and peninsulas surrounded by frozen ocean. It was therefore difficult to spot, but I was not too concerned. Our automatic direction finder (ADF) should lead us to the station's small radio beacon without any problem.

There turned out to be a serious problem, however, because this archipelago, the broken ice on the Arctic Ocean, the irregular coast itself, and the night effect were all causing our ADF to move in every direction with the same enthusiasm as the magnetic compass. I knew we must be close to the station, and I decided that if these famous DEW Line stations every 100 miles were sophisticated enough to detect the unexpected arrival of hostile bombers from Russia, which could appear in the stratosphere at supersonic speeds without warning, surely they could also detect slow commercial aircraft at low altitudes.

I contacted the Americans by radio. Yes, they could indeed see us on their radar screen, and they kindly guided us to their base. We were about to miss the station by some 10 miles! Rather embarrassing; a rookie private pilot would have failed his licence had he navigated so poorly.

The night landing was interesting. A 40-knot wind was blowing at a 60-degree angle off the runway, and the snow blowing around close to the ground was hiding the gravel and lights of the narrow strip. We landed on one wheel at high speed and almost without flaps, and everything went just fine.

These US stations were as comfortable as New York's top hotels. The buildings were connected by a system of corridors and closed walkways, so one did not have to go out in the cold and the night.

On the menu, tender and juicy steaks with crispy fries. The meals were rich and the comfort extreme. We spent the evening playing pool and listening to Bach. Outside, the blizzard intensified, and the coaxial cables leading to the radio antennas were slamming against their masts.

My passengers retrieved the tide recordings, making sure, as always, to change the machine's paper, and repaired their measuring station. The next day we left for Tuktoyaktuk, farther west, near the mouth of the Mackenzie River.

As I wondered how I would find the hamlet in the dark, I remembered a bicycle trip around England when I was 15. Pedalling through the delightful British countryside, I occasionally became totally lost and asked my way around. The adorable little old ladies who tried to help me with endless instructions would always conclude with "you can't miss it." Well, I did miss it, many times, as I had nearly missed Cape Parry the day before. But Tuktoyaktuk was lit up in the night and quite visible from a distance. We did not miss it. If we had not seen the hamlet in the dark and carried on for an hour farther west, we would have ended up flying along the north coast of Alaska.

In Tuktoyaktuk the Inuit were living in a relatively modern environment: snowmobiles backfired in the night, often tipping over into snow mounds, much to the locals' enjoyment. These kinds of snowmobiles were particularly unstable, but they had the advantage of making a lot of noise, and the faster they went the more fun it was. Others still preferred the good old dog sleds—which had the advantage of rarely breaking down.

The storm carried on through the night, and the next day visibility was less than 300 feet. We took the opportunity to go to the cinema, since a movie was being shown in town that

Inuit family at Char Lake, Victoria Island.

Tuktoyaktuk, along the Arctic coast, in December.

week. The whole of Tuktoyaktuk gathered in the assembly hall, all dressed up. The ladies looked beautiful, carrying their babies under their parkas. The children sat down on sealskins brought along for the occasion. The men looked magnificent in their caribou skin clothes. Everyone was wearing warm mukluks, boots of caribou skin and sturdy moose-hide soles, with duffle linings and thick insoles.

Sitting on the ground or on the few benches, probably borrowed from the church, all these lovely people watched with great interest as camel caravans made their way across the desert of Israel, and men died of thirst and heat. It must have been a coincidence, but it seemed that every time I went to see a film in an Inuit church or town hall, the story always took place in the desert.

The projector made so much noise that it was difficult to hear the music, and there were many intermissions, every time the film snapped or derailed. Some businessmen had managed to sell refrigerators to Inuit who used them to prevent their supplies from freezing too hard, but no one had yet had the idea of selling them ice cream cones during movie intermissions. There's a market there worth looking into.

After Tuktoyaktuk our journey became easy as we were heading back south, seemingly coasting along without effort as we flew down the map toward the sun. We stopped in Inuvik to take water measurements, then crossed the Arctic Circle discreetly near Fort Good Hope, without a sound, continuing south, upstream along the Mackenzie River. At exactly noon that day, up at 10,000 feet, we got to see the sun for the first time in nearly two weeks, barely reaching over the horizon. It was shy and only revealed its upper edge to offer a very short burst of sunlight before disappearing again. Still, we felt warm and comforted, and could not help but smile.

At Norman Wells, 100 miles farther south, we had almost reached civilization. There were trees, a little sun at noon, and a bit of town. It was a small community, from which, during World War II, the Canol pipeline had channelled light fuel oil to the Whitehorse refinery in the Yukon to supply US fighters and bombers flying to Russia via Alaska. The pipeline, which crossed the Mackenzie Mountains, had employed 52,000 men for two years, and some people later wondered whether all these men would not have been more useful elsewhere.

The next day, almost following the Arctic Circle, we flew east over Fort Franklin and across the entire length of Great Bear Lake

Inuit children in Tuktoyaktuk. The red building is the Nursing Station.

Fort Franklin in July, at the west end of Great Bear Lake.

to Port Radium again. There was fog, as usual, but we managed to land on the mine's small dirt strip.

Christmas was only two days away, which was too bad for the last two stops we were supposed to make at the outflows of Clut Lake and Point Lake. Bad weather was on its way, and if we landed in the wild to take more measurements over the next 48 hours, we would no doubt get stranded by the snow and low stratus. We therefore headed south instead and flew the last 250 miles to Yellowknife on instruments.

Thus, no one will ever know what the flow rate was, on December 23 and 24, 1968, under the ice of the two small rivers that run out of Clut Lake and Point Lake, nor whether this water was at 31° F or 30° F. Al and Brad would be home for Christmas, and by flying a little less than expected, I was saving the government some money. It was a win for everyone.

11. Around the Pole with a Guitar

Yellowknife, July 1967, Cessna 185 on floats.

John Daykin, the manager of Gateway Aviation's floatplane base in Yellowknife, came up to me with a big grin on his face—always a bad sign.

"Are you a Beatles kind of guy?" he asked. "We've got a trip for two young fellows and a young woman to celebrate Canada's centenary. The government of the Northwest Territories and the Canadian Centennial Commission have decided to entertain the Inuit across the Arctic by sending them three singers with their guitars. There'll be a lot of ice, some snow, and fog in many places. You may find a few barrels of fuel here or there, but there's no guarantee. As far as the weather is concerned, you'll have to go see for yourself. Are you game?"

"Well ... Umm ..."

"Great! I knew you'd be keen. You'll be leaving this afternoon. Try to be back within a month or six weeks. I'd much rather not have to go searching for you across a few million square miles."

I first went home to pick up the World War II British Enfield .303 rifle that I had bought the previous year from the Hudson's Bay

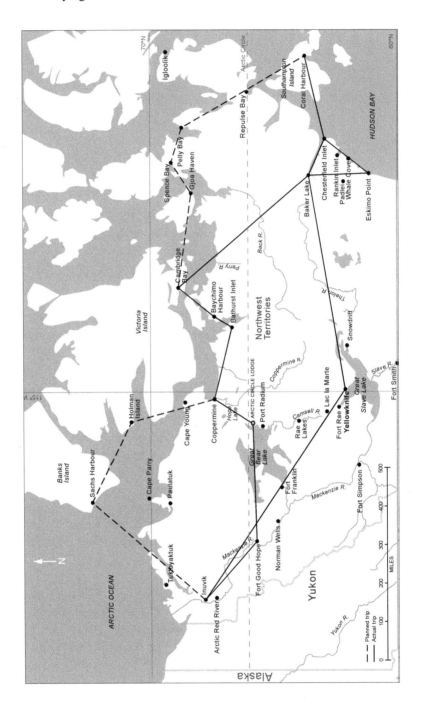

Ted Wesley in 1967.

Company trading post in Yellowknife as if it were a pair of socks or a toothbrush. Such a thing is handy when one tries to survive on caribou meat and fight off polar bears. I then assembled an emergency location transmitter portable distress beacon, my sleeping bag, all my survival gear, and the 80 aeronautical charts needed for the trip.

Meanwhile, husband and wife Ted and Leslie Wesley, 23 and 21 years old, and their friend Andy Steen, 24 years old, started piling their gear into the Cessna 185. There was no way to fit in three passengers, their belongings, and two guitars, so I took the two rear seats out and we tried to load it all in again. The passengers were now sitting on their luggage, obviously without any seat belts. One of my colleagues at the dock had to force the door shut, as one would with a suitcase that is too full. It reminded me of the Tokyo subway attendants who push passengers into the coaches so the doors can close.

Ominously, the backs of the floats were sinking into the water. We tried to take off but couldn't, and unloaded some gear. We tried again and still couldn't—back to the docks again. The third attempt was successful, and we set off.

The concert tour began at the west end of the Canadian Arctic coast, in Inuvik. My passengers spent the evening entertaining the locals by singing and playing guitar at the Eskimo Inn, also known as "the Zoo," Inuvik's big cafe-restaurant-bar-hotel.

At 11 p.m. the sun was still high in the sky. My immediate problem, while my passengers were singing and amusing the population, was to find out about the weather and the state of the ice in Sachs Harbour on Banks Island, our next stop, 450 miles to the northeast.

A ski plane from Aklavik Air Services, the local airline, had landed on the ice in Sachs Harbour three weeks earlier. "It's bad," said the carrier's founder and chief pilot, Mike Zubko. "Very bad. There surely won't be enough water for your floatplane." I tried the Mounties, but they had no information about Sachs Harbour. I went to the church to ask Father Fournier, the Inuvik priest. He usually contacted the Sachs Harbour mission by high-frequency radio twice a week, but he was out seal hunting, and the next radio call was not scheduled for another three days. At the church, a woman from the congregation told me, "Our priest was in Sachs Harbour a few days ago. Apparently, the weather was atrocious. It was snowing at first and then there was fog. Anyway, the ice hadn't melted at all."

That settled it. We would not go to Sachs Harbour.

The next stop, scheduled for the day after our canceled engagement, would therefore be Holman Island, 200 miles east of Sachs Harbour on Victoria Island. But the information I managed to glean during the rest of the night was no more encouraging: there was no open water in front of Holman Island, and the ocean was completely frozen. Without a ski plane, we would have to cross out Holman Island too, which was a shame. I really liked this lovely little hamlet, known for the quality of the Inuit clothing, drawings, and sculptures sold by the cooperative.

We would thus be forced to go straight to Coppermine, even farther away: 500 miles east of Inuvik. I returned to the Department of Transport's centre in Inuvik, since it occasionally communicated by Morse code with American DEW Line radar stations along

Fort Good Hope on the Mackenzie River near the Arctic Circle.

Downtown Fort Good Hope.

the Canadian Arctic coast. Once again, weather was a problem: Tuktoyaktuk and Paulatuk were completely overcast, and fog and snow engulfed the whole coast. We would have to reach Coppermine by taking a detour to the south, inland.

We headed south, upstream on the Mackenzie River, to Fort Good Hope, where we turned left toward the east, flying along the Arctic Circle across the full length of Great Bear Lake to Arctic Circle Lodge, the luxurious log hotel for rich American fishermen. It's amazing how often pilots within a 100-mile radius of the lodge encountered such terrible weather that they were forced to make a detour via the lodge to have dinner and spend the night. We were always wonderfully received, and so were our passengers. I regularly landed at the lodge, either because of the alleged bad weather in the area, or to bring food or customers.

That evening, to the bafflement of the folks isolated at the edge of the boreal forest, their entertainment descended from the sky. After dinner my passengers

Josh Manuel, Fort Good Hope.

took out their guitars and young voices, to the great delight of the American fishermen, the guides, and the waitresses.

We were not on holiday, however, and the next day we painfully wrenched ourselves away from this luxurious lifestyle to head to Coppermine. One hundred miles northeast of Great Bear Lake, we flew over Hope Lake, on the tundra, where everyone was bustling about looking for copper (see Chapter 10). The weather was fine and the flight was easy.

We soon reached the Arctic coast and landed without difficulty in front of the small Inuit village of Coppermine, on a narrow strip of open water between the shoreline and the edge of the frozen ocean. Planes could land in front of the village on floats during the two months of summer and on skis during the eight months of winter. They could also land on wheels all year round on a sandbar on the banks of the Coppermine River, near its mouth. It was just long enough for a DC-3.

At the edge of the small village, on the beach, husky dogs were tied to pickets and barked when strangers passed by. They ate one fish a day, which they swallowed head first, some of the fish still wriggling their tails. Each family lived in a tent or small plywood cabin surrounded by caribou antlers, rusty rifles, fuel barrels, and sealskins.

Father Lapointe was hosting us in Coppermine. The Catholic priests in the Arctic were French, including many from Brittany. At the cooperative opened by Father Lapointe, the Inuit sold bearskin mittens, sealskin boots, caribou skin parkas and pants, and small, primitive, but sometimes beautiful sculptures carved from serpentine stone. I took the opportunity to buy a superb soft white wolf hide.

From there we went over to the small Hudson's Bay Company trading post, but it did not have much left to sell at the end of winter, and the first supply boat of the season from Tuktoyaktuk had sunk about two weeks earlier, crushed by the ice.

That evening my passengers naturally offered an impromptu concert, to the surprise and delight of the residents. The next day we filed a Flight Notification with Gary and Bryan in the small radio cabin of the Department of Transport, then left Coppermine for Bathurst Inlet, more or less following the Arctic coast east for another 250 miles.

Alan Kuluk, Baychimo Harbour.

The vast metropolis of Bathurst Inlet was made up of five or six abandoned plywood cabins and an old wooden church (see Chapter 7), but everybody was gone, probably to Baychimo Harbour, 100 miles farther along the coast. Since there was no one to listen to us, appreciate us, and cheer us, we too left for Baychimo Harbour.

The small bay of Baychimo was covered in ice. I spent 10 minutes flying around in circles over the tents and few cabins, looking for a one- or two-mile-long strip of open water that would give me enough space to take off after our concert. I eventually decided to take a chance and land, then slowly steered the plane between the ice blocks to the shoreline, a mile from the village.

A young Englishman came to greet us. He was the new manager of the tiny Hudson's Bay Company post that traded shells, food, and warm clothes to the Inuit for seal, polar bear, caribou, wolf, and fox skins. He had recently replaced Duncan Pryde, a Scotsman who now lived in Yellowknife after having been elected as the local Member of the Legislative Assembly.

An Inuk child, Alan Kuluk, came to say hello. He was the younger brother of Jerry, a boy who had been shot in the stomach one night the previous year. At the time of this accident, one of the pilots from my company, John Langdon, was in Baychimo Harbour, stuck with a total electrical failure: no engine starter, no radio, no automatic direction finder, no gyrocompass, no landing light—not even a cabin light. John and Duncan managed to get the engine going by swinging the propeller by hand, carried the injured child to the plane, and then took off after sunset. This was in September, when the sun disappeared below the horizon at 6 p.m. They followed the coast and then crossed a branch of the Arctic Ocean to reach Victoria Island. Every few minutes, Duncan, holding the child in his arms, would light a match to illuminate the instruments. He was sure the child was dying. John managed to find Cambridge Bay and landed at night, by guesswork, on the black water of the bay. The local nurse, Betty Lester, watched over the child until dawn. Willy Lazerich's DC-4, based in Cambridge Bay, then took him to Yellowknife, 600 miles to the south. The small wooden hospital had just burned down, so they continued on to Edmonton, another 900 miles farther south. Two weeks later, we learned that the child had been saved.

When I arrived with Ted, Leslie, and Andy, I told them they would have to play quickly, because if the wind changed and the ice moved back into the bay, it would prevent us from leaving and we could end up stuck there for days. As it was, there were only three women and about 10 children in Baychimo at the time; the men were away hunting or fishing. Thus, the concert was cut a little short anyway.

The Inuit may have been wondering why we had come to offer them a concert—these white men were really unfathomable—but they were also delighted, smiling, nodding their heads, and bursting out laughing when my passengers were playing the clown.

However, the drift ice was now seriously encroaching in the bay, inspiring the seals to climb on it and dive or slide into the water, obviously just for fun; we had to get going.

Our floatplane, overloaded since the start of the trip, set off heavily in a beautiful spray of water, gaining speed

Betty Lester, Miss Cambridge Bay, 1968.

as it zigzagged through the ice debris, shaking all over, and desperately trying to get on the step of the pontoons, but to no avail; it seemed that the engine had lost power. The situation was hopeless, so I decided to leave my passengers in Baychimo Harbour and take off with all the luggage. I rushed over to Cambridge Bay, refueled from Gateway Aviation barrels scattered near the beach, and came back for my musicians. We finally arrived in Cambridge Bay at 11 p.m., with our poor engine doing its best but clearly struggling.

Edith Oyakyoak, of Baychimo Harbour, at Arctic Circle Lodge.

In the High Arctic the sun never sets in summer, and the Inuit sleep only when they have nothing else to do. The people of Cambridge Bay thus gathered in the middle of the night in the community hall to listen to my singers, who by now had their act down to a T. For a little over an hour, Ted and Andy sang and played, accompanying Leslie. They chose Canadian folk songs about the North and played some more fast-paced and upbeat traditional country music. The band was reminiscent of Peter, Paul and Mary, one of the most popular folk groups of the time.

The Inuit were leaning forward, attentive, drawn by the guitars and the singers. Sometimes, in the middle of a song, Ted would act silly and the Inuit would burst out laughing, all together, beaming. They were enjoying themselves like children at a puppet show, and were amused by this strange performance. Inuit have an admirable philosophy, courage, and endurance, and enjoy every moment of life, no matter what the next moment might bring. I have only ever seen them get angry at their dogs, and they always gave the impression of not being afraid of anything, accepting the most difficult situations in good spirit. In the Cambridge Bay community hall, they listened and observed, wondering at the commotion, having fun, and laughing.

I spent the rest of the night taking my engine apart—spark plugs, magnetos, fuel nozzles—to try to find out why it was not running well. I checked everything. The bottom spark plugs were dirty, and

DEW Line station, Tuktoyaktuk.

one of the nozzles was clogged. The wind was blowing in off the ice pack, and I struggled to hold the small screws with my frozen fingertips.

At last, at 6 a.m., the engine had recovered the 50 horsepower it had lost, and I set off in a jeep to pay the DEW Line radar station a visit. I needed to find out whether there was any open water and 100/130-octane aviation fuel farther east along the Arctic coast in Gjoa Haven, Spence Bay, Pelly Bay, Igloolik, and Repulse Bay. This represented over a thousand miles of coastline about which no one knew anything because of the lack of communication.

The next day I was given the weather forecast from each DEW Line station to the east. Everyone agreed: there was snow and fog almost everywhere, and the ocean was completely frozen. It was nice to know but not very helpful.

I managed to get further details from the French priests of the Catholic missions, who chatted to one another several times a week on their personal high-frequency radio sets: there was no fuel in Pelly Bay or in Igloolik. There were 20 barrels in Spence Bay, but no one knew what was in them, and there was no oil. These fuel drums are ordered most of the time by airlines intending to serve the community during the year, or by one branch or another of the government. They are delivered by barge once per year in the summer, and the owner's name is usually marked on them so that an itinerant pilot can ask local representatives if he can use some of their fuel, or just take what he needs, asking his company to pay the owner.

The priest in Gjoa Haven was out hunting: no information there. The one in Igloolik had not replied in 15 days; I later found out that his microphone was broken.

The Mounties also used their own HF radio system, and I soon learned from them that there was no fuel in Gjoa Haven. They had no information on the other stations.

Finally, through the radio network of the Hudson's Bay Company's trading posts, I was told that there was no fuel in Repulse Bay either. Gjoa Haven had been icebound the day before, but the wind had turned and cleared the bay so that there was currently almost a mile of open water. Of course, if the wind changed, the ice would return. Spence Bay had fuel but was completely frozen, although the lake behind the hill was open: it was surrounded by hills and was in a crescent shape perhaps one mile long, maybe a little more. Floatplanes had landed there from time to time in past years, but no one knew whether they had been loaded at takeoff. At Pelly Bay, the bay had been clear the previous week for 48 hours, but the wind had turned and the ice had now returned. Igloolik and Repulse Bay were trapped in the ice.

Four days later, we were still in Cambridge Bay, and I was starting to get an idea of the situation along the coast: it was snowing

Inuit summer camp at the mouth of the Perry River.

basically everywhere, there was a lot of fog, the ocean was frozen in front of all the communities except where the wind had turned and cleared the coast a little for a few hours, and there were sometimes one or two barrels lying around on the beach, but nobody knew whose they were and what was in them, if anything. It was all rather nebulous. Our problem was that although we had six hours' worth of fuel, we could not afford to go to a community, check it out, and then come back if it was socked in, if we could not land because of ice or waves, or if it turned out there was no fuel there to continue our trip.

I decided to change our route completely: instead of continuing east from the middle of the Arctic coast, we would fly diagonally toward the southeast, over the open tundra, until we reached the middle of the west coast of Hudson Bay. We would then head north along Hudson Bay, continue to the Arctic coast, and follow the coast from east to west to return to Cambridge Bay. Then we would go south to Yellowknife. We would simply fly the route counter-clockwise, the reverse of the original itinerary.

The weather was fine now, and we left Cambridge Bay. We soon crossed the south coast of Victoria Island, heading southeast. We ascended to 10,000 feet, above small cumulus clouds. What a delight to be able to climb so high and see so far! I was thrilled. We were even rewarded with the sight of a magnificent rainbow.

Rainbow over the tundra.

Flying in the Arctic tended to be rather stressful, with pilots often having to thread their way between low hills, sneaking under the stratus clouds right above the tundra. This segment of our trip, however, was a delight: we flew for an hour and a half over the frozen ocean, eventually reaching the Arctic coast at the mouth of the Perry River. This was where I had spent two weeks counting Ross geese with American researchers one summer. The researchers had ultimately found the 30,000 geese they had counted in California the previous winter. "I recognize them," John Ryder shouted with enthusiasm. John was an American PhD student who was writing his thesis on the Ross geese migration. The geese approximately follow the 40° F isotherm as they fly north in the spring, then lay their eggs in nests on the ground on small lake islands, protected from the foxes on the tundra by a foot of water while the bottoms of the shallow lakes are still frozen.

Four hundred miles later we reached Baker Lake, west of Hudson Bay but far inland. The wind was calm that day, but whenever it blew, the lake became so violent that many floatplanes had sunk there over the years. The latest one, earlier in the season, had flipped over in the waves near the shore.

We were now in the Eastern Arctic, where the Inuit wore brighter clothes, embroidered with more vivid colours. The back of their parkas ended with a train that reached all the way down to their ankles. Here, babies had their heads out and sat in a large pouch on the back, which the mother would swing over to her front when the baby was hungry. In the Western Arctic, babies straddled their mothers directly against their skin, and were held by a belt that tightened the parka at the waist. It was even easier to get to their mother's front side for feeding.

Our concert in Baker Lake that evening was another huge

Counting the 30,000 Ross geese near the Arctic coast during two weeks in July.

Young Inuit mother in Pelly Bay. Note the long trains in the front and back of the parka, typical of the Eastern Arctic.

success. To thank us for our performance, the locals offered us a drum dance. On a large flat rock, a small toothless woman in a long dress struck a drum almost as big as she was. The drum was made of a sealskin stretched over a large, circular wooden frame. She held it in one hand, hit it on one side, flipped the drum over with her wrist, then hit it on the other side. At times the Inuit men, crouching in a circle, let out a long, monotonous moan, slowly swaying their bodies.

Later that night another old woman came to sing what seemed to be an endless monotone where not a word was articulated. It was a song from her land, in memory of her Padlei ancestors who had been decimated by the 1950 famine when the caribou failed to appear along their traditional migration route. Richard Harrington, a photographer from southern Canada, was there, and he later published a book of very moving photos of this people in distress.[7] The hunters had gone to intercept the caribou on their way south at the end of the summer but had returned exhausted and hungry a few weeks later. Many Inuit in the area had starved to death that winter, too weak to reach the Hudson Bay coast to hunt seals and polar bears. The old woman burst out laughing at the end of her song, not because the ending was funny, but she had sung well and she liked the story, so she was happy. The second song seemed even sadder and more monotonous to us. After the final burst of laughter, for it was also a beautiful song and she liked it too, we learned that this was a more joyful story about the triumphant return of one of the men of the hamlet dragging a polar bear and four seals behind his dogs.

[7] **Richard Harrington**, *The Face of the Arctic* (New York: Abelard-Schuman/Toronto: Thomas Nelson & Sons, 1952).

For what was left of the night, the administrator, Peter Green, invited us to play bridge with Father Choque. There I learned that half of the fleet of vehicles in Baker Lake had been wiped out the previous day by a terrible traffic accident. There were no cars, naturally, and only two trucks in town, so traffic jams were limited, even at rush hour.

Drum dance in Baker Lake, west shore of Hudson Bay.

Still, when the two trucks had quickly maneuvered to avoid bumping into each other at the corner of a plywood cabin, one of them had slipped on the mud and piled into the ditch. The disaster of the year!

Our next stop was Eskimo Point, on the west coast of Hudson Bay, 250 miles to the southeast. The weather was bad; it was snowing along the route, and visibility was barely a mile. We flew right above the tundra all the way to the coast, where we were finally able to get our bearings and determine where we were.

The bay at Eskimo Point was not very sheltered, and the waves were impressive. I hesitated for a long time before landing, but there were no lakes in the area, so we had no choice and were forced to land across the bay, facing the wind and the waves but parallel to the swells.

While I was taxiing on the water, wondering what to do next, a man came to greet us in a canoe and showed us the way to a floating dock. It was impossible to moor the plane near the coast or drag it onto a beach, the man told me, for the range of the tide was 15 feet. The previous summer the wind had snapped the mooring line of the floating dock, which had drifted away with a floatplane attached to it and had ended up in the rocks across the bay. The dock had been put back in place and firmly anchored, but sometime later the wind had caused another floatplane to bang against the dock all night long, and it had sunk at dawn.

"Moor your plane with two ropes, with the nose of the floats facing the dock, and let the wind push it away from the platform.

Rankin Inlet.

It's still the least risky option." The local administrator was full of wise advice.

At the end of a quick dinner at the administrator's home, a man came to join us. Timidly, his face radiant with the legendary Inuit smile, he announced that he remembered having seen a barrel of fuel a little farther along the coast. We went to take a look. On a 45-gallon drum, we could just barely make out English writing: "100/130 aviation fuel, US Navy, 1943." The barrel had remained sealed for 25 years, but if the engine ran well on it, it would spare me a sleepless night and the six-hour round-trip ferry flight back to Baker Lake to get fuel.

We loaded the barrel onto his canoe and pumped the fuel into the wing tank. One turn of the engine starter and the propeller began to spin nicely: perfect. I got back to town just in time to catch the end of the guitar concert. The Inuit, crouching in front of the singers, were beaming, smiling, and nodding their heads to the rhythm.

The next morning the wind was fierce, and I dared not venture into the bay with my passengers for fear that the plane floating in the waves would be hit by a gust of wind and would capsize in the cold water.

By 2 p.m., however, the weather had improved a little, and we decided to try our luck. We returned to the plane by public transport: in a Bombardier, a tracked vehicle fitted with skis or wheels at the front, depending on the season, and which comfortably propelled itself over the tundra, snow, or ice with six or seven passengers aboard. The hatch in the cabin roof allowed passengers to escape through the top if the vehicle fell through the ice. The manufacturers had thought of everything, and this was reassuring.

Some of the planes I was flying were designed with the same escape system in mind: in autumn and spring, when the ice was fragile, I would always explain to my passengers in the Otters on skis that the panel in the roof of the cabin opened easily and provided an emergency exit in case the plane fell through the ice. This set the mood, and my passengers often stared at each other with a vaguely concerned look.

We set off, rolling in the downwind waves across the narrow bay. With this strong wind we should have the necessary distance to take off. Taxiing downwind was always very unpleasant, for I feared that when the plane went down a wave, the wind would catch the tail and lift it up, causing us to pitch forward. But the most critical moment was when we reached the other side of the bay and had to turn around to come back into the wind. As we turned slowly crosswind, the plane rolled strongly left and right in the waves, and the windward wing, when it was high, was at risk of being lifted by a gust and tipping us over to the side. Everything worked out well, however, and we took off across the bay with 1,000 feet to spare before flying over the rocks on the shore. The gusts of wind shook the plane and kept us close to the ground for a while in the turbulence of the nearby hills, but we eventually gained altitude and followed the coast to the north.

Our next stop, Whale Cove, was not far away, just 100 miles. It was a typical small Inuit village along the beach, with tents and small plywood cabins scattered among the rocks. We set ourselves up at the home of Father Trebaol, another Frenchman from Brittany, who

The Bombardier used for year-round transportation in Eskimo Point.

had gone sealing for a few days. That evening, when I heard that an Inuk was going whaling the next day at dawn, I signed myself up too.

At 4 a.m. he gave me a tour of his boat, of which he was very proud, and we headed off. In the cockpit, standing tall at the helm, he scrutinized the coast with a telescope. Every morning for the last 10 years he had traveled to a group of islands 20 miles away. I could not communicate with him or his two assistants, so we took turns smiling at one another.

The boat stopped as we reached the islands. The captain scanned the horizon after climbing the mast as merrily as the 70-year-old who once invited me to his hut in the far reaches of Indonesia and nimbly climbed a huge coconut tree to offer me something to drink. From the top of the mast, our captain cried out loudly and extended his arm. We all turned our heads and saw the water bubbling furiously a mile away: a white whale, a beluga, was caught in one of the nets.

We lowered the big canoe down to the sea and rushed to the trapped whale, the captain at the helm. Standing in the canoe, he threw a harpoon. The whale started bleeding and struggling even harder. The canoe got closer, and one of the assistants pulled out a huge knife that he thrust several times behind the whale's head. The movements slowed down and then stopped. Following one last convulsion, the whale rolled onto her side. We tried to pull her out of the net, but the whale suddenly came loose, turned downward, and slowly sank.

We promptly returned to the boat and fetched a large four-pronged anchor. The whale was resting on the sand, barely visible at a depth of 30 feet. The anchor quickly hooked onto her, and we brought her back to the surface and tied her to the side of the canoe. We returned to the boat to attach the whale to its side and hoisted her on deck with the crane. The captain climbed up the mast again, but the ocean was calm and there were no other whales in sight. We headed back.

At the helm, the captain picked up his telescope and chart again, regularly examining the compass while smoking a large victory cigar. We were following the coast, as we had on the way out, and the captain, standing tall and proud, grew silent. His face conveyed the quiet happiness of the Inuit returning home after a good day of hunting or fishing. Once back in Whale Cove, our captain asked a few men to pull the whale ashore and then to cut it up. The meat would feed the community for weeks. Meanwhile, the singers and guitar players had given their concert, which, as always, generated thunderous applause.

We had enough fuel left to reach our next stop, Chesterfield Inlet, also nearly 125 miles away. The next day we flew to the village without difficulty, but the very large waves in Hudson Bay forced us to land on a small lake nearby. The village administrator, John Parkin, welcomed us and invited us to his home. He had summoned the Inuit elders to discuss the expansion of the village: they needed to decide

The Inuit skipper hoists the beluga whale he has just caught near Whale Cove.

where to put the two or three prefabricated plywood cabins that had just arrived by barge and which they wanted to set up. But our landing changed everything, and the official program was swiftly replaced with a concert by the "Tundra Folk Band," which the children readily announced to the whole population. Yet another triumph.

On the shore of the lake where we had landed, a local airline had left a few drums of aviation gasoline and a note explaining that they had put Father Fafar and Father Henri, also Bretons, in charge of this fuel cache. I therefore went to tell them that I had taken 75 gallons, and gave them the coordinates of my company so they could send the bill.

Our journey now carried on northeastward to the far north of Hudson Bay, to Southampton Island. The weather was terrible. The 600-foot ceiling, the snow, and the strong winds were starting to worry me as we sneaked under the stratus clouds in very poor visibility. On Hudson Bay itself, the waves were certainly over 30 feet high, and I estimated the full crosswind at about 30 knots. Our plane was flying at 120 mph, so I mentally calculated a drift of 15 degrees.

After an hour of flying over the water, I started to wonder if we would ever find Southampton Island or if we were heading toward eternal glory. A polar bear came swimming quietly across our route, heading directly for the coast. It must have had solid guts not to feel seasick, and I wondered how it could possibly navigate through the storm. It had probably let itself drift lazily on an ice floe that eventually melted, forcing it to swim back. We also came across a few pods of whales blowing in the waves.

The ceiling dropped to 150 feet, and I hesitated to pursue the flight. For a few minutes we continued on instruments. What worried me was that we should soon be reaching the edge of Southampton Island, yet the two-toned map did not give any indication of relief: the ocean was shown in blue and the ground in white without any contour lines, and I feared that we might hit a hill when we got to the coast. A while later we came out of the stratus, still at 150 feet. The air was relatively calm now, despite a strong but steady wind. Visibility improved and reached over one mile. The ceiling also rose, and we ascended back up to 300 feet, which is always very comforting; the piloting became far less tense, although we were still in conditions well below the legal limits for visual flying.

Together, my passengers and I spotted the shoreline of Southampton Island just before crossing it at 120 mph. It was flat as a pancake, and the whole region seemed to be just a few feet above sea level and perfectly barren: a little yellowed grass, snow patches, and rocks. Lakes were scarce and certainly less than three feet deep.

Only 150 miles left. I tried my luck calling the Department of Transport's high-frequency radio station in Coral Harbour. After three attempts I heard a surprised voice: "Where are you?"

"We have just crossed over the southwest coast of the island."

"On instruments?"

"Euh ... not officially. We're supposed to be flying by sight. But the ceiling is very low, it's snowing lightly, and visibility is quite limited."

Soon the weather improved and we were able to climb to 500 feet. Everything seemed to be going very well, and I now felt perfectly relaxed.

The men from the Department of Transport in Coral Harbour told me over the HF radio, "It has been snowing almost non-stop for three days here, but the snow is melting on the ground. Dark sky, indeterminate ceiling, visibility less than one mile."

Forty-five minutes later we descended just above the ground again, but we still could see very little. The flight was becoming dangerous, not to say foolish, and I would very much have liked to land on a lake in the tundra and wait for the weather to clear a little, but that was not an option—the lakes were too small and too shallow. Fortunately, we were now getting reeled in by the Coral Harbour radio beacon, and all I had to do was follow the needle of the automatic direction finder to get to the hamlet.

A little later the weather improved again and we went back up to 500 feet. Visibility was much better, up to at least two miles. Conditions were still below the limits for flying visually, but the flight was getting a lot easier. The tall mast of the radio beacon appeared in front of us, at the end of a short strip of dirt road along which a few prefabricated houses were carefully aligned. We landed without difficulty in a tiny and well-sheltered bay just in front of the village, and dropped the anchor. A canoe came to get us.

We had reached Coral Harbour, the easternmost point of our adventure. Three weeks earlier, in Inuvik, we had been close to the north coast of Alaska. We were now at the north end of Hudson Bay, and Greenland was only 750 miles away.

The first barge of the season had just arrived that morning from Churchill, Manitoba. Churchill is a small town far to the south, on the western shore of Hudson Bay and at the northern end of a private railway line, affectionately called the "Muskeg Express," that brings food and supplies for the North.

The men on the barge in the small bay at Coral Harbour had almost finished unloading hundreds of barrels of fuel onto the beach in front of the village. *Thank you.* The barrels were stacked next to a US ship that had run aground there during the war, 25 years earlier.

Dick Kaip, the administrator, invited us for dinner at his house, and the next day my musicians' concert was once again a huge success. I now had to prepare for our return.

The plan was to head north to the eastern end of the Arctic coast and then follow it west toward Cambridge Bay. At the beginning of our journey we had only covered the western half of the Arctic coast, and we still had half a dozen small Inuit communities to visit along

Welcoming committee at Coral Harbour.

the eastern half. All these settlements had been notified by telegram that we would be passing by toward the end of the summer. So, with the help of the manager of the Hudson's Bay Company trading post, the head of the Mounted Police, and the priest, Father Mascaret, I organized a high-frequency radio communication network to try to get an idea of the weather farther north, to find out if there would be enough open water to land on the ocean in front of each community, and to determine whether there was aviation fuel anywhere.

Two or three days later the answers started coming in. They were not encouraging: all the planned stops were still frozen, which meant we could not land with floats. The only fuel was in Spence Bay. Everywhere we were planning to go, the radio operators reported snow or fog, and a local pilot from Coral Harbour ultimately convinced me that trying to fly north across the tundra to reach the Arctic coast was absolutely not an option.

We had left Yellowknife three weeks earlier, on July 25, but now I realized we should have waited until the middle of August for the ocean to thaw and the villages to be resupplied with fuel by the annual barge. So we headed back home, directly west across northern Canada, over the tundra, without trying to reach the eastern Arctic coast.

Following the concert in Coral Harbour, appreciated as always with an enthusiasm bordering on delirium, I spent a peaceful evening listening to the good stories of Father Mascaret. He was born in the

Vosges and had lived in the Arctic for 30 years. The tales of his adventures, and his thoughts on the way of life, the philosophy, and the character of the Inuit, were fascinating.

As I left his house around 3 a.m., I noticed the magnificent orange light shining above his door and congratulated him on it. "It's the anti-collision light of a plane that missed its takeoff," he explained. It reminded me of the beautiful aluminium door of a cabin in Pelly Bay that I had come across the previous summer: the door had once been attached to a DC-3 that missed its landing.

The return to Yellowknife was much easier, if only because I now knew where we could land and find

Hudson's Bay outpost in Rankin Inlet.

fuel. We returned to Chesterfield Inlet, then headed inland to Baker Lake. The weather was noticeably improving there: 3,000-foot ceiling, visibility 10 miles. After a final 500-mile hop, we reached the treeline northeast of Great Slave Lake. It was moving to see trees again after more than three weeks of tundra and ice. The weather was great, without a cloud in sight, no wind, and unlimited visibility. Yellowknife, the small town at the end of the world near the edge of the forest, now seemed like the heart of civilization to me.

Ted, Andy, and the young Leslie left me on the dock and faded away into the distance on the gravel road to town, their guitars under their arms.[8]

---

[8] **Ted Wesley** subsequently became quite famous: he released several excellent albums about the North, of which he is reported to have sold 70,000 copies, including *Straight North* and *Blackflies and Mosquitoes.*

12. Another Mayday: Totally Iced Up and Falling out of the Sky

Great Bear Lake, July 1969, Single Otter on floats.

Bud Golder, from Arctic Circle Lodge, guiding two American fishermen who just caught an Arctic char.

The day along the Arctic Ocean had been long but successful, and my 10 passengers had caught some beautiful Arctic char. We had taken off from Arctic Circle Lodge, the comfortable log hotel on the northeastern shore of Great Bear Lake, around 6 a.m.

The staff at Arctic Circle Lodge was mostly made up of boys and girls from Fort Franklin, a small Indigenous community 200 miles to the west, at the other end of Great Bear Lake. The others were students from Winnipeg for whom a two-month stay in this lodge was

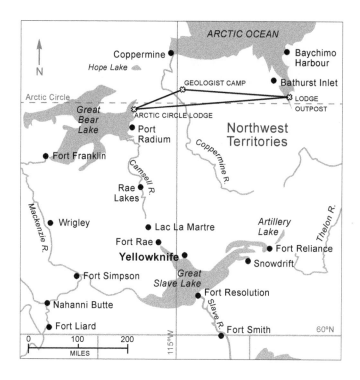

a treasured summer job. The boys worked as guides and took the
tourists fishing two at a time in aluminium canoes along the shores
of the lake. At lunchtime they would fry fillets of trout caught that
morning and serve them, with a side of potatoes and onions, to their
customers, who were sitting on the large flat rocks by the lake or on
a small pebble beach at the foot of the spruce trees, in the peace and
quiet of the North. The girls, like Skinny Pat, the tall, slim one, and
Fat Pat, the short, plump one, took care of the rooms and the kitchen.
Georgina and Sarah, from Fort Franklin, were barely 20 years old
and made all the boys swoon with their dark complexion and long
black hair, almond eyes, and disarming smiles.

The guests were wealthy Americans who loved fishing and
would come to the lodge for a week every summer, usually in a group
of men but sometimes with their wives. Some were so dedicated to
their work that they brought their young secretary along.

Every Friday they would fly in to Yellowknife from the United States in a Boeing 737. From there, they would carry on to Arctic Circle Lodge in a Twin Otter on floats, chartered for the occasion, completing the 300-mile journey in about two hours. Another plane, the Single Otter on floats that I was hired to fly that summer for the six weeks of the season, was based at the lodge itself and was sometimes used to carry luggage or a few extra passengers. Mostly it was used to take tourists from the lodge to more remote fishing areas, outposts along the Arctic coast where they might catch 25-pound Arctic char, a delicious type of salmon that turns red and swims up rivers in the late summer, and puts up a very tough fight. Customers would take the biggest fish back to the United States and have them stuffed as trophies for display above their mantelpiece.

On this day we had left the lodge early to make the most of the 24 hours of daylight in these latitudes at that time of year, flying my company's old Otter, CF-OVN, which made so much noise that the only way to communicate inside the plane was in writing. After flying 300 miles over tundra dotted with limpid shallow lakes, we reached the Bathurst Inlet outpost camp on the Arctic coast without difficulty and landed on the small nearby lake.

Flying very slowly because of the awful drag, I try to move two aluminium boats from Arctic Circle Lodge, at the east end of Great Bear Lake, still frozen solid, to an outpost on the north shore of the lake for the American fishermen in July.

This outpost had been set up near the mouth of the little stream through which the lake emptied into the ocean. This was where the char swam upstream—and where the lodge's guests were hoping to catch some stunning specimens to exhibit back home. We were welcomed by Bud Golder, a young ginger-bearded adventurer hired by the lodge every summer, and by his charming young wife, Jane, who was a schoolteacher during the winter. They lived in the camp for a few weeks, completely cut off from the outside world, sleeping in a small tent and hosting the occasional fishermen from the lodge in another, much larger tent that served as a dining room and kitchen.

I refueled with a hand pump, filtering gasoline through a chamois skin to remove the water and rust from the 45-gallon drums, and waited for my fishermen. The weather was starting to turn, with low stratus clouds already hanging along the coastline. I was particularly concerned, as these clouds announced a whole system coming from the west, a front that we would have to cross to get back to Great Bear Lake. We needed to take off soon, especially seeing as we had nearly three hours of flight time back to the lodge, and I would rather land before 11 p.m.—that is, before the sun set below the horizon and the shadows of the hills around the lodge prevented us from seeing the rocks under the surface.

Needless to say, my passengers were reluctant to go home and wanted to carry on fishing, but I threatened to leave without those who did not get on board with their gear, and we soon took off, heavily loaded with fish. None of us imagined for a moment that we were embarking on an adventure that was both brief and utterly astounding.

As we flew over Bathurst Inlet, with its barren rocky islands, the first low clouds were already forcing us to fly rather close to the ground and the waves. The passengers were curious, looking out the window and taking pictures. A few of them, happy and tired, were sharing a bottle of whiskey. Soon the ceiling dropped, forcing us to descend further. We were approaching a region of small hills on which the stratus clouds were resting. At 120 mph, our slaloms over the tundra between clouds and rocks were getting increasingly tight.

We surprised a herd of a dozen muskoxen. They galloped up a small hill to gather in a defensive circle, with the females and young at the centre. The passengers were thrilled and asked me to circle back to take pictures. I found them a little reckless—I was getting more and more worried and tense, struggling to avoid obstacles as I tried to sneak under the clouds. Still, we did another lap. After all, they had come from Chicago for the show and had paid a fortune.

We carried on for a few minutes, but visibility was deteriorating rapidly and the ceiling was still dropping. We got to a point where we just could not go on: there was close to zero visibility and we risked hitting the ground. I made a tight U-turn to try to go back, but the weather was now completely overcast in all directions. We made a few quick moves to avoid one hill and then another, and found ourselves trapped in a shallow basin, turning around in circles, as often happens when the weather is so appalling. In a split second we had lost our freedom and could not even return to the coast we had flown along just half an hour earlier. Cornered, defeated, livid, furious with myself for getting caught in this trap, I shot up at full throttle and began a long ascent through the clouds toward the west.

I knew this was another trap. When we got up there, suddenly bathed in light and dominating the world above the clouds, for a moment we would experience the high of total freedom, unlimited space. But at the same time, we would lose all the landmarks on the ground that would have allowed us to navigate. And upon arriving in the vicinity of Great Bear Lake, we would no longer be able to descend without the risk of hitting the hills, since the clouds went all

Muskoxen in a defensive circle, Victoria Island. Photo Bob Warnock.

Baychimo Harbour, the small community to the right at the head of the third bay.

the way to the ground. The only navigational aids were the Inuvik radio beacon, far to the west along the Arctic coast, the beacon at Cambridge Bay on Victoria Island, and the one at Resolute Bay, next to the magnetic pole. Pilots had to navigate visually, with a finger on the map—provided, of course, they could see the ground. Sometimes you had to open the side window to find your way around when there was too much frost or rain on the windshield.

The cloud cover was not very thick, and soon we could make out the sun above us. Shortly after that we came out of the clouds. My neighbour in the cockpit, a heavy man, blinked repeatedly, dazzled by the intense light reflecting off the top of the clouds. The layer was even bigger than I had imagined, and it extended to the horizon in all directions. Cloud systems in the Arctic often covered hundreds of miles, sometimes thousands.

I thought to myself that we would fly without any landmarks for two and a half hours, not knowing exactly in which direction we were headed because we had no astrocompass, and then we would go around in circles, looking for a hole in the clouds to descend. Then, not knowing where we were, I would have effectively lost control of the flight. Surrounded by clouds, I would slowly descend at random until we hit a hill.

But we were not there yet. The gyrocompass was still giving

a fairly accurate indication of our flight direction but would start precessing because of the rotation of the Earth. In mechanics classes we called this the Coriolis force, which is not a real force, just like centrifugal force. Go figure.

We were flying at an altitude of about 6,000 feet, guided very approximately by the sun. The passengers settled in as best they could. They were laden with parkas and bags. The large tubs of fresh fish blocked the central aisle. The back of the plane was packed with their fishing gear and the rest of their belongings. Some were reading, others dozed off or looked out at the top of the clouds. After an hour or so, two or three of them shared some sandwiches. My neighbour in the cockpit lowered the visor of his baseball cap to shield his eyes from the sun and fell asleep against the window. The flight would be quiet—at least until we had to start worrying about the descent. I settled into my seat.

After a while the cloud cover began to thicken and reach a higher altitude, and my hopes of finding an opening at our destination to start our descent were quickly fading. I slowly increased the engine power, but at about 10,000 feet the aircraft had reached its ceiling, given its heavy load, and could no longer ascend. Soon the cloud cover thickened before us again, and we could no longer fly over it. I reset my gyrocompass one last time, estimating the direction of the sun based on the time, and we entered the clouds for good. Things were becoming more complicated: we had already lost our bearings on the ground when we ascended over the top of the cloud layer, and now we were losing the sun that had allowed us to keep an approximate heading. As well, flying in the clouds was tiring.

I constantly had to check all the instruments to keep the aircraft level. First I would look at the attitude indicator to keep the wings horizontal, then at the turn and slip indicator to maintain a straight flight path, then at the air speed indicator, the altimeter, and the vertical speed indicator to make sure I was not ascending or descending, and then again at the attitude indicator. From time to time, I also needed to check the engine instruments.

I started to feel the cold seeping into my bones. Above the clouds, the sun had kept us warm. Most importantly, it had reassured me. Now I was starting to feel scared, for everything around us was uniformly grey and dreary, and I was not sure where we were going and how our flight would end. The clouds around us were getting thicker and darker, but there was no turning back: behind us, the clouds went all the way down to the ground and would prevent us from landing. I took slow deep breaths to try to relax. For the moment everything was going very well, and I knew I should be grateful for the tranquility of the current moment rather than worrying about the future. I tried to look perfectly content and relaxed to keep my passengers happy.

I had been stressed to begin with, but things were now getting worse. The outside temperature was rising: from about $-10°$ F when we were flying in clear skies, it had risen to $15°$ and was now close to $25°$. We had reached an area of the clouds where the tiny ice crystals we were flying through would give way to super-cooled water droplets, ready to freeze on impact as they hit the leading edges of the propeller and the front of the wings. When the ice builds up, the profiles of the propeller blades and the wings deform, the propeller thrust decreases and so does the wing lift, and the weight and drag of the plane slowly increase, a real conspiracy. Thus would begin our inexorable descent to the ground. Icing on poorly protected or unprotected propeller planes without enough power to quickly pass through dangerous cloud layers was probably the most serious risk pilots had to face.

Until this point, the situation had been troublesome: we did not know exactly where we were, and we only had an approximate idea of our direction. I was thinking that we would probably end our flight with a blind descent through the clouds, and we seriously risked ending up in the hills. Nevertheless, for the time being, everything was fine and there was no immediate problem to solve: I was just worrying about the future, but that was my problem and that was what I was paid for. However, if the ambient temperature did not drop, the situation would become far more serious: the aircraft would freeze over and start losing altitude, at the risk of crashing on the tundra.

A few minutes later the windshield was, in a split second, covered in light frost, followed by another layer, still thin.

That was it, we were catching ice. Wave after wave, the frost attacked us without a sound. Ice was certainly also forming on the propeller blades. Through my window, I could see the front of the left wing strut rapidly turning white, along with the gear holding

Unable to climb over the frontal system.

the floats.

    Soon the plane started to descend. I increased the engine power, slowly so as not to wake anyone up. Passengers are always very sensitive to variations in noise and aircraft attitude. A few minutes later I had to increase the engine power again. For the time being we were managing to maintain our altitude, a little below 10,000 feet. The waves of frost kept coming, more intensely every time. I could no longer see through the windshield, but since there was nothing to see in the clouds, this curtain of ice was not an immediate problem.

    The throttle was now at full power and the propeller was almost in fine pitch, as it would be for takeoff. I dropped the flaps a bit to increase the lift of the wings, then dropped them a little more again. When the flaps reached 20 degrees, there was nothing left to do. The ice was still building up, and the plane started descending again on its own. Not very fast, about 100 feet per minute, which gave us plenty of time to meditate before hitting the ground. The plane had decided to do its own thing now, to go down and head back to the hangar like a horse wanting to return to the barn after a long day. It had given up on me, and I thought to myself that our flight would soon be over.

    I made a radio call. I tried the frequency of the company, which had one of its bases in Yellowknife and the other in Edmonton, another 900 miles south. No reply. I tried again several times, but to no avail. On the Department of Transport frequency, often used in the Arctic, I now tried calling Coppermine's radio station on the Arctic coast. I knew one of the operators there, Bryan, but I had only seen him use Morse code to communicate with the outside world, and I was not sure he had an HF radio. No reply from him, either. So late in the evening, he had probably gone home. I then tried Cambridge Bay, far behind us on Victoria Island. It was one of two or three major airports in the Arctic islands, and a Boeing 737, specially equipped for gravel runways, landed there once or twice a week. They had a radio and the airport was always open, but even they did not reply.

I absolutely had to talk to someone. We were falling, and I wanted to tell somebody. The man to my right was very friendly, I had chatted with him a little at the lodge over the previous days, and at the camp where we had just spent the day, but I could not wake him up to tell him about my problems and share my concerns. The loneliness in these planes that one flies unassisted in difficult places is often hard to bear: you have to keep your troubles to yourself and

Entering a region of thick stratus clouds.

always look calm, serious, and confident, even when the situation seems desperate.

We were slowly losing altitude and soon reached 8,000 feet. It was a little after 8 p.m., and my neighbour woke up for a moment. He looked ahead but couldn't see anything through the frosted window in the clouds. He noticed the altimeter, which he took for a clock, and pointed to it, looking at his watch. He leaned toward me, shouting over the noise of the engine, "Are you sure it's 8 p.m.? My watch says 8:15." When he saw the needles gradually turning anti-clockwise as we continued to lose altitude, he understood his mistake and, embarrassed, sank back into his seat and closed his eyes.

This brief interlude took my mind off our situation and amused me. Well, so far so good, and we were doing well, but things were going less and less well, and soon they wouldn't be going well at all.

Since no one seemed to want to answer my calls, I decided to send a distress message. "Mayday, Mayday, Mayday." It was always moving to send out a distress call: this was a serious matter and meant taking some responsibilities. Only a select few pilots ever made such a call, and not very many of them lived to tell their stories.

Here I was, calling the whole world. I announced who we were and gave our estimated position, very approximately. Not that I hoped someone would rush to help us: there was no longer time for a rescue, and I was under no illusion. But I wanted to talk to someone, anyone, anywhere. Even a Turk or an Australian. In principle, my call should reach far beyond the horizon if the radio waves did, indeed, refract in the vagrant layers of the ionosphere, as the radio manuals explained. By giving our coordinates, I was also trying to avoid having too many people spending too much time and taking too many risks looking for us across tens of thousands of square miles of tundra. But by that stage, this would not be my problem anymore.

I sent out the message several times, but no one bothered to reply. The long radio antennas, stretched over the fuselage between the wing tips and the top of the tail, must have been covered in ice, and I was probably wasting my breath. So I put down the microphone. If that was how it was, if no one was interested, then we would manage on our own. See if I care.

In the meantime, my neighbour had opened his eyes again and watched me making regular calls. He had not heard anything I was saying because of the noise from the engine, but he seemed to be wondering if something was wrong.

For a moment I wanted to write him a note, to tell him that we were slowly falling and that there was nothing I could do. Sharing my concerns with him would make me feel better. He would be very worried, however, and I would then have to reassure him, comforting myself in the process: "No, no, don't worry, it's not very serious. We're descending, but very slowly, there's no reason to be concerned for the time being." Eventually I put together a forced smile, shrugging my shoulders and raising both hands in a gesture of helplessness to convey that the radio did not work but it did not matter. I then quietly sat back in my seat. It seemed to reassure him; he leaned back against the window and closed his eyes.

We were now descending at the rate of 300 feet per minute. Fortunately, we still had about 6,000 feet to go before we reached the ground, which gave us about 20 minutes of peace and quiet.

There was no reason to get upset for the moment, and I tried to relax. The situation could hardly get any worse; I did not have any unpleasant surprises to deal with, or a spate of critical decisions to

Difficult navigation: only some of the lakes are shown on the map, and their shape is often wrong.

make. This monotony made the flight almost reassuring. I was now out of the loop. I almost felt like I had finished my day and could go home soon. At 120 mph, we would hit the tundra with our pontoons. Or perhaps the rocks. Anyhow, we would soon find out. Unless, of course, we did not see anything at all and crashed directly into the side of a hill or a rock face. Ultimately, I was bored and felt useless. I wanted to have problems to solve. There was nothing to see outside, and nothing to do inside, other than blindly fly the plane.

So, to keep my mind occupied, I thought back to my math and physics classes and tried to recall the old trigonometry formulas. "Cosine p plus q"—one had to know that. And the ballistic galvanometer equation. That was also an important one for calculating the angle that the light mobile frame mounted on a torsion wire would reach when sent a small electrical pulse. How could one do without it? And what about the formula to get the size of the smallest object visible under a microscope when illuminated with a beam of wavelength lambda? I regretted ending my life in the tundra before I could really use the knowledge that I had suffered so much to memorize.

I eventually roused myself from my melancholy by thinking about my passengers' sad fates. It was not absolutely impossible to land on the tundra with floats: the floatplane would slide a little, stopping abruptly, and would normally tip over onto its back. If that happened to us, the Otter would certainly be very damaged, and passengers would find themselves hanging in their seats, upside down, in a hodgepodge of luggage, fish, bags, and gear. They would be suspended, head down, under a hundred gallons of fuel that would start to run from the inverted tanks. Even if a few of them were still relatively mobile after the accident, they would hardly have time to get out and escape.

I felt guilty and turned to them, as if to ask them for forgiveness. But everything was quiet; they looked perfectly peaceful, dozing away. Admittedly, there had been no turbulence, and the flight had been very calm from the start. For the passengers, this was simply a long, monotonous, and boring journey. They must have thought that they had a very good pilot who had organized a very smooth trip for them.

These rich Americans were between 50 and 70 years old, and mostly came from Minneapolis and sometimes Chicago or even

Texas, wearing cowboy boots and hats. They would arrive aggressive, demanding, and impatient at the start of their stay, but would often calm down a few days later when it finally dawned on them that they were really at the end of the world, like a small group of castaways.

I remembered one woman, the previous summer, who had suddenly become very agitated about her health. When she arrived at a fishing camp on the Arctic coast, similar to the one we were returning from, she realized that she was very far from home, from what she called civilization.

"Is there a hospital nearby?" she asked me.

I told her that the nearest one was in Yellowknife, a six-hour flight away, not accounting for a detour and stopover for fuel.

"Is there a telephone?"

It was very quiet out here, I reassured her. No one would disturb her.

"So what do I do if I have a heart attack? Or a blood clot?"

I explained to her that life here was very healthy: this was not New York, and no one had ever had a heart attack in Bathurst Inlet. This was true, although a year earlier one of the fishermen had died, overwhelmed from wrestling with a huge trout on Great Bear Lake. They had to bring him back to the lodge to be kept in one of the fish freezers until the next flight south.

Finally this woman resigned herself to spending 24 hours away from the civilized world that so reassured her.

Another time there was a man who was shouting very loudly. We were at the same Bathurst Inlet camp, after a trip that had ended quite eventfully. We had been flying over the ocean in strong winds when, 10 minutes before landing, our Otter's engine started to sputter. The wind was fierce, and I was pretty miserable above the big waves, thinking that we were going to flip over into the cold ocean waters. We had somehow managed to drag ourselves to the camp, and I had spent the rest of the day with my head under the hood, looking for the problem, which turned out to come from one of the magnetos. A colleague from Yellowknife, whom I had managed to reach by radio from the plane, told us that he would come with a mechanic to bring us a spare part, but it took them two days to get there because of the terrible weather. Naturally, during all this time, my passenger was

Even in the summer, without the use of a compass so close to the North Pole, navigation is really difficult.

screaming, and no one could calm him down.

"I demand that someone bring a spare part immediately."

"I ordered it by radio. It will come with a special plane and a mechanic when the weather improves."

A little later he wanted fresh vegetables and a good dessert. "I want a proper meal."

"We're going to cook you the char you caught. You'll see, it's delicious."

Of course, there was nowhere to sleep in the camp.

"I need a bed."

"There are none. Why don't you have a rest in the floatplane?"

As he needed to share his frustration with someone, he wanted to make a call. "I have to call my wife."

"You can call her as soon as you get back to Great Bear Lake, if the lodge's radio-telephone is working. It depends on the height of the ionosphere."

He punctuated each of his demands by banging his fist on the table in the tent. Fortunately, all these good people did eventually calm down, once they realized that these noisy protests were not impressing anyone and had no effect. Later, some of the passengers, including the one who had been so demanding, even helped to load the plane and refuel.

For the time being, no one was complaining as my Otter sank slowly through the icing clouds, and no one was demanding anything. They even seemed very satisfied. I started to wonder if I should warn them. How would I go about it? I could tear up a piece of my map, which was now completely useless, and write them a message that they would pass around.

Ladies and gentlemen, this is your captain. I regret to have to report that our plane is completely covered in ice and we are inexorably descending toward the tundra. In 10 minutes, we'll hit the ground at cruising speed. Please ensure that your seat belts are fastened, say your prayers, and wish your neighbours luck.

I could picture their dismay. Some of the passengers would be devastated by this sad news, while others would rush to the back of the plane to look for something on which to write their last words and wishes. Some of them would remain very calm and would ponder the vagaries of distant travels and the surprises that life had in store. In the meantime, the delicate balance of my plane would be offset by all this movement in the cabin, and I would quickly lose control. It was best not to say anything. I could not even tell my neighbour: his wife was in the back, and he would go straight to her. Then everyone would know.

So there was still nothing to do, and we kept descending, now at 400 feet per minute. We were just over 3,000 feet above sea level, probably 1,500 or 1,800 feet above the ground. I waited. I had been flying on instruments for an hour, manually piloting, and we had been descending for 20 minutes. I was tired. It was not as cold at low altitude, and the temperature had climbed to just above freezing. The frost would start to melt now, but it was too late: we were covered in thick clear ice and still descending. The aircraft was not flying well at all and was becoming unwieldy.

When we reached 1,800 feet above sea level, a little above the hills, I straightened up in my seat: we had reached the end of our journey and would be arriving soon. The ground must be around here somewhere. Strangely, I still did not feel any fear. Maybe I would have an interesting piloting problem to deal with, if we had time to react a little when we reached the ground. For me, this was an intriguing new experience.

I lowered the side window, as I could not see through the windshield. Everything was dark grey; you could see nothing to the side either. It was 8:30 p.m., the sun was already quite low, and we were under more than 6,000 feet of dense clouds, which were absorbing the light.

Suddenly, through the window, I saw the cloud under the plane darken, becoming almost black. Here we go, this is it, the ground is coming. Reflexively, I pulled on the yoke to absorb the impact and ducked my head. The plane was still a little maneuverable thanks to our high speed, and its descending trajectory was becoming more rounded.

Through the window, for a split second, I saw the tundra whizz past at great velocity just under the floats. Visibility was almost zero, but this corner of the tundra looked pretty flat and we had not hit anything yet. I pulled on the yoke further, very slowly, to finish the landing.

I wish I could have seen the look on my passengers' faces. They were certainly surprised to suddenly see the ground so close. Maybe they thought that the pilot could have warned them we were about to land. The speed was slowing down a little, but we were still going much faster than usual for a landing.

We reached a strip of rocks, large grey blocks strewn right across our path. I was furious about this bad luck. A few seconds earlier I had hoped that maybe we could make it, that perhaps we would land on the tundra without too much damage, even if the plane flipped. These rocks were going to crush us.

The engine was at full throttle, the propeller in fine pitch, and the flaps partially down, but the aircraft continued to slow and soon started dropping. I figured the passengers were tense; they must have sensed that this full-throttle, high-speed landing was not normal.

With my head turned to the side, through the lowered window I saw a surface of water emerge from the fog: the strip of rocks marked the edge of a lake or river. I thought to myself, "The back of the floats will hit the last rocks, and we're going to topple into the water." The plane came down a little, and I once again pulled the yoke toward me. But it wouldn't go back any further. We hit the water at high speed but, surprisingly, not too hard.

I pulled the throttle lever back to slow the plane down before we hit any rocks that might be in front of us. It was hard to tell how much water there was, since visibility was nil. The plane slowed down and almost came to a halt. We had not hit anything. Amazing!

But I could feel the back getting heavier. Through the window, I saw the heel of the floats sinking into the water. The floatplane, overloaded with ice, was tipping backward and was about to sink. Really, you just never got a break in this business. I increased the engine power to move the aircraft quickly across the surface of the water. To my left there was only water and fog. I asked my neighbour to stick his head out his window and guide me to follow the shoreline so we could find a place to stop.

Suddenly my co-pilot called out, "On the right, there's a small beach."

This was unhoped for. A quarter turn to starboard, and we beached on the sand. We were going fast, and the arrival was a little abrupt. My passengers could not have been impressed.

Now that there was no longer any risk of sinking, I slowly brought the engine back to idle and let it cool down gently. It had been working almost at full throttle for half an hour, from the start of the descent. That brave engine had done a good job. The plane also deserved a compliment. I thought it had given up on me earlier, but the slow descent had occurred just to remind me to pay attention to it and treat it gently. I gave it a friendly pat on the top of the dashboard. She and I got along well. We had been working together for years.

The flight was over. We had arrived. I had no idea where, let alone how we had gotten here, but it did not matter. I felt perfectly calm, though totally dumbfounded. I must have had my mouth open and my eyes wide with surprise. In the end there was nothing to worry about, and everything had gone very well. We were on a lake, on a pretty little beach, in the tundra. The weather was not great—in fact, we could not see anything at all—so the situation could only improve.

My neighbour was staring through his open window. I couldn't see anything because of the frost on the windshield, but I assumed he had spotted a caribou on the tundra.

"What's there?" I asked.

"I was just looking at the tents," he replied.

By this point, nothing surprised me anymore. He could have told me that there were cows or a young girl riding a bicycle, and it would have seemed perfectly normal to me. I leaned out the window. Indeed, about 60 feet from us, at the top of the shore above our little beach, two white tents were pitched.

I started laughing. Now that it was all over, it was the incongruity of this flight that delighted me, the absurdity of the blind descent in our plane covered in ice, and our amazing fall on the corner of an unknown little lake lost in the fog, landing us by a lovely quiet little beach, in front of the local cafe, a thousand miles from the nearest settlement. It was always the nonsense, the highly improbable sequence of events, that was the most amusing. Perhaps courage is simply the ability to see the absurdity of a situation before it unfolds, finding humour in it and remaining calm. But our story was over, and there had been no dramatic decision to make: everything happened on its own, in the proper sequence, by chance. All we had to do was be patient and wait for the end of this string of absurd events. As the young hotel manager Sonny says in the film *The Best Exotic Marigold Hotel*: "Everything will be all right in the end. And if it's not all right, then it's not yet the end." Admirable!

Prospectors, geologists, and botanists used this type of tent when

A typical biologist camp in the tundra.

Prospector's camp in the tundra.

they spent a few weeks on the tundra in the summer. Often, two men would do their research in the area, a university professor and a PhD student, accompanied by a third man who would stay at the camp and prepare the meals. One of the tents was usually used as a kitchen and living room, while the other had two or three camp beds. In July and August there would be a camp like this by a lake every 500 or 1,000 miles throughout the Arctic. Two or three summers earlier I had spent a week with two biologists who had come to study the habits of Ross geese and count them. With our floatplane, the researchers and I flew around over the lakes, finding all the 30,000 geese they had counted in California.

But I knew there were hardly any animals where we had fallen out of the sky. Perhaps a few isolated caribou or small groups of muskoxen. The men whose tents were pitched in front of us must have been geologists or prospectors. The Precambrian shield of the Canadian North is rich in metals. The Inuit had always collected raw copper from the ground to make arrowheads, and 50 to 100 miles northwest of here, in the Coppermine area, a great copper rush was in full swing around Hope Lake. A little farther east a geologist had once showed me a vein of pure galena, about five feet wide and 150 feet long, jutting into the ocean from the coast. In Yellowknife, three gold mines had been in operation for about 30 years. In Port Radium,

A typical prospectors' camp near the Arctic coast.

near the lodge we were coming from, silver had been mined for a few years by Echo Bay Mine, now that the uranium was depleted.

The weather was so bad that our geologists would certainly not have been able to leave their camp that day. In any case, it was close to 9 p.m. and they should be home. At that moment, one of the tents opened and a bearded face appeared. The sound of the engine still running must have caught his attention. Just then a passenger, who was probably starting to wonder what we were doing, clambered over the fish trays and bags blocking the corridor and came to find me in the cockpit. She seemed happy.

"Have we landed at the lodge?"

"Oh, no, ma'am. We still have at least 150 miles to go."

"So where are we?"

It is always embarrassing for a supposedly serious pilot to admit that he has absolutely no idea where he is. So, looking at the bearded man who had just shown his face, I smiled at my passenger, avoiding her question: "The weather is so bad that I thought we could stop for a bit to have some coffee."

"What a great idea," she replied, her face lighting up. "I was just thinking I'd like to stretch my legs. Can we get off now?"

"Of course, ma'am. Just a second. Let me open the door for you. Give me one or two minutes to let the engine cool down. But stay close to the camp. You can't really see anything: even the seagulls are traveling on foot."

All this seemed perfectly normal to her. Back in the cabin, the passengers started to get up. They could not leave through the rear door, as the water covering the heel of the floats reached up to the foot of the cabin ladder, and the tops of the floats were covered in bare ice. This was no time for them to fall into the water or twist an ankle. I therefore opened the cockpit door to see if it was possible to alight from the plane that way. There was a solid half inch of clear ice on the rungs of my ladder; I clung to it so as not to slip. When I got down to the float, still over three feet from the ground, I invited the passengers to follow me and helped them down with one hand, holding myself with the other. They disembarked in line, amused by the contortions they had to make to pass through the cockpit and around my seat, then slipping and skidding on the frozen rungs of the pilot's ladder to the pontoon, sliding from there to the ground. What an adventure! They would have a lot to tell their friends.

Once my flock was ashore, I jumped down onto the beach in turn.

Near the Arctic coast by my Cessna 206, feeling cold and miserable on a foggy day.

The three men were standing in front of their tent and waiting for us. They seemed both delighted with our visit and surprised to see all these American tourists show up, each with a camera slung over his or her shoulder. Our hosts must have been especially surprised that we had found them, for, in the greyness, we could not see more than 300 feet away. It was barely a few degrees above freezing outside, and we were soon soaked in the light drizzle.

The first passengers had already reached the kitchen and were invited in. I followed them. This tent was very pleasant and warm, and I felt safe there. We were a little crammed with over a dozen of us, but it was good human warmth, and my fellow travelers were delighted with the stopover. The cook brewed a large pot of coffee. We were even offered biscuits, freshly baked bread, powdered milk, and sugar. The visitors shamelessly served themselves, and within a few hours they had swallowed up provisions that could have lasted the three men another 15 days. Clearly my passengers had no idea of just how isolated we were.

None of the passengers wondered how we had gotten here. The landing in zero visibility, in front of a tent where we were served coffee and small biscuits, all seemed perfectly normal to them. A man had just landed on the moon; surely we could land on a lake.

I started getting a little impatient and wanted to yell at them: "Do

Bringing supplies to prospectors in the tundra.

In July, the larger lakes are still frozen.

you realize where we've come from? Fifteen minutes ago we were all supposed to die, crashing into the tundra at high speed with no visibility! You should be blown away with amazement, or on your knees thanking the Lord." But there they were, delighted, quietly chatting and trading fishing stories.

Pierre, the cook from Montreal, was not too sure what he was doing there. But Joe, the geologist, and Bob, his assistant, both came from Edmonton and were relatively familiar with the North, having been there several times. They eventually came up to me, visibly astonished. I was glad someone was interested in my aviation exploits.

"How did you find us?"

"Oh, you know, I've been flying in the area for years, and I had spotted your camp a while back." I remained vague, having no idea how long they had been here.

"But what about this awful weather ... ?"

"That's precisely why I decided to stop for a bit until it clears up."

On that note, still perplexed, they once again welcomed me to their modest abode. But what I really wanted to know was where we were. I tried to get them to talk about the geology of the North in the hope that they would take out their maps to show me. Geology was right up their alley, so they were delighted. I told them of my many flights with geologists across the tundra and the Arctic islands, the minerals we had found there, the prospectors who had stumbled upon a vein and blown their millions on alcohol and women. I told them about Fred, who I had often flown with around Great Slave Lake and who, at over 60 years of age, would set out every summer with his tent, his rifle, his canoe, his box of dynamite, and a ton of gear, in hopes of finding a gold mine as large as the one he had discovered 30 years earlier by Giauque Lake, which was named after him. I spent ages telling all kinds of geology stories to gain the geologists' trust so they would tell me a little bit about what they did and, therefore, reveal where we were. But I was also telling stories to distract my passengers, who were used to being entertained and were naturally impatient when they were no longer being looked after.

The geologists beat around the bush without ever telling me just what they were looking for, but they eventually agreed to explain the geology of the area to me. They needed their maps and soon laid them out on the table. Finally! But the coloured geological areas on their map did not mean anything to me. At least I could see a few signs around a lake and a large cross penciled in. I decided that the spot

The treeline just north of Great Bear Lake.

Arctic Circle Lodge in July, with Great Bear Lake in the background. There is barely enough room to land by the lodge, but not enough to take off.

must be the camp, and I memorized its coordinates. Later I slipped out to the plane and found the lake on my own map, discovering we were not so far from our direct route, barely 20 miles away.

The ice was slowly melting on the fuselage, floats, and wings. Completely de-icing the plane would likely take several hours. Outside it was dark, cold, and humid, but visibility was already improving a little. I headed back to the tent.

By 2 a.m. the drizzle had stopped and the surrounding hills were starting to clear. An hour later the ceiling was only around 150 or 200 feet, but visibility was unlimited. The tundra was relatively flat, and we could see the horizon clearly in all directions. I gathered my passengers and off we went.

The flight back to the lodge was easy, and I had a lot of fun. We flew between sky and earth, just above the ground and just below the cloud cover. The tundra was deserted; there was not a single caribou, not a muskox or a wolf in sight. This region was like a prehistoric world, empty, wild, infinite. The largest lakes were still frozen in the middle, their blue-grey surface reflecting the dark base of the clouds. The snow had completely disappeared, though, and the colours of the sparse, short grass and the grey rocks covered with a little lichen were restful to the eye. Nature seemed gentle and peaceful, almost welcoming.

We soon crossed the Coppermine River. It was interspersed by rapids and waterfalls at the north end of a very narrow and steep valley. The valley cut across the tundra, forming a stunning green strip of small spruce trees slightly shielded from the wind and the cold. A few summers earlier I had dropped off a group of adventurers and their canoes on the river, far to the south. They planned to travel down the river to Coppermine, at its mouth, where another floatplane would pick them up. As we said our goodbyes, they had a moment of hesitation as they realized they were going to be alone in the middle of the tundra for over a month. One of the young women then asked me, tentatively and with a little embarrassment, "How do you make a distress signal?"

"You prepare three fires in a triangle. It's the international signal, but you certainly won't need it."

She smiled as she thanked me, and I watched them paddle away before taking off to return to Yellowknife.

The most beautiful part of the Coppermine River was farther north, about 10 miles from the coast, in the Bloody Falls area. That is where Samuel Hearne, a young employee of the Hudson's Bay

Vegetation in the tundra.

American fishermen board a chartered DC-6 at Sawmill Bay after a week at Arctic Circle Lodge.

Company, arrived in 1771. He walked from Fort Prince of Wales trading post, on the west coast of Hudson Bay, across northern Canada from east to west to Great Slave Lake, and then headed north, accompanied by a group of Chipewyan people. He reached the Coppermine River and journeyed downstream, thus becoming the first European to discover this small stretch of the Arctic coast. On the way, at Bloody Falls, they met an encampment of Inuit, whom the Chipewyans promptly massacred. Samuel Hearne later recounted that one of the Chipewyan men expressed surprise when his spear pierced the naked body of a young girl crawling out of her bag of caribou skins, exclaiming that Inuit women looked exactly like their own women.

After another 50 miles of tundra, we crossed the treeline, soon reaching the edge of Great Bear Lake. We flew over the lodge, landed, and pulled up to the pontoon dock. It was about 5 a.m., and the sun was already high. The students were just starting to wake up to prepare breakfast and organize the boats, as the fishermen liked to leave early.

The manager came to us, unsurprised but happy to see his clients in good spirits. We had been expected the night before, but in the

Arctic people only start to worry when the plane is more than 48 hours late. I explained that we had to make a pit stop because of the bad weather, and had spent some time at a camp of geologists, where we were very well received. On one of our next flights, I suggested, we should give them back some food and gift them a bottle of whiskey. The fishing had been good, the manager and his guests were happy, and everyone went off to take a shower before breakfast.

That evening, before dinner, my fishermen offered me a drink. They were delighted with the highly successful day of char fishing and the peaceful flight back—"Excellent pilot, very smooth flight!"— and asked me for more stories. All these very civilized people liked to feel fear listening to horrible stories in living rooms, warm in front of a wood fire, whiskey in hand.

The next day I returned to the geologists' camp to replace the food we had devoured and bring them some alcohol to help them get through the rest of the summer in their tents on the tundra. And until now, I have never told anybody what really happened that day.

13. Typical Insane Flights

On many occasions, a single event in an otherwise long trip or in a series of flights was particularly striking. The short stories that follow describe some of these situations.

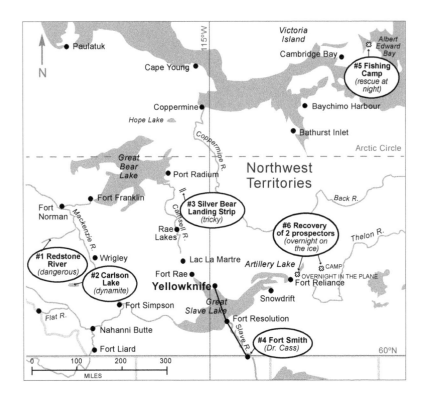

1. Redstone River

Yellowknife, July 1969.

The Redstone River, in the Mackenzie Mountains northwest of Yellowknife, flows into the Mackenzie River between Wrigley and Fort Norman, 150 or 200 miles north of the Nahanni River. The Redstone was one of the rivers that Water Resources regularly monitored to determine its flow rate over the seasons and the years.

The area available for floatplanes was shallow and short, hemmed in downstream by a tall cliff, at the foot of which the river took a right-angle turn, and upstream by fierce and shallow rapids. One really has to be an acrobat to land here in a floatplane, and several of my colleagues had rolled their airplane into a ball on landing or takeoff.

For landing, the passenger seated to the right of the pilot had to help adjust the flaps. The pilot guided the airplane in line with the landing area, descending as slowly as possible to fly just above the edge of the cliff without the tail hitting it, then diving toward the stream with the engine at idle and all flaps extended, and landing facing the current—with luck, stopping before the plane reached the rapids. Passengers who enjoyed a rush of adrenalin definitely got their money's worth, and the pilot felt like he was earning his wages. The plane could only be parked along the shore against a pebble bank, hitting a few rocks in the process as the river was very shallow.

To get out of this place, the pilot had to reduce the load to a minimum and make four or five trips, taking either a bit of gear or a passenger on every rotation and dropping them off about 10 miles away on a lake. From there, one could take off with a full load.

The takeoff manoeuvre involved turning towards the rapids from the pebble beach, facing the current, and then, with the engine completely idle, drifting back with the current to the base of the cliff where the river turned at a right angle. One would hit a few rocks here and there as the floatplane slowly drifted back, but at low speed this caused no damage to the pontoons. At a higher speed, during both landing and takeoff, the aircraft was on the step and did not need much depth.

With the Water Resources Department on the challenging Redstone River.

Loading and refueling a Cessna 206. The author, in red shirt, is talking to the base manager, John Daykin (right).

When you got to the foot of the cliff, you would increase the engine speed a little to stop drifting backward with the current; say a quick prayer to Saint Christopher, the patron saint of travelers, and ask for his blessing; then push the throttle wide open, make yourself as light as possible, and wait to see what happened. Were you going to take off before the rapids and fly over them without touching the rocks? It all depended on the wind and the temperature. To reduce the friction from the water, you would first lift off the float that was naturally a bit lighter because of the engine torque, then lift off the other. Once in flight you had to hold the wheel tightly as you traveled over the 1,000 or 1,200 feet of rapids, just above the rocks, trying not to hit anything in the process. It was only when you finally ascended a little upstream of the rapids and gained speed that you could breathe a sigh of relief.

Two years earlier, John Daykin, an excellent and very considerate pilot who always helped and encouraged me, had flown to Redstone River with two Water Resources men in a Cessna 206 on floats. The landing was a great success; however, for the return he managed to take off before the rapids but did not have enough speed to ascend, so he hit the water and the rocks while trying to gain altitude. The plane tumbled down the stream, crumpling into a ball as it bobbed along the river to the cliff. John and his passengers did manage to get out and reach dry land by swimming and walking across the cold and shallow water. They were all unharmed, just wet and cold, but had to wait several days before anyone realized that they were missing and went looking for them. That experience tempered John's enthusiasm, and he decided not to return to the Redstone River.

John was not the only one at the company to wreck a plane there.

The following year, in June, another pilot tried to drop off two Water Resources men and their gear on the Redstone River in an Otter on floats, CF-LAP. On landing, they hit a gravel bar and ripped open the underside of the floats. The insurance company put salvage mechanic Denny McCartney in charge of pulling the plane out of the water and getting it back into working condition.[9] Unable to fully repair the floats underwater, Denny called for help by radio. A helicopter came the next day and brought a powerful sprinkler pump from the fire department. Together with Gateway Aviation pilot John Langdon, Denny attached the pump to the rear of the damaged float, set the pump's fuel tank on the small ladder that passengers used for boarding, attached it with ropes, and started the pump to remove 120 gallons of water from the float. They kept the pump running at full power during takeoff so as to keep as much water out of the pontoon as possible. The Otter, empty except for the pilot, took off without any problem, and Denny returned to Norman Wells in the helicopter.

Then my turn came. When John Daykin—who in the meantime had become the manager of the Yellowknife station—first sent me to Redstone River, he told me that he had once been there himself. This was to reassure me and boost my confidence. It was indeed the truth, but certainly not the whole truth: he failed to mention that he had crashed his plane in the process. And it was only long after my own trip that I learned the next pilot, the following summer, had also demolished his plane.

These stories of previous accidents remind me of one I heard from a helicopter pilot. He was reluctant to land in a small mountain clearing, but then his passenger said, "I was dropped off right here two months ago." The pilot felt vexed at the implication he didn't

---

[9] **Denny McCartney**, *Picking Up the Pieces* (Victoria, BC: Trafford Publishing, 2002), Chapter Two, "Redstone River."

measure up to this previous pilot, landed, hit a tree with the tip of a rotor blade, and broke the helicopter. "It's funny," said the passenger, "that's exactly what happened to the other pilot."

Moral of the story: when pilots tell you "Don't worry, I have landed there myself," you should always ask how the flight ended.

2. Dynamite in the Mackenzie Mountains

Fort Simpson, April 1969, Otter on wheels and skis.

Prospectors would often take dynamite with them, but usually in small quantities; one or two boxes was typically enough. If it blew up, there would be nothing left of the plane, but it probably would not hurt the beavers and muskrats on the ground. However, on this flight I had to carry a really heavy load of dynamite, plus a large cardboard box full of electric detonators. This was to supply a one-week seismic survey being carried out for an oil company on Carlson Lake in the mountains west of Great Slave Lake. For eight days the plane would be based on the small dirt landing strip in downtown Fort Simpson on the Mackenzie River, and I would have to fly every day of the week to rotate the men and bring over more dynamite.

Long seismic trenches, tens of miles long, had already been

Unloading seismic crews and supplies at Carlson Lake.

opened through the forest, and my passengers would be spending every day blowing up charges so that their geophones could detect the waves reflected by the subsoil layers and recorded on batteries of seismographs. This would provide a vertical cross-section of the ground, which made it possible to determine where to drill wells to look for pockets of gas or oil. The men were using a snowmobile and sled to pull miles of electrical wires along trenches opened through the forest, and to transport the geophones and seismographs.

I had often transported explosives. The previous time had been for the mayor of Fort Simpson, who worked with Ace Explosives: 1,000 pounds of gunpowder and eight yellow canisters, each containing 2.5 gallons of nitromethane. That time we had made it back in one piece, but I was more worried about this heavy load of dynamite because the electric detonators had to be transported at the same time in the Otter on wheels and skis, CF-OVN. I remembered learning in high school that when a strong enough radio signal is emitted, it creates an electric current in nearby conducting wires—which I thought might cause the detonators and their long copper leads to go off. It just goes to show, you never know when something you learned in class might come in handy. Since we had the electric detonators on board, we would not be able to use the radios to report a problem. Then again, if the airplane blew up, we probably would not need a radio to call for help.

I pondered over how to distribute the explosives. At the front of the plane, on the engine side of the firewall, were whole bundles of electrical wires, including the alternator to recharge the battery, the two magnetos, and the 18 spark plugs, the purpose of which was precisely to produce strong sparks to keep the engine running. As for the rear of the cabin, it was hardly more reassuring: there was a large battery and all the radios, connected with more bundles of wires. Thus, not only would the radios have to be kept off to maintain peace in the tail section, but the power on board also had to be completely cut off to avoid the risk of electrical surges among the instruments and electronics in the cockpit.

We therefore loaded the plane, starting with the snowmobile, the sled, and all the seismic gear, and then very gently put the boxes of dynamite in the back. I had always lacked a little boldness and decided to put them as far away from me as possible—a sure sign of innocence and childish naivety. I then set the box of detonators, which I felt was far less dangerous, at the front of the airplane, just behind the cockpit, told one of the passengers to sit beside me, and positioned the other two behind the bulkhead, on either side of the box of detonators. If it blew up, my passengers would blow up with me, which offered some kind of consolation.

I had discussed this series of flights with the men at the Department of Transport cabin in Fort Simpson. Pilots usually called the DoT men by radio at the beginning of a flight to say where they were going and when they planned to return if everything went well, and then called by radio again, generally a few days later, to let them know that they had returned safely. I had told the DoT that I would be going to Carlson Lake with three passengers every day for eight days but would not be calling them on the radio on the way out, and that I should be flying back every night if all went well. I added, "For this series of flights, if one evening we don't come back, it's not really worth going searching for us." This had made them smile, as it was the first time they had ever been asked to do nothing for a group failing to return from a trip. We agreed that when I took off, in lieu of a radio call, I would buzz their office. On the way back, with no more explosives on board, I would call them during landing.

"Don't fly too close to us when you leave," the manager recommended with a slightly worried smile.

We took off from the small dirt strip downtown, and I immediately made a wide turn to avoid the frail log houses of Fort Simpson, thinking of how distressed the inhabitants would be if the plane were to explode in flight over the village. When I reached the Department of Transport cabin, I made a commendable effort to fly close enough that they would hear me, but not too close in case the airplane blew up.

The weather was fine, and we arrived safely at Carlson Lake an hour and a half later. It was early April, so I hoped the surface would still be strong enough for us to land on skis. We could see small puddles of water on the thin layer of snow, and the ice was already melted in some places along the edge of the lake. As the centre of the lake was always the safest, at least in the spring, that is where I landed and stopped. My passengers had their snowmobile and sled to get to shore, and I would stay near the plane all day. This would be safer for me than trying to help with the handling and moving of all that dynamite.

The explosions started promptly. Soon there was dynamite blowing up all over the place. The mountains were high around Carlson Lake, and the multiple

Connecting the wires to blow up all the seismic charges.

echoes reverberated from all directions. It reminded me of the US tank attack on my family's castle in eastern France in September 1944. The Germans had been there for weeks, and US shells were raining down while we took shelter in the castle cellar. Most of the villagers came up the hill to join us in the basement, as they had probably done in medieval times. The battle lasted three days. As I waited by my plane in the middle of the lake, I expected to see shells blowing up water everywhere. The vibrations in the air were so strong that I was afraid the ice would crack and my plane would sink.

Eventually, calm returned in the evening. We seemed to have won the battle, and we easily returned to Fort Simpson with an empty plane, radioing the good news to the Department of Transport officers.

Early the next day we were ready to start all over again, without the snowmobile or seismic instruments, but with just as much dynamite and detonators. One got used to that kind of operation very quickly; in fact, I soon realized that it would be easy to become negligent when nothing happened day after day. This was particularly serious as aircraft explosions should always be avoided: they tend to inconvenience scores of rescuers from faraway places, and the searches are usually long and difficult because an aircraft pulverized by a load of dynamite produces tiny pieces of debris that are extremely hard to find. This time, however, all went well and we didn't need a search party to collect the small fragments.

3. Tricky Landing on a Mountainside

Yellowknife, June 1970, twin-engine Beech 18 on wheels.

Near the northeast corner of Great Bear Lake, not far from Port Radium, a mining company, Silver Bear, had a small dirt and gravel landing strip on the side of a mountain. I flew in there only once, but I still remember it vividly.

The strip was very short and very steep. In fact, it was so short that, had it been horizontal, there was no way a Beech 18 aircraft could have landed there, let alone taken off again. A twin-engine Beech required a 1,500-foot runway, and this mountainside track was nowhere near that length. Fortunately, it was so steep that you could stop very quickly by landing uphill.

As with all these acrobatic mountain landing strips, you got only one shot at it. I knew there was no way I could open the throttle again and go around if I wasn't happy with my approach, because I was flying directly towards the mountainside.

The approach was scary: Having no horizon to use as a reference, I simply could not tell whether we were coming in towards the inclined strip at an angle that was way too steep or way too shallow. Rounding off over the threshold and bringing the nose of the aircraft right up towards the top of the ridge for landing seemed totally insane. We ended up touching down about a third of the way up the strip. I then pushed the throttles to wide open on both engines. This would get us as far up the landing strip as possible before I stopped and turned the plane to a 90° angle across the runway to prevent it from rolling backward down the slope. Running the engines at full throttle on a gravel strip is very poor airmanship because it causes whirls of gravel that will destroy the propeller blade tips, but there are situations where you have no choice.

We had landed safely, and my passengers seemed perfectly content. They had thought nothing of the approach and landing, and disappeared for a few hours to blast some rocks, collect ore samples, and check progress on the new silver mine. Finally, they returned.

Now we had to take off. The strip was so short that I had to face

The steep rocky strip has been carved along one of these hills by the Camsell River, near Great Bear Lake.

the plane downhill and immediately open the engines to over-boost, accelerating rapidly but knowing that I wouldn't have enough time to get airborne. As with the approach, I could not change my mind during takeoff. We were gaining speed so quickly on the downhill slope that stopping was impossible. When we reached the bottom end of the strip, the plane had not attained flying velocity, and we rolled over the edge into the valley to finally gain enough speed to start flying.

My passengers may not have realized the kamikaze nature of our landing, but as the plane barrelled down the short landing strip at full throttle, with the edge of the mountain racing towards us, they were breathless. I know because I heard them all gasping for air, and breathing very strong sighs of relief when the plane was finally flying again down in the valley.

4. Frozen Feet with Dr. Cass

Fort Smith, February 1969, –40° F, Beech 18.

During a stopover on a scheduled flight with a twin-engine Beech 18, I called the terminal on the ground frequency to announce that the plane was ready and that my passengers could now board. The good Dr. Cass came to sit next to me. She was a remarkable eye doctor, particularly dedicated to her work, well-known, liked, and respected by all, who had spent her life traveling the Arctic to treat and help people who had problems with their eyesight. A book has actually been written about her.[10]

That day, she was going from Fort Smith to Yellowknife. As the schedule was quite tight, with a stop in Fort Resolution each way, I had quickly refueled after disembarking my passengers. That had taken me 20 minutes, during which I stood outside without moving following two hours of flight in this plane without much heating. I was cold.

In fact, even in my thick woolen socks and my lovely caribou mukluks with a big felt sole, I could no longer feel my feet. This was not the end of the world, but I was still uneasy as I preferred not to lose my toes. As well, I really did not see how I could steer the plane on the ground, as the brakes were at my feet, on the tips of the rudder pedals.

Good Dr. Cass saw that I was hesitant and worried, alternately moving each leg about a little to see if I could operate the brakes.

"Is something wrong?" She thought it was a mechanical problem.

"No, everything is fine, thank you. It's just that I can't feel my feet anymore, so I'm not sure I can manage the tight manoeuvre in the parking between the other planes. That's what I'm a bit concerned about. Once we get on the taxiway it'll be easier."

"This is insane! Go to the terminal immediately to warm your feet."

"But, Doctor, the plane is full, the door is closed, and we have to take off and maintain the schedule."

---

[10] **Renate Wilson,** *Thank God & Dr. Cass* (Yellowknife: Outcrop Ltd., 1988).

The Beech 18 in Fort Smith used for scheduled runs.

"That's out of the question. Get off now! Hurry up!"

"But ... the passengers ... ?"

"Get out immediately, you hear me? I'll talk to the passengers. Come on, quick, get out! Go warm up!"

I hardly had a choice, doctor's orders, so I got off to head to the terminal building, walking past my flabbergasted passengers. After 20 minutes in the terminal with my feet against a heater, I got back onto the plane. The passengers were amused and asked, "So, are you feeling better? Can we go now?"

Indeed, I was doing much better and we soon took off. Everything went very well, and the plane returned to Yellowknife as planned, albeit a little late.

5. A Fisherman in Distress at Night on Victoria Island

Victoria Island, August 1967, Otter on floats.

Late one afternoon I took a dozen American fishermen from Cambridge Bay, on Victoria Island, to a campsite in Albert Edward Bay, about 100 miles to the northeast, where they would spend a few days fishing Arctic char. At this latitude of 70° north there was still daylight quite late at night, but within a month the sun would set at 6 p.m., just as it did everywhere else on Earth at the equinox.

Willy Laserich's DC-4 in Cambridge Bay.

My passengers had arrived in Yellowknife around midday on the regular Boeing 737 flight from Edmonton, and had carried on to Cambridge Bay in the afternoon in Willy Laserich's DC-4, which was based there.[11] That evening I was handling the last leg of their journey, from Cambridge Bay to the campsite on the tundra, with my Otter on floats.

Once at the fishing camp, everyone was tired but glad to have arrived—including me. The summer had been really hard and I had spent months flying every single day, basically non-stop since there was no night. I was exhausted and it would soon be getting dark, so

Willy Laserich in his DC-4.

I decided to stay at the fishing camp and return to Cambridge Bay the next morning at dawn, especially since the wind was piercing and cold, and the cloud cover really low. Pilots usually only pass by, so no one at the camp thought about feeding me, let alone putting me up for the night.

I could always sleep on the kitchen floor, but the kitchen would probably stay open virtually the whole night for the American tourists. Sleeping in the plane was also an option, and I was used to it,

[11] **Willy Laserich** was inducted into the Canadian Aviation Hall of Fame in 2010.

but it would be noisy and not very comfortable because of the wind and the waves. With my sleeping bag under my arm, I left in search of a tent that someone might agree to share with me for a night. All the tents seemed to be occupied already by two people, until I reached the wide-open tent of a beautiful Inuit girl, who must have been 15 or 16 years old, breastfeeding her baby. Her tent was lit up by a kerosene lamp, and she gave me a disarming smile as I walked past, stopping for a moment to admire this charming nativity scene. Encouraged, I began to wonder if she would take me in as a bodyguard for the night. The baby's crying would be annoying, but it would hopefully be compensated by the charm and interesting conversation of the smiling young mother.

I was about to open my mouth and ask her if she would consider inviting me in when I heard someone shouting out loudly in the camp: "Pilot? ... Pilot?"

What did this mean? I was here, but I was done for the day and was busy looking for a place to sleep.

The shouts started again: "Pilot!"

The callers seemed impatient and persistent, which made me think the situation might be serious. I figured my floatplane, jostled against the rocks by the wind and the waves, might have sunk in front of the camp, or perhaps it had unmoored and floated away on its own into the Arctic Ocean—which would indeed have been serious.

I therefore headed back toward the camp to let everybody know that I was here, no need to shout so loudly, and found myself surrounded by a pride of excited and scared fishermen, all talking at the same time.

"We have to go to Cambridge Bay right now. You need to take a passenger there!"

"Sorry, but it's already nighttime, the weather is lousy, the cloud cover is very low, and there's a range of hills between the camp and Cambridge Bay so we can't get through. In any case, I can't take off from here at night when I can't see the rocks or the shoreline, and I won't be able to land in the dark on the water in front of Cambridge Bay. Goodnight."

"But this is an emergency!"

"It doesn't change anything. The flight is impossible, and I don't want to kill anyone."

Inuit staff at Char Lake, working for the fishing outpost.

On that note, they brought me the emergency passenger. He was tall and skinny, and must have been at least 70 years old. At any rate, he seemed very nice, and he looked at me anxiously. He seemed to have a bad cold. He could not breathe, and his closed mouth was very swollen.

"He has two fish hooks in his lips."

I got closer and saw that his mouth was completely shut by a fish hook that had pierced his upper lip and got stuck in his lower lip from the inside, and by a second hook that had pierced his lower lip and got stuck in the upper lip from the inside. It was all so tight and swollen that surgical instruments were obviously needed to relieve the unfortunate man. In the meantime, the poor soul was suffocating, and he clearly would not make it through the night.

I wanted to ask him how on earth he had managed to get himself into such a compromising situation, or at least why he had not done it during the day when the weather was fine and we could still fly.

"All right! I'll try. But this is a very risky flight and really very dangerous. You don't take off facing the shoreline when you can't see anything, and you don't fly at night on the tundra in such conditions under low stratus, especially when you know you can't land at the other end. All this is completely irresponsible."

"I'll come along to help him," said one of his friends.

"No, absolutely not. That's out of the question. Only the two of us are going, period. That's non-negotiable."

We all headed to the plane. His friends helped him into the right-hand seat, I untied the ropes, and we sailed backward, facing the wind like a weather vane, the waves getting stronger and stronger as we moved away from the shore. It was now completely dark, and I could see nothing at all, not even a few lights from the camp over the dunes. The ocean was very shallow, and the steps of the pontoons regularly bumped against rocks.

I could not see the shoreline or the rocks, but after a while navigation became smoother and we were not hitting the bottom anymore. I let the large tri-blade propeller turn very gently as we slowly continued sailing backward, facing the wind. Twenty minutes later I figured we should have enough space in front of us, and I pushed the throttle wide open. I was afraid to hit rocks or the shore, so I jerked the plane out of the water as soon as possible, and we were off, flying over the tundra, maintaining an altitude of 150 feet to avoid the clouds and the risk of icing, and making a long detour around the end of the range of hills between the camp and Cambridge Bay. I was sure I would find Cambridge Bay because of

Cambridge Bay.

its powerful radio beacon. That was not a problem, but we had to get there without hitting the ground, and then land in the bay without being able to see it.

Ninety minutes later I spotted the lights of the small town. I called the control tower to let them know someone should come to pick up my passenger, and I also asked if they could have some cars drive to the docks to try to light up the water surface a little. I laughed when I spotted the procession of cars heading toward the docks, lining up along the shore to show me where to land.

The landing was very smooth, and my fisherman was quickly taken to the clinic, where a visiting doctor, certainly very skilled, spent over an hour cutting the flesh and taking out the fish hooks.

The next day, my passenger and I, well-rested, fed, and fresh, returned to the fishing camp. He was welcomed as a hero, carried away in triumph, and the whole camp took great interest in his story, asking for the details of the surgery. My charming little Inuit girl, still just as cheerful and smiling, was in the kitchen doing the dishes, her baby on her back. Finally, the cook, even though he had long since finished breakfast, offered me an omelette before I left for Cambridge Bay and other missions.

A bit later, when most of the people in camp had gone fishing, I went alone to find my Otter, unmoored it from the rocks, let it drift backward with the wind, and took off for Cambridge Bay. I was totally by myself.

I never found out the name of the fisherman with the fish hooks in his mouth, and have no recollection of meeting the campsite manager. But then, when a patient is rushed to the hospital, does anybody ever care about the ambulance driver?

6. Two Tough Prospectors

Yellowknife, November 1968.

It was cold and overcast, and the thick layer of low stratus clouds was keeping everything in darkness. I spent my days worrying at the thought of having to fly: every time the phone rang I panicked, my breathing stopped, and my heart started pounding. I found this environment very stressful. Luckily, the days were short and we could go home by around 3 p.m., when it was getting too dark to fly anyhow.

All the trappers and prospectors had been brought back in float-planes before freeze-up. Well, not quite all. We had realized there were two men in the tundra to the east of Great Slave Lake that we had forgotten to pick up. Now that we had skis and could land on the smaller lakes, the first ones to freeze, it was time to try to find the two prospectors. There was some urgency because they had probably run out of food a while back, and they would not be dressed for winter.

The pilot who had dropped them off during the summer was now flying elsewhere, and since most lakes had no name, the description of where he had left his passengers was rather vague. To add to the challenge, we could realistically fly only between 10 a.m. and 2 p.m. The snow and ice were hiding landmarks and would make the prospectors' little white tent very difficult to find. And, of course, it was fairly dark and overcast all the time.

One of our pilots, John, had spent all the useable flying time one day trying to find the missing prospectors, and Paul had done the same thing the next day. Neither of them had been successful. Now it was my turn.

The little white tent that nobody could find on the tundra.

After an hour and a half of flying, I reached the area where the prospectors should be but soon realized that the prospect of finding the tent was pretty hopeless. The clouds were down to the top of some of the hills, and the landmarks were hard to identify under the snow in the absence of shadows.

I started a search pattern: flying around between the shallow hills just below the clouds, and trying to spot the little tent among the snow-covered lakes and rocks while passing by at 120 mph. I soon lost track of where I was and was ready to give up: these two poor fellows would never be found before spring.

Going around a hill to try another opening, I caught a glimpse of a small tent that I was passing by at great velocity. I came back to be sure. Yes, that was the tent! White and partially covered with snow. Two men jumped out and started waving frantically. Another miracle, another success!

Elated at the thought of having finally found them, I landed and stopped the plane close to the tent.

The men had big smiles on their faces and did not even complain about having been forgotten. They were obviously thrilled to see me, and I felt really welcomed and useful.

The two prospectors were skinny but in relatively good shape physically and mentally. They looked pretty rough with their beards and dirty clothes, and they obviously had not washed for weeks. There was no food left at all, but they had shot a caribou about six weeks earlier. Miserable from the increasing cold, they had made a stove out of an aluminium suitcase, in which they had burnt caribou fat, skin, bones, and damaged meat until they ran out. They made the chimney out of a bunch of tin cans piled one atop the other. Their tent was a nice cozy corner of the frozen tundra, except that they had nothing to eat and nothing to burn for heat. Yet they were laughing and joking. These were two tough men, physically and emotionally!

We spent a good half hour at their camp while they were explaining how they had survived, but it was beginning to get dark. Time to go home. They gathered a few belongings, leaving their tent and all their gear behind. I started the engine, watched the instruments, and stretched my arm to unlock the gyrocompass, now that it was spinning nicely and holding its heading.

My jaw fell. I couldn't believe it. In my excitement at finding the prospectors, and distracted by their frantic waving, I had totally forgotten to lock the gyrocompass on the heading it was indicating when I shut down the engine. The direction it would be giving now would bear no relationship to reality.

Daylight was fading when we finally took off and started wandering around the hills. My problem was twofold: I didn't have a clue where we were within a radius of 20 or 30 miles, and I had no idea in which direction we were flying.

This was silly, and I decided to look for a flat surface where we could land. I had long lost the frozen lake from which we had taken off 15 minutes earlier and was searching for another one. I was concerned because this was exactly how people got hurt—flying at a low altitude in deteriorating weather conditions during the evening.

Turning around the corner of a shallow valley, we stumbled upon a wide flat area, most of it black, which meant open water. It was a very large lake that appeared long and relatively narrow. Our end of it was frozen, forming a fairly wide bay. I just hoped the ice would hold. Even if it did on landing, it might not support us through the night.

First, though, I had to call the base and let them know we were going to try landing on the ice. Flying over the open part of the lake was easier, and I was finally able to take a quick look at the map. The only rather big lake I could find in the whole area was Artillery Lake.

"Yellowknife, JWT, we are landing at the south end of Artillery Lake."

After a few seconds I recognized the voice of Bob Warnock, the station manager: "Roger, JWT. Say again the name of the lake?"

The transmission was weak and garbled.

"Artillery. Cannons shooting together. Remember Waterloo."

My message was followed by a long pondering silence.

"JWT, can you spell it out?"

"Alpha, Romeo, Tango..."

"Roger. Check. Artillery Lake. Thank you. Out."

Bob didn't even wish me happy landing and good night. How uncivilized!

We landed, the ice held, and the world became very still and very quiet. I set up two small catalytic heaters under the hood and covered the engine with a tarp for the night. It was around 3 p.m., so we had 18 or 19 hours to wait in our little airplane until there would be enough daylight to take off. The temperature was reasonable for the season, around 5° or 10° F, and we each had a sleeping bag, so we were fine.

From my personal emergency bag I handed each of my passengers some chocolate bars for supper. Not having eaten for days, they were thrilled to chew on something. We probably each got at least some sleep, although I was brutally dragged awake and jumped off my seat in a panic each time the ice cracked around us. The open water was not far away!

At around 9:30 or 10 the next morning, nothing much had changed, but it was now daylight, so I removed the engine tent and the two heaters, and off we went. I reset the gyrocompass along the shore of Artillery Lake, flew below the clouds as long as I could, then in the clouds, and finally caught the Morse code signal of the Yellowknife radio beacon, which pulled us in nicely for the end of the trip. We came down over the airport and flew to Yellowknife Bay, where we landed on skis and parked at the company docks.

Bob did his public relations job with great talent to comfort and appease the prospectors, celebrating their return with enthusiasm, cheering them, patting them on the back, and offering them a well-deserved shot of whiskey. I felt a bit left out of the celebrations, but I was happy about the flight and finding the prospectors.

Epilogue

Most of the flights described here occurred at the limit of what a pilot and an airplane can do. I was certainly lucky at times— like the day I fell out of the sky in an Otter loaded with ice and landed in the fog on a small lake near the geologists' camp. But I believe I survived where many of my colleagues did not because of the long, intense, and thorough training available at the time in France at a few National Flight Centres open to all. We came out of these two-week sessions feeling as comfortable flying upside down, falling to the ground in an inverted spin, or stalling at great speeds as most people feel flying straight and level. In addition, we thoroughly understood the mechanics of flight and knew exactly when trouble would start.

Unfortunately, these years of ecstasy in the North came to an abrupt end. On a Friday evening in December 1971, I returned from a flight with a Beaver on skis with a few prospectors, investors, and a geologist. They had spent the short winter day checking a number of rocks and quartz veins some 150 miles northeast of Yellowknife. It was cold and dark, and we were happy to be back in civilization, in the warmth and light of the airline office.

When I walked in, the manager, a former trapper who was also the mechanic maintaining the Gateway Aviation aircraft in

Yellowknife, handed me an envelope from head office in Edmonton: my services were no longer required. This manager had always felt that I had too many diplomas and licences, and that I complained too much about the maintenance, having lost one engine or the other on the Beech 18 at least 13 times on scheduled flights in November, usually when crossing Great Slave Lake, which was still partially open and where the patches of ice were not sturdy enough for emergency landings.

I immediately turned to one of my passengers to tell him that our flight had turned out to be the last one for me. Always positive and cheerful, he reacted with a friendly pat on the back and a great smile: "Why don't you come over this evening to celebrate. My boss is organizing a party at her office."

I joined him and was introduced to Pat Carney, who had just opened Gemini North, an economic consulting firm studying the impact of the proposed Mackenzie gas pipeline. In the 1980s she was to become the federal minister of Energy, Mines and Resources, then minister of International Trade, president of the Treasury Board, and finally senator.

"What do you do in life?" she asked, handing me a glass of bubbly.

"I fly airplanes. Or, rather, I used to fly them until half an hour ago. I just lost my job."

"Well," she said, "that's too bad. We don't need a pilot, but I am desperate for an economist with an engineering background."

"You are in luck," I answered. "I am that too."

"Can you start on Monday?"

"I'll be there."

I spent Saturday buying a folding chair as well as a door and some two-by-fours with which to build a table. I dropped a glass in the hole for the door handle to hold pens and pencils. The job was fascinating and Pat was a brilliant and kind boss, but my part of the work was completed in a couple of

Nordair DC-3 at Pangnirtung, Eastern Arctic.

years. I then wrote to Nordair, a large regional air carrier based in Montreal, and they answered, "Come over," so I did, eventually becoming vice president of marketing. I flew privately there on occasion but was mainly behind a desk or standing up at McGill in front of MBA students who wanted to learn about microeconomics.

Nordair was later purchased by CP Air, whose president asked me to come to Vancouver to be their VP marketing. Being disciplined and obedient, I agreed.

A year later CP Air was purchased by Pacific Western Airlines, a regional airline based in Calgary. Within a year PWA had eliminated Don Carty, president of Canadian Airlines and a great fellow. He had

Canadian Airlines B-737 in Northern Quebec.

an MBA from Harvard, and I had been working closely with him. Since he was the one who had hired me, I knew I would be next and, sure enough, a year later I was kicked out too, together with a few other VPs and a number of directors and

managers. We all started our individual aviation-consulting firms in Vancouver, and I did well through all my airline contacts.

One ousted director started a travel agency, and I ran into him downtown one day.

"You won't believe where I just came from," he said. "I was in East Africa for a few days, in Tanzania. The World Bank is looking for somebody to turn around and manage the national airline, which has been bankrupt since its inception, for 17 years. Absolutely unbelievable," he added, shaking his head in amazement. "Nothing works, nobody does anything, no one cares, and electricity as well as telephone lines have been essentially cut off at the head office. There is little or no running water, and most of their airplanes are grounded, B-737 jets, F-27 turboprops, and a few Twin Otters. There is no place for a consultant to stay anyhow, other than at the decrepit hotel downtown where there is often no water or electricity, and the sinks come off the walls."

"Whoa," I said, "exactly what I was looking for!"

He gave me the coordinates, and I traveled to Tanzania and saw that it was even worse than what he had described. Management asked me to join and, as usual, I said I would but only in three months, at the end of the university year: I was teaching at UBC and Simon Fraser University.

Air Tanzania B-737 in Dar es Salaam, Tanzania.

Tanzania was another paradise, but a warm one this time, with wonderful people who were always happy and smiling, perfect weather, and nice beaches with coconut trees. I worked virtually around the clock for six months, seven days per week, sometimes sleeping on the floor in the office. Later I could take one day off every few weeks, and I was able to gradually shorten the work days to about 12 hours or even less. The job was relatively straightforward—the airline just needed proper management and cost control. I was helped by two dedicated and efficient Indian fellows, residents of Tanzania and also on the World Bank payroll: one was looking after the finances and the other doing audits. The domestic debt was gradually repaid, the aircraft overhauled, the foreign debt reimbursed, and an official schedule was published and maintained, to replace the practice of making daily announcements of flights depending on how much cash was available to buy fuel.

After three years I was able to produce the first annual report that made sense and was accepted by the auditors. Until then, nobody had bothered converting the dozens of currencies used by Air Tanzania: the German marks and US dollars were simply added, in the books, to the millions of Tanzanian shillings or the billions of Zimbabwean dollars.

After five years, Air Tanzania was running smoothly, had no domestic or international debt left, was making good profits, and had a fleet of aircraft that were freshly overhauled and working like new. I had to admit to the World Bank that I could no longer justify my presence there, and I came back to Vancouver to retire as a sailing instructor and publish navigation books. Only then could I work on my old flying stories.

Glossary

Ailerons: Small surfaces at the end of the trailing edge of the wings. They can pivot down or up, increasing or decreasing the curvature of the wing and thus increasing or decreasing its lift. One aileron on one wing tip goes down, while the aileron at the tip of the other wing goes up. This produces a rolling movement of the aircraft along its longitudinal axis. The pilot activates the ailerons by rotating the wheel (yoke) clockwise (to roll the aircraft to the right) or counter-clockwise.

Angle of attack: The angle at which the air reaches the wing, i.e. at which the wing moves through the air. As the angle of attack increases, in the beginning, lift increases too. However, beyond a critical angle of perhaps 10 to 20 degrees, the air flow can no longer follow the curvature of the top of the wing and starts an increasingly turbulent movement above the wing. Lift drops dramatically and the aircraft "stalls"—i.e., falls out of the sky. Prompt action by the pilot allows recovery, but only after a significant loss of altitude. Otherwise, a stall traditionally results in a spin to the ground.

Astrocompass: A sighting device mounted above the dashboard. It allows a pilot to measure the bearing (relative direction) of a celestial object from the axis of the aircraft. Knowing the absolute direction of the celestial object, which is given in Sight Reduction Tables depending on the time and the approximate position of the aircraft on earth, and knowing the celestial object's relative direction as seen from the aircraft, which can be read from the base of the astrocompass, one can determine the direction of the flight. In the regions close to the magnetic pole, a sighting with an astrocompass on a celestial object is used to regularly re-set a gyrocompass, which would otherwise precess about 10 or 15 degrees per hour to the right in the Arctic because of the rotation of the Earth.

Automatic direction finder (ADF): A radio compass that automatically points toward the origin of a radio transmission. These compasses allow a pilot, when arriving relatively close to a transmitter without any visual reference, to find the station and either land or simply note his position and continue. This navigation system requires either a dedicated transmitter identified by its Morse code, or a public broadcasting radio station.

Blow pots: Small heaters used to warm up the oil and engine block before startup in winter. They can use aviation gasoline, which makes them very handy for pilots.

C4 compass: A gyrocompass automatically corrected for precession. A C4 compass can retain for several hours its orientation, which thus needs to be determined only once, initially, from the direction of a landmark or a celestial body whose relative direction is measured with an astrocompass. The C4 compass was, in the '60s and early '70s, the only way to keep a course near the pole, where the magnetic compass cannot be used, where landmarks could not be identified because of ice and snow in winter, or where the ground was not visible because of clouds or darkness.

Dock boy: Young fellow working around the aircraft at the docks, responsible for loading, unloading, and refueling. In the summer, the dock boy pumps any water off the pontoons before the flight. In the winter, he looks after the engine tent and heaters and removes any frost from the wings.

Elevator: Small surface at the back of the horizontal stabilizer, at the end of the tail section, that controls the up-and-down pitch of the airplane by decreasing or increasing the lift of the tail. The pilot activates the elevator by moving the wheel (yoke) back (to pitch the aircraft up) and forward.

Emergency Location Transmitter (ELT): Small battery-operated portable transmitters operating at 121.5 MHz (VHF range, emergency frequency) and 206 MHz (UHF range for detection by satellites). They typically last around 24 hours, but significantly less in winter. In order to determine the direction of the source in VHF, the Search and Rescue aircraft needs to be equipped with a VHF direction finder. Satellite signals give a position within a radius of a few miles. ELTs, once armed before a flight, are usually triggered automatically at impact, but can also be turned on and off manually.

Fin: Vertical surface at the tail of the aircraft, above the fuselage, to maintain lateral stability. On some floatplanes, the fin is slightly extended below the fuselage.

Flaps: Sections of the back of the wing that fold down to increase the curvature of the wing and thus provide more lift during takeoff and landing at relatively low speeds.

Float: See "pontoon"

Floatplane: A regular plane on which the wheels, on the fixed undercarriage, have been replaced by floats (pontoons) to allow operation on water. Some pontoons contain a retractable wheel for landing on runways. Floatplanes are tricky to operate on water because they tend to weathercock into the wind like a weather vane, cannot be slowed down when the engine is running, and have small and rather inefficient water rudders at the back of the pontoons. Landing on glassy (extremely smooth) water is dangerous because the pilot has no perception of depth.

Gyrocompass: A dial on the dashboard indicating the direction of the airplane, usually in degrees True (i.e., counted clockwise from True North) when navigating close to the magnetic north. The gyrocompass has no way of establishing its orientation—i.e., where north is—and must always be set by hand initially, by comparison to the direction of a landmark or a celestial object (e.g., the direction of the sun at noon, or 180° S, as established with an astrocompass). The orientation of the gyrocompass is maintained for a while by its gyroscope but needs to be reset after some time, perhaps every half hour. This is because the gyroscope precesses as a result of the rotation of the Earth, at a rate which varies with latitude. Near the North Pole, where the effect of the Earth's rotation is maximum, precession is 15 degrees per hour clockwise. Following a course straight north (000° True) near the North Pole on a gyrocompass without regularly re-setting it on a landmark or on a celestial object would mean actually ending up flying in a direction of 45° toward the northeast after three hours (3 x 15°/hour).

High Frequency (HF); Very High Frequency (VHF); Ultra-High Frequency (UHF). HF radio waves require long antennas (typically 30 or 40 feet in length) for distant communications. These long antennas can be unfurled from a drum to trail behind some of the planes, or stretched from the wing tips to the tail. HF radio waves travel beyond the horizon and are refracted by the ionosphere, which allows communications over even further distances. The strength of the signal transmitted and received depends on the orientation of the airplane antenna with respect to the ground station, and on the ever-changing height of the ionosphere. The "**Single Side Band**" technology introduced in the mid-'60s amplifies the HF signal and reduces atmospheric interference. **VHF** radio waves are much shorter and require small antennas (typically around five or six feet). They are used for short-range communications and provide a very clear signal, virtually free of static. **UHF** waves are even shorter and are used for communications with satellites.

Horizontal stabilizer: Horizontal surface at the back of the fuselage to maintain longitudinal stability. This surface can often be adjusted manually (see "trim") to increase or decrease its angle of attack and therefore its lift depending on the location of the centre of gravity (which depends on the distribution of the payload) in order to control the attitude (pitch) of the aircraft. On some airplanes, trimming is done through a very small mobile surface on the elevator.

IFR (Instrument Flight Rules): Rules which apply, typically, when visibility close to the ground is below three miles and/or the ceiling is less than 1,000 feet. Aircraft under IFR need to fly at specific flight levels within defined airways, following instructions from Air Traffic Control to ensure aircraft separation.

Navigation in the Arctic: In the '60s and early '70s, navigation in the Arctic was conducted mainly by sight, with one finger on the map and using rulers, dividers, and square protractors. South and west of the treeline, and relatively far away from the magnetic north, navigation was fairly easy as long as the ground could be seen and there was enough visibility forward. Over the tundra, however, and closer to the magnetic pole, navigation was challenging. Direction of flight had to be determined with a gyrocompass, which needed to be reset fairly frequently because of precession from the rotation of the Earth, as determined by the direction of landmarks or a celestial body.

At the time, pilots used white and blue maps that showed no contour lines, gave little or no indication of elevations, and often completely misrepresented the size and shape of lakes because the maps had been drawn from aerial photographs taken when the lakes were still partially frozen. Navigation was hard enough during the summer, when lakes and rivers were visible. However, during the winter, navigation over the tundra was extremely difficult. Ice and snow covered the landmarks, and features such as rivers or lakes could no longer be identified.

There was virtually no way to establish one's position. In winter over the tundra and in the absence of visible sunlight, there was no way to determine one's course either. Many pilots became lost, and some of them were found only many years later. A few communities and some of the large mining and oil exploration camps had small private radio beacons, which helped pilots find the station with their ADFs (automatic direction finders) once they had approached to within 50 miles.

Pitch: a) Movement of the plane around the lateral axis—i.e., the line across the aircraft from one wing tip to the other. When the wings are level, pitching the plane up or down means raising the nose or bringing it down. The pitch is usually controlled by the elevator.

b) The angle of attack of a propeller blade. The propeller pitch is set to "fully fine" for takeoff, which is equivalent to putting a car in first gear. The engine then runs at its full speed, and power is maximized. After takeoff, the pitch is progressively increased, slowing the engine and reducing power but allowing the plane to cruise faster through the air. This is equivalent to moving to second, third, and fourth gear in a car.

Pontoon: An elongated and aerodynamic aluminium flotation device fitted on a fixed undercarriage, replacing wheels, for operation on water surfaces. Pontoons usually have a flat top for easier walking and are divided into watertight compartments. On larger pontoons, some of these compartments can have a tightly screwed-in opening on their upper surface to allow some storage. Small, round openings on the top of the pontoons, typically closed with rubber half-balls, enable the pilot, before takeoff, to pump out the water that occasionally leaks into the pontoon. A "step" is built at approximately mid-pontoon, along the bottom of its keel, to reduce friction of the water and facilitate takeoff.

Precession: The small change in orientation of a gyroscope or pendulum due to the rotation of the Earth. Precession is largest close to the poles (15 degrees per hour) and nil at the equator.

Rolling movement: Movement of the aircraft around its longitudinal axis—i.e., the axis along the fuselage, from the nose to the tail. This movement is usually controlled by the ailerons.

Rudder: Small mobile surface along the back of the fin to control the yaw (movements of the aircraft to the left and the right). The pilot operates the rudder with the rudder pedals. Pressure on the left rudder, for instance, makes the aircraft yaw to the left.

Ski plane: A regular plane on which a ski has been fitted around or to the side of each wheel. Some planes are fitted with wheels OR skis but not both. When wheels AND skis are fitted, a hydraulic system allows the skis to go up to the level of the hub of the wheels for landings on dry runways. Landing on snow on an overcast day or in the dark, when there are no shadows, is dangerous because the pilot has no perception of depth.

Stall: Sudden loss of lift when the angle of attack reaches a critical value (see "angle of attack").

Step: A "step" is a discontinuity of an inch or two built at approximately mid-pontoon along the bottom of its keel: the back half of the pontoon is suddenly not as deep as the front part. The aircraft needs to "climb on the step" before takeoff can occur. Once the aircraft is gliding smoothly on the step with hardly any spray, instead of ploughing its way through water, it usually accelerates rapidly. Wind and choppy water help a plane get on the step, while glassy surfaces or an excessive load make it a lot more difficult.

Trim: Temporary adjustment of the controls, usually the elevator, to compensate for the tendency of the aircraft to climb or descend depending on the distribution of the load along the fuselage. A centre of gravity slightly to the back, for instance, tends to make the airplane fly "tail heavy"—i.e., nose high—which is dangerous because of the higher risk of stall. Before takeoff or immediately afterward, the pilot would, in this case, adjust the trim "down." Otherwise, he or she would have to continuously push the wheel forward to keep the airplane level.

VFR (Visual Flight Rules): Rules which apply when the weather is good enough to fly by sight with reference to the ground, typically when visibility is more than three miles and the ceiling above 1,000 feet. In the Arctic, these weather conditions are quite rare in winter.

Yaw: Movement of the aircraft around the yaw axis, which is perpendicular to the lateral and longitudinal axes. The yaw axis is vertical when the aircraft is flying horizontally in a straight line. This movement is normally controlled by the rudder.

Water rudders: Small aluminium rudders at the back of the pontoons, designed to help steer the floatplane on the water. The water rudders are typically not very efficient, and the airplane tends to weathercock into wind, which makes it difficult to control on water. In an effort to reduce drag during takeoff, water rudders are usually lifted up by hand from the cockpit with a cable, and stay up during the flight.

Indigenous Names of Communities

Aklavik	Aklavik	**Holman Island**	Ulukhaktok
Baker Lake	Qamani'tuaq	**Inuvik**	Inuvik
Bathurst Inlet	Qingaut	**Lac La Martre**	Whati
Baychimo Harbour	Umingmaktok	**Norman Wells**	Tlegohli
Cambridge Bay	Iqaluktuttiaq	**Padlei**	Padeli
Coppermine	Kugluktuk	**Paulatuk**	Paulatuk
Coral Harbour	Salliq	**Pelly Bay**	Kugaaruk
Eskimo Point	Arviat	**Rae Lakes**	Gameti
Fort Franklin	Deline	**Repulse Bay**	Naujaat
Fort Good Hope	K'asho Got'ine	**Resolute Bay**	Qausuittuq
Fort Liard	Echaot'l Koe	**Sachs Harbour**	Ikahuak
Fort McPherson	Teetl'it Zheh	**Snowdrift**	Lutleslk'e
Fort Norman	Tulita	**Spence Bay**	Taloyoak
Fort Rae	Behchoko	**Tuktoyaktuk**	Tuktoyaktuk
Fort Resolution	Deninu Kué	**Victoria Island**	Kitlineq
Fort Simpson	Liidlii Kué	**Whale Cove**	Tikiraqjuaq
Fort Smith	Thebacha	**Wrigley**	Pedzeh Ki
Gjoa Haven	Uqsuqtuuq		
Hay River	Xatl'odehchee		

Bibliography

1. Books about Bush Flying

Boer, Peter. *Bush Pilots*. Edmonton, AB: Folklore, 2004.

Canadian Bush Pilot Book Project. *Uncharted Skies*. Edmonton, AB: Reidmore, 1983.

Evans, Harvey. *From Fox Moths to Jet Rangers*. Madeira Park, BC: Harbour Publishing, 2009.

Fader, Sunny, and Edward Huntley. *Land Here? You Bet!* Surrey, BC: Hancock House, 2005.

Godsell, Philip. *Pilots of the Purple Twilight*. Allston, MA: Fitzhenry & Whiteside, 1955.

Grant, Robert. *Bush Flying*. Surrey, BC: Hancock House, 1995; *Great Northern Bush Planes*, Surrey, BC: Hancock House, 1997; *Wheels, Skis and Floats* (with E.C. Burton), Surrey, BC: Hancock House, 1998

Hamilton, Donald. *Flying Overloaded*. Kelowna, BC: Aspire Media Works, 2007.

Karram, Kerry. *Four Degrees Celsius*. Toronto, ON: Dundurn, 2012.

Lamb, Bruce. *Outposts and Bushplanes*. Surrey, BC: Hancock House, 2005.

Liefer G.P., *Broken Wings*. Surrey, BC: Hancock House, 2003.

Lopaschuk, William. *They Call Me Lopey*. Smithers, BC: Creekstone Press, 2009.

Matheson, Shirlee Smith. *Flying the Frontiers*. Calgary, AB: Fifth House, 1994.

McCallum, Jack. *Tales of an Old Bold Pilot who Lived to Tell his Story of Flying the North,* Sicamous, BC: John Elvin McCallum, 2004.

McCartney, Denny. *Picking up the Pieces*. Victoria, BC: Trafford Publishing, 2002.

Metcalf-Chenail, Danielle. *Polar Winds*. Toronto, ON: Dundurn, 2004.

Schofield, Jack. *No Numbered Runways*. Winlaw, BC: Sono Nis Press, 2004.

Tadman, Peter. *The Survivor*. Hanna, AB: Gorman & Gorman, 1991.

Turner, Dick. *Wings of the North*. Surrey, BC: Hancock House, 1980.

Vlessides, Michael. *The Ice Pilots*. Vancouver, BC: Douglas & McIntyre, 2012.

White, Howard, & Jim Spilsbury. *The Accidental Airline*. Madeira Park, BC: Harbour, 1994.

Whyard, Florence. *Ernie Boffa*. Whitehorse, YT: Beringian Books, 1984.

Williams, Al. *Bush and Arctic Pilot*. Surrey, BC: Hancock House, 1998.

2. Books describing the Inuit in the 1950s and 1960s

De Poncins, Gontran. *Kabloona*. New York, NY: Reynal & Hitchcock, 1941.

Metayer, Father Maurice. *Tales from the Igloo*. Edmonton, AB: Hurtig, 1972; *I, Nuligak*. Toronto, ON: Peter Martin Associates, 1966.

Mowat, Farley. *The Desperate People*. Boston, MA: Little Brown & Company, 1959; *People of the Deer*. Vancouver, BC: Douglas & McIntyre, 1952.

3. Books Describing Adventures in Northern Canada

North, Dick. *The Lost Patrol*. Edmonds, WA: Alaska Northwest, 1978.

Turner, Dick. *Nahanni*. Surrey, BC: Hancock House, 1975.

Index of names

Other books published by Dominique Prinet

Celestial Navigation
using the Sight Reduction
Tables Pub. No. 249,
220 pages

**Celestial Navigation
Exercises** for Class and
Home Study, 242 pages

Coastal Navigation
for Class and Home Study,
135 pages

**Coastal Navigation
Exercises**
based on the Canadian chart
*Strait of Georgia, Southern
Portion*, 140 pages.

These books are available from the publisher FriesenPress in
Victoria B.C., from Amazon, and from a few large retailers
such as Indigo or Barnes and Noble.

The author can be contacted at:
Dominique@MarineNavigationBooks.com

About the author

In the 1960s, Prinet worked as a commercial
bush pilot in the Canadian Arctic and High
Arctic, often navigating with an astrocompass.
He holds an airline transport pilot licence and
has more than 5,000 hours of flying. He worked
as V.P. for Nordair in Montreal while teaching
economics at McGill for 12 years, and then

moved to Vancouver in 1988 as V.P Marketing for Canadian Airlines. He has
spent his retirement years as a sailing instructor and has published several
books on celestial and coastal navigation. The stories in this book describe
some of the adventures he experienced in northern Canada.

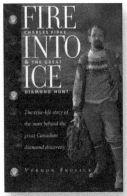

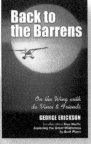
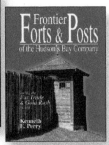

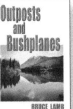

CPSIA information can be obtained
at www.ICGtesting.com
Printed in the USA
LVHW072319191222
735584LV00031B/701